Reading Circles, Novels and Adult Reading Development

Also available from Continuum

Learning to Teach in the Lifelong Learning Sector, Ewan Ingleby, Dawn Joyce and Sharon Powell

Perspectives of Quality in Adult Learning, Peter Boshier

Reflective Teaching in Further and Adult Education (3rd edition), Yvonne Hillier

Reading Circles, Novels and Adult Reading Development

Sam Duncan

continuum

Continuum International Publishing Group

The Tower Building   80 Maiden Lane
11 York Road   Suite 704
London, SE1 7NX   New York, NY 10038

www.continuumbooks.com

British Library Cataloguing-in-Publication Data
A catalogue record for this book is available from the British Library.

ISBN: 978-1-4411-7315-7 (hardcover)

Library of Congress Cataloguing-in-Publication Data
A catalogue record for this book is available from the Library of Congress.

Typeset by Deanta Global Publishing Services, Chennai, India
Printed and bound in Great Britain

Contents

FIGURE 1 Eye-Balloon by Odilon Redon, 1878

Acknowledgements

I would like to thank all my friends and colleagues at City and Islington College and the Institute of Education, as well as everyone at Continuum, for your kind support. Thank you in particular to Irene Schwab, Peggy Aylett, Monica Duncan, Brian Duncan, Alice Kaye, Steven Cowan, Tom Woodin, Sophie Yarde-Buller, Vanessa Tyrell-Kenyon, Yvonne Hillier, Jane Spiro and Ron Barnett for your advice and feedback on aspects of this process, and to Jay Derrick and Amos Paran for your detailed and extra-ordinarily generous help throughout this entire project. I also owe you, Amos, a lifetime of thank-yous for supervising the doctorate work this book is based on.

Thank you to all those I interviewed in my reading and reading circle research, particularly the members of the *Passenger* reading circle; it was such a pleasure to read with you. A huge thank you also to Billy Cowie, author of *Passenger*, for coming to talk to our reading circle. Finally, thank you to Marco and Eva for more than I would ever have time to put on paper.

List of Figures

Introduction

We read rotas, train tickets, political manifestos, signs on the doors of public toilets, funeral cards, wedding invitations, biology school textbooks, love letters, shop signs, novels, newspapers, receipts, recipes, prescriptions, notes passed in secret, emails we do and do not want, letters from banks, prayers, food packaging, letters on headed paper from debt-collection agencies and tax offices, posters on walls and windows, calendars, community newsletters, Tube maps, draft notifications, flyers, leases, job-application forms, menus, slogans, fridge warrantees, trial transcripts, telegrams, diary notations written months ago in messy handwriting, websites selling nappies and DVDs, road signs and address labels, books about birds, holy books, repair manuals, poems, cinema listings, court summonses and washing instructions. Some of us, like Truman Capote, read 'too much' and 'anything' (editors of the *Paris Review*, 1957, p. 26)

We read in the mornings and in the middle of the night, when we are busy, lonely, bored, tired, eating breakfast and on the go. We read at home and in workplaces, in bedrooms, toilets, offices, and on factory floors and balconies. We read on buses, trams, trains and cable cars and occasionally on bicycles, horses and mules. We read in meadows and public squares, in coffee shops and on mountaintops, in prisons and on beaches. We have even read in trenches and on the moon.

This is a book about adult reading practices and pedagogies, about novels, reading circles and adult emergent reading development. It is about using reading circles to develop adult emergent reading. It is written by an adult literacy teacher for other adult literacy teachers. It is also for adult literacy teacher-educators; for those with academic, professional or personal interests in adult literacy or reading development; and for those interested in novel reading processes and practices. Though aspects of this book may (I hope) be of interest to anyone teaching or studying literacy or the novel in any language, its focus is on literacy practices, pedagogies and adult literacy provision in the Anglophone worlds.

As an adult literacy teacher I searched for ways to help adults with their reading, and was struck again and again at how every book, every course, every trainer and every teacher seemed to be working from their own particular definition of reading. But, what about the learners' definitions? How can we help adults with their reading if we don't know what *they* mean by reading? This led to research (Duncan, 2009) posing the question: 'What are we doing when we read, according to adult literacy learners?' I gathered adult literacy learners' ideas of what reading is, what it involves and how best we can develop it. This taught me that researching the conceptualizations of adult literacy learners can yield invaluable insights into the learning and teaching of reading. It also indicated that the relationship between fiction and individual reading development warrants further – and closer – exploration. I decided to research what adult literacy learners can tell us about novel reading and what novel reading can tell us about adult reading development.

However, in searching for literature on the novel and reading development, I found large amounts of data on 'reading circles': people getting together to read and discuss novels (or other texts) as a group. Most of this research is either historical/ethnographic research into the circles formed autonomously by groups of adults in the past and present, or educational research on the reading circles formed by teachers within compulsory schooling or English as a Foreign Language (EFL) provision. It was hard to find any research on the use of reading circles within adult literacy provision, despite the fact that the research conducted in the school and EFL contexts has found that the reading, thinking and discussion generated by reading circles can develop reading and discussion skills, independent study skills, confidence as both readers and members of the community, the exploration of personal identity and the development of personal reading practices – all arguably goals of adult literacy education. I became increasingly interested in what reading as a group involves, why it appeals to individual readers, and how it relates to both adult literacy development and novel reading. I therefore decided to set up a reading circle in an existing adult literacy class, give the group control over what they read and how they read it, and use this reading circle as a research case study. *Reading Circles, Novels and Adult Reading Development* is based on this case study, placing it within a larger investigation of reading circles, adult reading practices, the novel and literacy education.

I aim to make one primary argument: that reading circles should be used in, and as, adult literacy provision. To make this argument, I will place the above-mentioned research case study of a reading circle within formal adult literacy provision alongside secondary research on how reading is conceptualized and researched, on past and present reading practices, on how adults and children have learnt to read, on the place of literature in literacy development, and on reading circles. In doing so, I will also make three secondary arguments: that to know more about reading we need to talk to readers; that adult literacy teachers should learn about the history of literacy practices and pedagogies; and that adult literacy provision should be located within a wider adult education offer based on adults' needs and goals.

Yet more than to make a linear argument (or arguments), my aim is to follow a train of thought around adult reading development, literature, novels and reading circles. This book is therefore an exploration, speculation or meditation on the issues which crop up along the way, such as how reading is defined and researched, the role of reading in adult life, the relationship between literacy and literature, whether reading is primarily an individual act or a communal act, and, crucially, what is actually going on – for any of us – when we read novels.

Chapter 1 examines how different disciplines claim, define and research reading; Chapter 2 inspects the role of reading in adult life, past and present. In Chapter 3, I have traced how we have learnt to read, from Ancient Greece and Rome to the late twentieth-century Anglophone adult literacy campaigns. Chapter 4 will analyse the relationship between literature and literacy (how and why literature has been used to develop literacy skills), while Chapter 5 investigates the reading circles formed in the past and the present, looking particularly at *why* people choose to read communally. Chapter 6 looks at how we formed a reading circle within an existing adult literacy class and how I used this as a case study for research. Chapter 7 is an analysis of the findings of this main case study: the assertion that reading is five distinct acts (educational, cognitive, imaginative, affective and communicative); the notion that we each have a 'reading identity'; observations on the relationship between decoding and vocabulary development; how the 'story' of the novel is built up by its readers; thoughts on the relationship between fiction, truth and learning (including ideas on 'the tenacity of the story' and corresponding 'disappearance of the author'); and five benefits of reading as a group.

Chapters 8, 9, 10 and 11 examine these findings in light of other literature in order to explore reading as experience, reading circles as ideal pedagogy, reading as an individual act versus reading as a communal one and, finally, the pleasures and politics of novel reading and reading circles. This includes investigations of heightened experience formation; collaborative learning, negotiated syllabi and open-ended pedagogy; how reading aloud can develop phonic decoding skills; the novel as an exploration of individual psychology versus the novel as the product of a mass-taste-led industry; the ethics of fiction; and the vital importance of 'what could have happened'. The hope is that readers will pick and choose the chapters, or the sections of the chapters, that are of particular interest to them. I have suggested further reading at the end of each.

In 2005 Margaret Atwood published a review of Azar Nafisi's *Reading Lolita in Tehran: A Memoir in Books* (2004). She writes: 'There is a book club in *Reading Lolita*, but it's more like a life raft than an after-work social gathering'(Atwood, 2005, p. 317). This one sentence contains four important and implicit messages. It indicates that the concept of a 'book club' is widely understood: book clubs are a common, accepted, 'normal' part of Anglo-North American lives. Second, it implies that book clubs can play dramatically different roles in these lives – from 'life raft' to 'after-work social gathering'. It also conjures the question of how anyone could possibly identify the role that a book club plays in someone else's life: what may seem like an 'after-work social gathering' may in fact be a 'life raft'. The individual reader's perspective is usually obscured. Finally, for anyone who has read *Reading Lolita*, or who goes on to read the rest of Atwood's review, this sentence raises the issue of the relationship between informal book clubs (or reading circles) and formal educational (and political) policy. These four messages are aspects of my rationale for this book. More than this, they are reasons why I feel that literacy – and literary – teaching and research will always be of critical cultural importance.

Chapter 1

The Charted Waters of Reading: How Reading is Claimed, Researched and Defined by Different Fields

If, as an adult literacy teacher, I want to feel better equipped to help learn-ers develop their reading, what should I do? The answer to this question seems to depend on the answers to so many more. What do I need to know? Who should I turn to? Who are the reading experts? What should I read? What are the 'key readings' for adult literacy studies? And what are the 'key readings' for reading development?.

The answers to these questions are not straightforward. There are many different traditions of reading research, produced by different groups of reading experts, each working from a different definition or understanding of reading. Very simply, reading is claimed by many different fields. What 'claimed' means and what exactly is being claimed needs further explana-tion. Three images come to mind. The first is James Gillray's famous carica-ture of imperialism, 'The Plum Pudding in Danger' (1805). Napoleon and William Pitt carve up the territories of the world like two greedy schoolboys carving up a large and tempting plum pudding. Yet this representation of 'claiming' suggests that the various parties are in cahoots, like Pitt and Napoleon, aware of each other's desires and so together dividing the spoils. The various experts busily claiming reading show little awareness of one another's existence, let alone one another's work.

Perhaps a more appropriate image would be that of the blind men touch-ing the elephant in the parable. As each man is touching a different part (a leg, the trunk, the tail, etc.), they each describe a different creature and a disagreement ensues. Like the various disciplines claiming reading, their descriptions do not match because they are each describing a different creature, a different 'elephant'. Yet this still implies that there is a complete, sharply delineated and independent creature called an elephant, waiting to be discovered if only the men could work together and share their perceptions. I do not believe there is one definitive 'reading' waiting to be discovered.

The final image is a group of fishing boats heading out into a rough and infinite ocean, each boat charting its own waters, each drawing maps and taking measurements, sometimes shouting over at one another but generally paying little attention to the rival charters. Hundreds or thousands of different maps are produced: at times the maps overlap, at times they agree and at times they contradict, but huge territories remain uncharted and no one really knows where the ocean begins and ends. Perhaps more significantly, their acts of exploration shape the very ocean they are hoping to 'discover'. This, I feel, is closer to representing the situation with reading and its range of busy expert explorers. There is, overall, little communication between the different fields, with their boats of contrasting colours and distinct measuring equipment (and separate journals and conferences and university departments). What they are charting is so vast, mysterious and ever-changing that though their charts may at times overlap, they will also always miss something. Their job will never be done.

This chapter presents five fields of reading experts: psychology and neuroscience (often called 'scientific studies of reading'), literary theory, social history, social practice theory and education. I will examine the concerns, research methods and some example findings of each, along with the definitions which both inform their concerns and are produced by their findings. I will then briefly discuss examples of interdisciplinary studies before turning to how adult literacy learners themselves have defined reading.

The Scientific Studies of Reading: Psychology and Neuroscience

Psychologists and neuroscientists are concerned with what have been termed the cognitive, physiological or neurological processes of reading. Al-Haytham was a Basra scholar working in eleventh-century Cairo. He used his physiological expertise to draw and theorize the processes of eye and brain, arguing that all perception involves inference based on a developing faculty of judgement. Importantly, he presented perception on a spectrum of increasing self-awareness, from involuntary to voluntary, from seeing to decoding (Manguel, 1996). Eight hundred years later, Javal conducted experiments in eye movements at the University of Paris. He observed that eye movements in reading are rapid and discontinuous. Reading, he noted, does not involve a continuous, smooth movement from word to word across a page (Huey, 1908/1968; Manguel, 1996). Both men could be considered pioneers of the scientific study of reading because they, like their many untraceable colleagues, saw reading as a potentially observable – and 'experimentable' – process of mind or brain.

The reading mind

The mid- to late twentieth-century field of cognitive psychology differentiates itself from behavioural psychology through its interest in those very cognitive processes which are not easily observable. Cognitive psychology aims to understand the hidden mental processes such as how we think, make decisions or use language. Its interest in reading is therefore in understanding how people learn to read, the cognitive processes of fluent reading and the causes of reading difficulties or disabilities. Research methods vary, from eye-movement observations to timed word-and-sentence reading experiments. The emphasis is on research as empirical, quantitative and reproducible. For example, Ren and Yang recently published an article entitled 'Syntactic boundaries and comma placement during silent reading of Chinese text: evidence from eye movements' (2010). This reported a research study into the influence of commas on the reading of Mandarin words, clauses and sentences. Their sample was relatively small – seventeen Mandarin speakers at the Chinese Agricultural University, all with normal or 'corrected to normal' vision. The researchers created forty-eight target sentences containing variations on comma use. Eye-movement monitoring equipment was used to track and measure eye movements as participants read the target sentences. Ren and Yang performed statistical analysis of their data to draw conclusions about when eye fixations were longer or shorter. They concluded that comma placement affects word identification when reading Mandarin.

  The findings of cognitive research into reading are of course many and diverse, but they include: charting the processes involved in decoding words and phrases; the development and role of phonemic awareness; the role of vocalization and sub-vocalization in fluent reading and reading development; sentence and text comprehension; and the nature of dyslexia. Researchers present models of the 'route' from the eye seeing a word on the page to the mind allocating a meaning to that word, identifying both lexical routes (where visual identification of a whole word leads to a meaning) and phonological routes (where identification of letters or groups of letters leads to the spoken word and then the meaning). Models differ in detail, including whether the lexical and phonological routes are parallel or sequential, and the role semantics plays in the path from print to speech, but they share a common shape from text to meaning and agree on the existence of potentially distinct whole-word and sound-based routes (Coltheart and Jackson, 2001; M. A. Just and Carpenter, 1980; Rayner and Pollatsek, 1989; Stuart, 2005a, 2005b).

Importantly, though, the concern and findings of cognitive psychology go beyond word-level reading and understanding. Just and Carpenter (1977) investigated eye movements in sentence and paragraph reading, observing that the duration of eye fixations reflects the semantic importance of words or phrases as the reader builds up an understanding of sentences and paragraphs through 'comprehensive computations'(1977, p. 137). Garnham (1987), and Garnham and Oakhill's (1992) 'mental models theory' presents how the reader processes each new word in the context of a mental model he or she has already built of the text, a model that is constantly added to and adapted. Noordman and Vonk (1992) present this 'building' process as an interplay between new information that the reader gathers from the text and the reader's existing world knowledge.

The reading brain

Under the broad category of 'scientific studies of reading', one could make a distinction between the above studies of the reading *mind,* and studies of the reading *brain.* Neuroscience, or rather the cognitive neuroscience of reading, is concerned with not only the cognitive processes of reading, but with how those processes relate to the physical brain, the rest of the nervous system and the eyes. The biggest difference between neuroscience and cognitive psychology are their research methods: cognitive psychology uses experimental methods to *surmise* the internal, hidden processes (for example, the 'route' from print to speech mentioned above), while neuroscience tries to open up what is hidden and locate those processes within the physical body (where, for example, could we locate those routes physiologically?). The concern of the neuroscience of reading, therefore, is to map function to structure and so better understand the cognitive processes of reading. Perfetti and Bolger (2004) break this larger concern into three key elements: the acquisition of reading skill (how we learn to read); the understanding of reading disability; and the cognitive processes of reading (what fluent reading involves).

Until the late twentieth century, the main opportunities for understanding the neuroscience of reading came from the study of those with brain lesions, work made famous by the French neurologist Dejerine in the late nineteenth century (Poldrack and Sandak, 2004). By studying damage to certain parts of the brain (particularly after accidents) and observing impairments in reading, researchers could draw conclusions about which parts of the brain were involved in particular aspects of the reading process. Over the past 25 years, this all changed as neuroimaging technology revolutionized the neuroscience of reading. Crudely, neuroimaging has opened up new avenues for reading research by measuring the magnetic or electrical products of brain activity or blood flow, indicating when and which neurons are active during different reading or linguistic processes.

Though neuroimaging research is very young, it is already beginning to produce significant breakthroughs in our understanding of fluent reading, reading difficulties and how people learn to read (Perfetti and Bolger, 2004). For example, neuroimaging research has demonstrated that the processes involved when one begins to learn to read are different to those of fluent reading because fluent reading increasingly develops a 'reading circuit' through distinct regions of the brain where activities related to orthography, phonology and semantics take place. Neuroimaging technology can also tell us more about sentence and text comprehension. For example, Caplan (2004) used neuroimaging to demonstrate that comprehension of written sentences occurs in the same areas of the brain as comprehension of spoken sentences.

Neuroscience also offers hypotheses of the potential relationship between reading and genetics. Kate Nation (2006) argues that though literacy is too recent in evolutionary terms to be genetically encoded in the same way as speaking and listening, there are nevertheless genetically encoded cognitive and linguistic capabilities which affect reading, such as lexical comprehension. Additionally, neuroscience and cognitive psychology can work together: neuroimaging and genetic research can test the existing hypotheses of psychological models of reading (such as the dual-route model), and psychological experiments can explore claims made by neuroscience.

Despite their differences in research methods, psychological and neurological studies of reading both define reading as a cognitive process and share a common concern for its identification and observation in greater and greater detail.

Literary Theory

Cognitive psychology and neuroscience are by no means the only fields concerned with reading as a process of mind. Literary theory is a vast and ancient field but has always included work focused specifically on the processes of reading and (going back further) spectatorship. Probably the most famous of these writings is Aristotle's *Poetics*, in which Aristotle begins by arguing that poetry (meaning both poetry that would be recited to an audience and drama performed on a stage) is of 'two causes', both born of 'the universal pleasure in imitations' (p. 6). The first is an innate human drive to imitate, and the second is the 'delight' we experience when observing and then understanding these imitations, because 'understanding is extremely pleasant' (p. 7). This second pleasure is the direct product of the mental processing involved in observing, decoding and interpreting the meaning of artistic representations: 'this is the reason why people take delight in seeing images; what happens is that as they view them they come to understand and work out what each thing is' (pp. 6–7). Aristotle's *Poetics* therefore begins with an analysis of the cognitive and affective processes of spectatorship.

Perhaps more famously, the *Poetics* tackles the processing pleasures of tragedy in particular. Addressing the old riddle of why audiences experience pleasure from observing acts on stage which would cause great pain in real life, Aristotle explains: 'Tragedy is an imitation … in language made pleasurable … effecting through pity and fear the purification of such emotions' (p. 10). Here are two more pleasures of cognitive and affective processing: first, observation and appreciation of the aesthetic quality of language; and second, *katharsis*, purification of excess pity and fear by experiencing versions of these same emotions in the tragic imitation.

On the Indian subcontinent (and at least two centuries earlier), Sanskrit dramatic theorists were equally concerned with understanding the processes which bring pleasure to audiences of dramatic productions. They decided that this pleasure is the result of a conveyance of combinations of eight possible *rasa* (flavours, tastes or moods): romantic/erotic, comic, violent/furious, peaceful/compassionate, repulsive/terrifying, heroic and marvellous/wondrous (Sastri, 1960). The audience experiences these *rasa* in a generalized or abstracted form, quite different from experiencing such emotions in our individual lives. Second, and integrally, the emotion generated by the drama is not new, but drawn from the existing experience of the audience, who *re-taste* it as the dramatic events proceed. One critic, Abhinavagupta, argued that the '*re*-tasting' is literal: we feel pleasure from experiencing the emotions of drama because we have actually *been* one of the characters in the drama in a former life (the belief in reincarnation was absolute). As we watch the drama, we re-experience the flavours of a past life and are moved by this fleeting link between past and present, thus 'tasting one's own consciousness'(Dundas, 1994).

This ancient desire to understand the literary experience is the basis of our more recent drives to understand the literary reading process. Literary theory, over the course of the twentieth century, shifted its concern from the author to the text and, finally, to the reader (Eagleton, 1996), to offer models of the reading process. In this way, literary theory, like cognitive psychology, is concerned with the route from text to meaning in the mind of the reader.

The term 'research methods' is not often associated with literary study, though of course the methods literary theorists use to develop their ideas are a form of research. The primary research methods of literary theory are textual analysis and philosophical exploration, with a wide-ranging borrowing of concepts from other disciplines, depending on the particular interest or school the theorist is working within. For example, some literary theorists use psychoanalytical theory, others social history. I would argue that all literary theorists are also using their own personal perspectives as readers, though this is often unacknowledged, even when the theory is explicitly focused on the reading experience.

Stanley Fish (1980) presents a model of the reading process from the American reader-response tradition, developed through a linguistic analysis of Milton's sonnets. Fish argues that purposely ambiguous lexis, syntax and punctuation force the reader into a highly active role:

> the making and revising of assumptions, the rendering and regretting of judgments, the coming to and abandoning of conclusions ... In a word, these activities are interpretive...not waiting for meaning but constructing meaning and continually in the act of reconstituting (pp. 158–159).

Similarly, German reception theorist Wolfgang Iser theorized the difference between the written *text* (the marks on the page) and the *work* of literature – 'a convergence ... virtual ... dynamic' (Iser, 1972, p. 212) – produced in the reader's mind by the connections he or she makes between sentences of text:

> each intentional sentence correlative [link to be made between one sentence and another] opens up a partial horizon, which is modified, if not completely changed, by succeeding sentences. While these expectations arouse interest in what is to come, the subsequent modification of them will also have a retrospective effect on what has already been read (Iser, 1972, p. 215).

Reading is therefore an active, interpretive process unique to each reader, and to each reading, which produces, through constant 'anticipation and retrospection', an 'individual realization' (Iser, 1972, p. 219) of the written text.

In making links between and within sentences written by someone else, the reader is also following in another's cognitive footsteps: 'The I which I pronounce is not myself' (Iser, 1972, p. 226). In producing the *work* of literature, the reader is 'oscillating' between 'the alien me and the real me' (p. 224). Elizabeth Wright, discussing Norman Holland's psychoanalytical theorizing of novel reading (Holland, 1978), calls reading 'a re-creation of identity ... an intersubjective process ... the overtaking of another's meaning'(Wright, 1982, p. 149). For these theorists, 'overtaking of another's meaning' characterizes the reading process.

More interested in *how* the work itself is built up, narrative theorists, such as Culler (1975), Perry (1979) and Rimmon-Kenan (1989), explore how the reader constructs and reconstructs the 'story paraphrase' (Iser's *work*). 'Frames' of meaning are formulated and revised or rejected throughout the reading process. While Culler builds on the work of structuralist linguistics, Perry and Rimmon-Kenan use the work of cognitive psychologists Asch (1946) and Luchins (1957) on the 'primacy effect' and 'the phenomena of adaptation' to theorize the reader's cognitive drive to hold on to earlier formulated interpretations, even when these are threatened by more recently read text, as well as the dynamics of when new information may finally overturn previously held interpretations/conclusions. The reader uses the *text* to construct the *work* in a highly active, interpretive reading process. To literary theory, reading is a cognitive process, as well as an emotional, spiritual and cultural one.

Importantly, although the research methods of literary theory differ dramatically from those of cognitive psychology, their findings are remarkably similar. They both emphasize the reader's activity of 'building up' and constantly revising meaning based on the decoding and interpretation of written code.

Social History

Social history is the branch of history concerned with people's daily lives. Its work on reading includes the social history of literacy, education and publishing, as well as the recently popular field of 'the history of the book'. Social history is interested in reading practices as they relate to larger cultural, religious, linguistic, educational, economic and political shifts.

The research methods of social history are those of history: policies, laws, treaties, letters, objects, buildings, paintings, photographs, textual evidence of all kinds, along with oral accounts. For example, Steven Cowan (2010b) argues that the 'incidental depictions of public reading which litter' Hogarth's paintings tell us just how common public reading practices were in eighteenth-century London. Similarly, Brown (2009) explains that the language and themes of two ninth-century prayer books made in Mercia (now the English Midlands) indicate that they were written by and for women, suggesting that at least some nuns, and possibly lay-women, wrote and read books in England at this time.

The findings of social history are naturally diverse, covering thousands of years of reading across the globe. To take three examples, Albin (2009) found that the art of Arabic bookmaking was born following the death of the prophet Muhammad. He argues that while Muhammad was living, the Holy Text was shared and preserved through memorization, but after Muhammad's death, his followers felt the text needed to be standardized in writing. Verses were collected, and by the eighth century the 'Universal Text' was established, along with 'the age of the Islamic manuscript' (p. 166). Stressing the significance of textual variation, rather than standardization, Murphy (1989, 1992) analyses (and then goes on to translate) the ninth-century Saxon epic *The Heliand*, arguing that it is a 're-imagining' of the Gospel created specifically to convert the Saxons to Christianity. Murphy argues that this 'northernization' of the Gospel within a Saxon cultural context (knights replacing shepherds and hill-forts replacing mangers) played a significant role in the conversion to Christianity of what is now northern Germany. Continuing the theme of the role of texts in religious worship, Houston (2002) reports the case of Arthur Chapman, a blacksmith ordered to appear before a church court in sixth-century Durham, England for 'misbehaviour in church' (2002, p. 246): reading a book aloud while the priest was speaking. He was asked to read more softly in future.

The examples are countless (and many more will be explored in the next chapter). For social history, reading is a cultural practice closely related to political, religious and economic trends, both local and global.

Literacy as a Social Practice

The field of social history most certainly regards reading as a social practice; that is, as something performed as part of social life. Literary theory and the scientific studies of reading would also agree that reading is, of course, a social practice. However, the terms 'social practice' and 'social practice theory' carry a specific association with a particular body of work within literacy studies. Influenced by the work of Shirley Brice Heath (1983) on the language and literacy practices of two distinct communities in the Piedmont Carolinas, New Literacy Studies (Barton, 1994; Barton et al., 2000; Gee, 1996; Mace, 1992; Street, 1984) emerged in the 1980s and 1990s, and is now the closest thing the United Kingdom has to an orthodoxy for adult literacy teachers. Within literacy studies, New Literacy Studies' mantra of 'literacy as a social practice' presented a move away from the study of literacy as individual skill and towards a more socially located perspective: literacy can only be understood in relation to a cultural context. This is social practice theory.

Social practice theory shares with social history its interest in the relationship between literacy practices and the wider political or cultural context, but, having more in common with sociology than history, examines (often globally) diverse contemporary practices rather than focusing on the past. While including the study of objects and texts which provide insights into literacy practices, the 'signature' research methodology of social practice theory is ethnography – the study of how people live. Barton argues that a defining element of ethnography is its concern with 'participants' perspectives' (2004, p. 29). For example, Mace's (1995) study of 'reminiscence' groups (gatherings of older people interested in sharing their memories and past experiences) is the product of around a decade of working with, observing and interviewing such groups. This allowed Mace to gain insights into key 'intersections' within these groups, how members' accounts influence, inspire and echo one another, and how oral work intersects with written.

As for each field I am examining, findings are many and varied. Ladaah Openjuru and Lyster (2007) studied the literacy practices of a Christian community in rural Uganda, finding that the drive to read the Bible was the primary motivator for literacy development. Ghose (2007) explored the 'everyday' literacy and numeracy practices in New Delhi, citing examples of wall writing on houses in Dalit (untouchable) communities, which 'included polio immunization messages, religious texts, names of family members, names of newly-wed couples [and] poetry' (2007, pp. 46–47). Gebre, Rogers, Street and Openjuru (2009) transferred Ghose's model to Ethiopia in order to encourage adult educators to work from existing community literacy practices, such as covering home walls with 'magazine papers and [...] religious, cultural and educative quotations' (p. 79), which families would read and reread over coffee. They also noted the increasing use of text messaging 'among people officially designated as "illiterate"'(p. 12) and friends writing and reading messages to one another 'using more than one language and indeed more than one script' (p. 121).

Perhaps most relevant to this book is Gregory and Williams's (2000) study of the social practices of reading and learning to read among the multicultural inhabitants of the London districts of Spitalfields and the City over a hundred-year period. They report a diversity of reading pedagogies and practices (seeing pedagogies as also practices and practices as potential pedagogies), along with how individuals felt about learning to read, reading and the role of reading in their lives. Their study also presents a clear and much needed rejection of 'the myth of the "correct method" of teaching reading [which] has become particularly powerful in Britain during the final years of the twentieth century'. They found instead:

> an array of methods in different contexts; for example, letter naming in school, chanting and blending sounds in their religious classes and reciting whole chunks of text at choir or drama classes (p. xvii).

Like social history, a social practice approach sees reading as inextricably linked to cultural context. The theorists of New Literacy Studies use their findings to argue for this to be taken into account in both the teaching of literacy and the development of educational policy.

Education

Education most certainly claims reading. Early years, primary, secondary, foreign language learning, university academic literacy support and adult literacy teaching – we all claim reading as our own. Education is concerned with the teaching, learning and development of reading as a skill or (less often) a practice.

Its research methods are varied, and include those of each field discussed above. Indeed, much of the research already surveyed in this chapter was performed in the name of education. Education also generates literature reviews or large studies surveying existing research on reading in order to apply these to current educational preoccupations. For example, the UK governmental Rose Review (2006) famously analysed the results of existing research (much of which could be classified as the work of cognitive psychology) in order to argue for the use of more phonics instruction in the teaching of early reading.

Educational research also includes research into what goes on in the classroom itself, both practitioner/action research (where a teacher investigates an aspect of his or her own practice with the view to improving it in some way) and studies where researchers go into educational settings to observe or work with teachers to evaluate different techniques. Burton's *Oral Reading Fluency for Adults* (2007a) reports on a small-scale research study. Over approximately 1 year, a small team of researchers worked with six adult literacy teachers and forty adult learners in nine classes. The teachers tried out a range of rarely used strategies related to 'oral reading fluency', such as choral reading and paired reading. The researchers and teachers worked together to evaluate these approaches through a combination of observation and talking to the learners, and concluded by suggesting that teachers take more risks to try out new or different strategies.

Findings of education research into reading usually concern what is done and not done in classrooms, what is effective or not effective for particular groups of learners, what should be done more often and what is often done but perhaps should not be. For example, Besser et al. (2004) reviewed the 'school-level' research on reading before using classroom observation, diagnostic materials, interviews and teacher focus groups to identify a range of adult literacy learner difficulties in reading (including phonological awareness, decoding and comprehension), advocating more classroom attention to these areas. Similarly, McShane (2005) analysed key adult reading difficulties, assessment tools and areas of instruction, calling for development in the assessment of reading and the teaching of alphabetics, fluency, comprehension and vocabulary development. Like Besser et al. (2004), McShane's research methods included a survey of existing research, teacher interviews and evaluations of teaching methods. Three years later, Brooks, Burton, Cole and Szczerbinski (2007) investigated the effectiveness of the methods used in adult literacy classes to develop reading skills, concluding that more work needs to be done on 'oral fluency, explicit comprehension strategies, reciprocal teaching, phonics and language experience approaches'(p. 10). For education, adult and school, reading is an area of constant debate, a political battleground.

Interdisciplinary Studies

The above disciplines may present significant differences in how they conceptualize and research reading, but I have also noted similarities in approaches and findings. There are indeed studies which aim to provide links between different worlds of reading research. Holland's *5 Readers Reading* (1975) is an unusual study of how an individual's identity influences how they read, and therefore their own individual reader response. This work is a departure from Holland's earlier literary theory in its far greater use of psychological and psychoanalytic theory, and in its focus on five real readers as case-studies. It is less a literary study influenced by psychology, and more a psychological study influenced by literary theory. Similarly, Zunshine (2006) unites key concepts from cognitive psychology and literary theory to analyse her title concern *Why We Read Fiction*. She finds that reading fiction allows us to exercise the pleasures of 'cognitive experiment' in imagining or interpreting a character's 'state of mind' (p. 25).

Looking away from psychology and towards child reading pedagogy, Meek (1988) uses literary theory to develop ideas on how children learn to read. She argues that only literary texts can provide young readers with the opportunity to develop their skills in interpreting the 'multiple meanings' which are the challenge and joy of reading. Taking an even wider stance, Wolf's ambitious and fascinating *Proust and the Squid* (2008) uses history, philosophy and literary theory alongside neuroscience/genetics to examine our reading development both as a species and as individuals. Finally, Purcell-Gates et al., (2004), and Green and Howard (2007) unite the often-opposed social practice and cognitive skills-based approaches to adult literacy pedagogy, sharing the view that skills are embedded within any literacy practice and practices are the wider purpose behind any development of skill. Both, they stress, need to be a part of adult literacy teaching.

The above studies demonstrate the fruitfulness – and necessity – of interdisciplinary reading research. They also highlight the gaps. Where, for example, are the studies connecting adult literacy teaching and literary theory?

The Reader Perspective

Social history often aims to represent what Rose calls the 'history of audiences': 'to enter the minds of ordinary readers, to discover what they read and how they read it' (2010, p. 1). Literary theory, as noted above, has an implicit basis within theorists' interpretations of their own reading processes. Scientific studies, social practice theory and education would also each argue that they are concerned with the experiences of readers, their processes, practices and development. Yet not one of these fields is primarily focused on the perspective of readers themselves.

I am interested in how readers (particularly adult emergent readers) conceptualize reading processes and practices. My primary focus is what reading is for the reader. This is a core argument of this book: the reader's perspective matters. More than this, it is integral. We need the reader's perspective if we are to get closer to charting the waters of reading more thoroughly. Neuroscience may be able to tell us that a particular part of the brain is active in a particular part of the reading process, or social practice theory may be able to tell us that certain people read for primarily religious purposes, but neither will be able to tell us what it *feels* like to read – what reading is, as an experience. Only readers can do this.

To access this perspective, researchers need to talk to readers. This is the approach taken in the main research case-study of this book (see Chapters 6 and 7) and is the approach, I am arguing, which can best integrate the ideas of the above disciplines. Several years ago I interviewed about fifty adult literacy learners at a large London further education college. I started each interview with the same question: *What is reading?* Here are some of their responses:

'It's knowledge and it's a way of escaping. I think that's what reading is, to me at least.'

'For me, reading is to get more ideas and it's a way to educate my family.'

'It's understanding letters and words.'

'Reading is learning new things.'

'Reading is very nice because sometimes when you get bored or you feel alone you read something and you like it and you forgot everything. So sometimes when I'm home alone or I feel bad, I just get a book and I read it.'

'Reading to me is trying to better yourself.'

Reading is the way to get letters together and then understand the meaning of letters and words.

'I get a picture of what I'm actually reading about, in your mind you get a picture of what you're reading about.'

'Reading is communicating with those people who can't be with you at this moment.'

'I don't really know what reading is, to be honest with you … See, I'm not much of a fan. I don't really read, but I know it's important to read, because I can't even sit at home and read with my son.'

'It's relaxing in your own private space.'

'Your eyes are looking at the words and then making the words.'

'You read to find out what is written inside.'
'I don't know who invented reading, but it's lovely.'

These responses relate to each of the fields explored above, and also provide something else: the reader's first-person perspective.

Chapter Summary

Reading is something different according to the context in which it is researched. Experimental psychology and neuroscience see reading as a process of mind and brain, researching the cognitive and neurological processes of learning to read, fluent reading and reading difficulties. Much literary theory shares this interest in reading as a process, analysing how meaning is built up in the mind of the reader. Social history and social practice theory investigate the diverse reading practices of different people in different contexts, while education commissions and plunders the work of each of these fields to better understand reading as something that is taught within formal educational settings. While much of the work of these fields is performed and received in isolation, interdisciplinary research does exist, serving to highlight the importance of bringing together insights from different perspectives. Another way to bring together different approaches to reading is to start with the reader him- or herself. Reading can be researched by talking to readers themselves, particularly to adult literacy learners, who bring the skills and experience of adult life to improving their own literacy and are therefore well placed to offer insights. At the beginning of this chapter I asked where an adult literacy teacher should turn for advice on developing adult emergent reading. My answer would be to all of these, to each of the above disciplines and perspectives – and more – as we strive to develop our understanding of 'the tangled story of the most remarkable specific performance that civilization has learned in all its history' (Huey, 1908/1968, p. 6).

Suggested Reading

Barton, D., Hamilton, M., & Ivanic, R. (2000), *Situated Literacies*. London: Routledge.
Barton, Hamilton and Ivanic's highly influential collection established the core of social practice theory. See particularly Chapter 1: 'Literacy Practices' by David Barton and Mary Hamilton.

Gregory, E., & Williams, A. (2000), *City Literacies: Learning to Read Across Generations and Cultures*. London: Routledge.

This is a study of the social practices of reading and learning to read among the multicultural inhabitants of London's Spitalfields and the City over a hundred-year period. It is an example of both a social history, and a social practice approach to reading research.

Houston, R. A. (2002), *Literacy in Early Modern Europe: Culture and Education 1500–1800*. London: Longman/Pearson Education.

Houston's social history of literacy in Europe (1500–1800) traces literacy practices as well as how, when, why and to whom literacy has been taught.

Lodge, D., & Wood, N. (eds) (2008), *Modern Criticism and Theory: A Reader*. London: Longman.

This literary theory reader has two useful contents lists (one arranged chronologically and the other according to schools of theory), making it an ideal place to start reading about literary theory. It includes seminal work on the role of the reader from both Iser and Fish.

Rayner, K., & Pollatsek, A. (1989), *The Psychology of Reading*. Englewood Cliffs, NJ: Prentice Hall.

A clear and detailed look at the psychology of reading, this book is suitable as both an introduction to the psychological study of reading and an opportunity for more in-depth exploration.

Chapter 2

Reading and Adult Life

We need to understand the potential roles of reading in adult life before we can understand and assess reading research and pedagogy. I started the introduction to this book by listing some of our present-day reading practices. We read political manifestos and food packets, websites to buy shoes, posters for concerts, street names and CD sleeves. We read because we want to and need to, because we are told to and sometimes because we are told *not* to. We read to learn, understand, escape, relax, be entertained, do our jobs, help our friends, communicate, cry, laugh and administer our lives. We read through arduous struggles and we read without realising that we have read anything.

I am using the pronoun 'we' to represent a range of common experiences of the majority of people on this planet right now. Yet what would this picture have looked like five thousand years ago? One thousand? Five hundred? Even fifty? A quick glance at the history of reading seems at first to reveal a logical and inevitable path from antiquity – when reading was something oral, social and public, performed by the few, male, experts reading from heavy pieces of stone or bulky scrolls – to our postmodern world, when reading is predominantly a silent, private, solitary act that everyone does, at all times of the day and night, reading from screens which will probably soon be implanted in our eyelids. In many ways this is not far from accurate, but these two end-points create the illusion of a smooth and homogeneous development, obscuring the many twists and turns, blips, revolutions and contradictions that can provide us with the greatest insights into the role of reading in adult life.

This chapter will try to follow some of these twists and turns, examining the inventions, technological advancements and shifting physicality of reading, interrogating the relationship between reading and writing, exploring the great dichotomy of reading aloud and reading silently, and investigating the relationship between reading, civil rights and constructions of illiteracy. The aim of this chapter is to paint a picture of the history and diversity of reading practices. It is just one picture, though: it will not and cannot be all-inclusive or exhaustive. I will highlight some examples to which the reader can add hundreds more.

Trade, Religion and Empire

Most historians agree that there were four independent birthplaces of writing: Mesopotamia, Egypt, China and Mesoamerica. From these, 'writing spread with trade and religion'(Coulmas, 2003, p. 201). Trade, religion and (I would add) empire, have spread literacy practices across the globe ever since.

Literacy practices moved to and from the Indian subcontinent through developments in religion and philosophy, as well as trade routes. Further west, the Phoenicians traded with the Ancient Greeks, bringing the alphabet which the Greeks, via the Etruscans, brought to the Romans and the Romans to much of Europe. Through both trade and religion, the Chinese brought their writing system to Japan, where the Japanese adapted it to write their evolving languages. The early Christians brought Latin and its alphabet to most of Western Europe, where the Celtic and Germanic peoples either converted or did not, started using the Latin language or did not, but, regardless, used the Roman alphabet to produce written texts in their own languages on an unprecedented scale. The Greek alphabet also spread with the Eastern Orthodox Church, leading to the development of Cyrillic to write the Slavonic languages, while Islam brought the Arabic language and writing system to its conquered territories in Asia, Africa and southern Europe.

The European empires of France, Portugal, Spain, Holland and England/ Britain brought their languages, religions and writing systems to their trading posts and colonies in Africa, Asia and the Americas. As happened in the Christian conversion of northern Europe, along with the imposition of the vernacular European languages, the Roman alphabet began to be used as a writing system for native languages, some of which had been predominantly oral, or had used other systems of recording – such as the Quipu knot system of Inca Peru and Ecuador (Coulmas, 2003, p. 20) – designed for administration rather than for narrative. With attempted religious conversion came new literacy practices, including the use of key religious texts translated into indigenous languages and written using the Roman alphabet. For example, to convert the Massachusett Native Americans to Christianity, the Puritan settlers of North America, and their Native American associates, translated the Bible into the Massachusett language using the Roman alphabet. This resulted in many Massachusett speakers using the Roman alphabet to write down their language, whether they converted to Christianity or not (Ostler, 2005; Wyss, 2000). In turn, the use of a new writing system brought with it new literacy practices, such as a style of autobiographical narrative described by Wyss (2000) as a 'bicultural' practice, neither wholly Native American nor Puritan.

The term 'bicultural' is a useful way of observing the influence of religion, trade and empire on literacy practices, and acknowledging that an older practice is rarely completely replaced by a new one. More often, older and newer practices merge. The Christian conversion of the northern European Germanic tribes was both a process of violent empire building and genuine cultural mixing: a meeting of Mediterranean Christianity (with its established tradition of written texts) and 'Paganism' with a strong oral poetic tradition. Caedmon, as described by Bede in the eight century, was a legendary Anglo-Saxon Christian warrior poet who fell asleep and had a dream in which he was told that he must sing of God's work. He immediately recited a poem in Old English that he had never heard before. The poem was a perfect example of the conventions of metre and alliteration of the Old English oral poetic tradition and, at the same time, an orthodox example of Christian theology. In the morning, when Caedmon awoke, he spoke of this dream in the monastery and recited his poem, 'Caedmon's Hymn'. It was agreed that Caedmon's dream was the product of divine inspiration. His poem was written down (in the Roman alphabet) and frequently recited to preserve this symbolic meeting of cultures (Howe, 1993). Invasion, religious conversion and political and economic-empire-building continue to influence what, how and why we read and write.

Invention and the Shifting Physicality of Reading

Leaving aside languages and writing systems, what – *physically* – were people reading in different historical periods? How did we position our bodies to read? What props did we use, and where did we read? How did we get from cave paintings to iPhones?.

The objects

The first writing was probably done in cuneiform on clay tablets in the fourth millennium BC (Coulmas, 2003), and for the next four thousand years we read from stone or clay tablets, walls of buildings and statues, engraved pieces of wood, papyrus scrolls and pieces of animal skin. The sixth-century (BC) Chinese read from *jiances* or *jiandus*, delicate rolls of bamboo or wood which were written on with a brush and ink, and were linked together with cord (Edgren, 2009). The Ancient Egyptian *Book of the Dead* is an anthology, pieces of which were first written on (and read from) the walls of tombs and sides of coffins, and later rewritten on papyrus for a larger, living audience to read (Roemer, 2009). Ancient Greek, Roman and Jewish texts were predominantly written on papyrus scrolls (*volumen*), while wooden or wax tablets (*tabulae*) were used for practising writing or taking notes (Brown, 2009). Reading from *tabulae* may have been part of an individual study or work process, while reading from *volumen* was a strenuous, physical, social process of performance, as the reader held each end of the scroll in an outstretched hand, declaiming to his audience (Cavallo, 1999).

The codex (the arrangement of bound sheets we now call a book) was less common in the West until the Roman Empire became Christian and:

> Books were no longer a cheap alternative favoured by a persecuted underclass [Christians in pre-Christian Rome], but honoured receptacles of sacred texts within a powerful establishment religion (Brown, 2009, p. 179).

Yet, as associated as it was with early Christian persecution, it is important to note that the codex was never a form exclusive to Christianity. Early Islamic writings were also in codex form (Albin, 2009).

The pages of codex were initially made of *parchment* (sheep or goatskin) or *vellum* (calfskin). When, from 1100 onwards, thinner parchment and paper became common materials (Clanchy, 2009), the codex became increasingly popular because it offered several practical advantages. Both sides of a page could be written on (making it cheaper), and parchment and paper could be produced fairly easily (unlike papyrus). The codex format was also easier to store, distribute and use. This ease of use, allowing the reader a greater range of body positions while reading, seems particularly significant in the development of diverse reading practices: 'transformations in the book and transformations in reading practices necessarily went hand in hand' (Cavallo and Chartier, 1999, p. 15).

These early books, or bound manuscripts, were painstakingly copied by hand by professional scribes and varied in size according to use. In the monastery or university, large 'bench books', intended to rest stationary on a surface, dominated. For private study, smaller, portable volumes were more popular (Cavallo and Chartier, 1999). Even smaller volumes (about the size of a modern hardback) which could be read in the warmth of a bed were particularly popular in late medieval England (Taylor, 1996). In 1935, when the chairman of the publishing house Bodley Head was returning from a weekend in the country with Agatha Christie, he stood at Exeter train station worrying about his business surviving the Depression and wishing that he could buy something interesting to read on the train. He was struck by an idea: to sell 'quality' fiction at cheap prices at railway stations. Penguin paperbacks and the commonplace practice of reading on trains was born (Trubeck, 2010). This, like any legend, is exaggeration, as pocket-sized books and pamphlets had been around since the advent of the printing press, if not before. Yet it did mark a dramatic increase in paperback production, in the type of texts published in paperback and in the sheer numbers of books read 'on the go'.

Kindles, iPads, smartphones, laptop screens and other electronic reading devices are probably even more revolutionary in terms of shifting the physical experience of reading, though it is still too early to say exactly how they have done this, and to what extent. Some (a laptop screen for example) combine the scrolling movement of the *volumen* with the portrait orientation of a codex page; others deliberately mimic the page-turning motion of a codex (including its difficulties), though electronic scrolling seems to offer significant advantages without its ancient disadvantages of bulk and weight. Many electronic reading devices also hold the potential to realise (or perhaps merely tempt) two long-standing reader fantasies: to be able to annotate and therefore take control of a text (so that the reader annotations and the original text are indistinguishable), and to have access to a universal library – all the texts one could ever desire within reach (Cavallo and Chartier, 1999). The possibility of accessing an almost unlimited number of texts means that one can be reading a particular text, see a reference to another, and switch to reading that text within seconds, without needing to get up, move around a library or make a note to search out that text elsewhere. We can explore a wealth of texts from one physical location, and even one body position.

Yet we certainly do not *only* read from screens now – or from books – but also from buildings, items of clothing, Zeppelins, the sides of trains and buses, one another's bodies (see Peter Greenaway's *The Pillow Book* [1996]), the walls of our homes and from billboards – Banana Yoshimoto first published her story *Newlywed* on a series of billboards on the walls of the Tokyo Underground (Figes, 1996). We read standing up, sitting down, leaning on walls, lying on the floor, at tables, on tables and under tables (Petrucci, 1999). The physical nature of the texts we read continues to determine how we position our bodies, and how, when and where we read.

The props

Other props affect how we use our bodies when we read. The 'reading wheel' was the pride of Renaissance inventors. A large mechanized wheel consisting of a series of gears, it allowed readers to keep ten or twelve books open and within reach at one time (Cavallo and Chartier, 1999, p. 29). Reading glasses were a much more significant invention, possibly dating from thirteenth-century Italy. They became a relatively common sight (though still not common or easy to own) in most parts of Europe by the fifteenth century (Clanchy, 2009). Their popularity lay in how they extended the 'reading span' of most readers: where previously deteriorating eyesight would have meant the end of someone's reading career, reading glasses allowed them to read on into old age. This remains true today, yet glasses are still not affordable for many people around the world. This means that even if someone knows how to read, they may be able to read only for a certain number of years and/or in certain light.

Reading also requires a light source, and so reading practices have depended – and still depend – a great deal on the light available. Being 'able to read' is therefore determined by whether one has leisure time when the sun is up (many did not and do not), on the presence or absence of windows (particularly at times of window tax [Watt, 2000]), and on the availability and affordability of candles, lamps and fuel. For these reasons alone, reading was (and is) easier for those with more money, more leisure time or for those people whose working situations include time and space to read. Watt (2000) and Fergus (1996) both note that servants made up one of the largest working-class reading groups in eighteenth-century Britain precisely because their workplaces provided light and books.

Printing

Many see our recent digital revolution as comparable to the revolution of movable type, the fifteenth-century technology which allowed for Guten-berg's printing press. Very simply, the printing press meant that books and pamphlets were produced more cheaply and in far greater numbers. A key example of the impact of the printing press is the large-scale printing and distribution of Martin Luther's pamphlets, so crucial to the Reformation

(Shaw, 2009). Printing altered reading practices by dramatically altering the ratio of texts to people: more texts allowed for more readers. (Yet printing was not the only influence on the ratio of books and people. Hamesse [1999] argues that the Black Death of the fourteenth century had a profound influence on reading practices: many people died throughout Europe, particularly the scholars gathered in cities, leaving more books for fewer people. This brought books and other printed materials closer to the lives of a greater proportion of the population).

In England in the 1630s, six thousand books were published; in the 1710s, twenty-one thousand; in the 1740s fifty-six thousand; and by the 1870s, three hundred and twenty-five thousand (Raven, 1996). The market for books and other printed matter increased dramatically in eighteenth-century Britain for three reasons: a sharp rise in population (which 'outpaced the death rate'); an increase in income across society, but particularly among the wealthy; and increased literacy levels across all social groups (Feather, 2009, p. 237). More texts had produced more readers, and more readers meant a need for even more texts.

Printing and the book trade quickly became symbols of national identity. This was particularly important in the 'New World'. In 1539, a press was established in Mexico City, the first in the Americas. Between 1638 and 1639 a press was established in Cambridge, Massachusetts, with Pennsylvania following in 1685 and New York in 1693. By the time of the American Revolution, the Colonial Presses were in full force and playing a significant role in the Revolution by producing patriot propaganda and 'official proclamations' (Martin III, 2009, p. 265). As with Luther's Reformation, even without the printing press, the American Revolution would most probably still have happened, but it would undoubtedly have been different.

Libraries

Increased book production did not mean that books were no longer expensive – they were. And because they were so expensive, a London bookseller, Francis Kirkman, in 1661 opened London's first 'circulating library', allowing customers to borrow books for a fee (Feather, 2009). Other booksellers followed, leading to a 'lending library' revolution. There were twenty lending libraries in London in 1760, but fifteen hundred by 1821 (Raven, 1996). These were generally small, privately-run libraries, but the eighteenth century also saw the birth of large city libraries: the Berlin public library in 1704, Philadelphia in 1731, Liverpool in 1758, the Royal Library in Paris in 1785 and York, Upper Canada in 1810 (Draper, 1989; Houston, 2002;

Raven, 1996). Additionally, throughout Europe and North America, the wealthy created libraries in their homes, displays of 'comfort, civilisation and choice taste'(Raven, 1996, p. 188).

Libraries were not new, of course; they had also been displays of power in the ancient world. 'They were manifestations of the greatness of the ruling dynasty ... [texts] were accumulated rather than actually read' (Cavallo and Chartier, 1999, p. 10). The early Christian era saw libraries in monasteries, as places where manuscripts were copied, maintained and read as part of religious worship, but, just as in the ancient world, removed from the population at large. The Scholastic age (from the twelfth and thirteenth centuries) brought libraries into universities, where texts were read in order for other texts to be written, for teaching, for knowledge to be 'generated' and discoveries made (Hamesse, 1999). University libraries, however, were still closed to the vast majority of the population. The eighteenth-century lending libraries were notable – revolutionary even – for being open to the public, or at least to those members of the public who could pay their fees.

Our present-day idea of libraries seems to include aspects of each of these models, perhaps because our libraries still represent this range: royal libraries, national libraries, religious libraries, university libraries, and the smaller, local libraries (council libraries, school libraries, postal libraries). We even have mobile libraries – from small vans to 'Biblioburros', rural mobile libraries on the backs of donkeys, a 1990 initiative of the Columbian Ministry of Culture (Manguel, 1996). For some libraries we need special membership, from others we are barred. Some we need to be searched to enter, some cry out for us to use them, and, no doubt, some are so secret that we do not even know they exist or what they could possibly contain.

Library buildings themselves, not merely the books within, have been seen as magical; or rather the buildings are magical in that they represent and magnify the ideas and ideals within their books. In the eighteenth century, library shelving represented the earthly and the tall library windows represented the heavenly, with the busts of great writers (and their embodiments as books) the in-between, the demigods (Raven, 1996). It seemed impossible for the very structure of a library – the bricks and glass – not to represent the ideals of its texts. Similarly, today the building of national libraries takes on a supreme importance in the public imagination: from the controversy about the (relatively) new British Library and its superhuman Newton sculpted by Paolozzi to the prestigious design competition for the rebuilding of the Library of Alexandria in Egypt in the 1980s (Manguel, 2006).

In the early twenty-first century Anglophone worlds, libraries hold a unique cultural status, managing to be both representations of the comically mundane and the powerfully mythical. Radway (1994) links the myth that reading is a primarily solitary activity with the cultural construction of the spinster librarian as a figure of fun – and pity. Yet Manguel has written an entire book about the heroic nature of libraries – *The Library at Night* (2006) – featuring chapters on 'The Library as Myth,' 'The Library as Identity,' and 'The Library as Home'. An even greater statement on libraries comes from Umberto Eco's *The Name of the Rose* (1983): a historical mystery, a religious analysis and a study of the meanings, fears and horrors libraries can hold. The Japanese novelist Haruki Murakami has set at least two of his novels in libraries. The protagonist narrator of *Hard-boiled Wonderland and the End of the World* (1993) uses the town library as his only place to go, as (quite literally) the location of memories and dreams, and as a role in life, a legitimacy. In *Kafka on the Shore* (2005) the young runaway Kafka finds similar refuge in a library, this time at the Komura Memorial Library, a library so comfortable and elegant that 'the whole place makes me feel as though I'm in some friend's house' (p. 39), or rather, with the ever-friendly Oshima at the desk and the beautiful older woman Miss Saeki in command, an old and recurring dream. If libraries for Eco are Bluebeard's lair, then libraries for Murakami are the dreams within Hitchcock's dreams.

Reading and Writing

Busy within these libraries, we read because we write, and we write because we read. Reading and writing are two sides of the same coin. Or are they? Raven, Small and Tadmore (1999) begin their anthology *The Practice and Representation of Reading in England* by stressing the importance of distinguishing between the two:

> If we discard assumptions of a simple overlap between reading and writing, we have to rethink fundamentally the means by which we appraise the history of reading (p. 9).

We must, they argue, discard these assumptions and reappraise the history of reading. Likewise, in her study *Literacy in American Lives,* Brandt (2001) emphasizes the separation between reading and writing. The nineteenth century, she argues, was only the 'century of mass literacy' if we see literacy as reading; the twentieth century was the century of mass literacy in terms of writing.

This distinction is not new; what *is* new is the assumption that reading and writing are twinned. The Romans and colonial North Americans were both very clear that reading and writing were distinct skills and activities, required by different groups of people, acquired separately and taught differently. The Romans felt writing was the primary skill, more important because it allows the recording of the spoken word. Boys were first taught to write and then later, if deemed necessary, they would be taught to read (Cavallo, 1999). The Puritans were equally convinced of this distinction, but felt reading was the primary and more basic skill. Everyone had to be able to read in order to read the Bible as part of Puritan religious worship. All children were therefore taught to read; only a smaller elite, usually boys, were taught to write. The teaching was also separate. Teaching reading was seen as an important, though not specialist, activity. It was taught by parents or widows in 'dame schools' and homes. Teaching writing, however, required specialist expertise. It was taught by male teachers and in school buildings (Monaghan, 1989, 2005). Similarly, in much of Europe during the early modern period, both boys and girls were taught to read, but only boys – and even then, only those belonging to certain social groups – were taught to write (Houston, 2002).

Reading and writing have also been presented as opposing pairs in at least three dichotomies of the cultural imagination: passive versus active, conformist versus subversive and divine versus earthly. A newspaper article, arguing for a wider recognition of what 'counts' as literary, is introduced with the subtitle 'Reading is passive. Writing is where the action is' (Howard, 2006). In the article itself, Howard makes an implicit argument for reading feeding into writing, but the provocative subtitle conjures up a clear opposition: reading is passive and writing is active. This opposition also appears in language teaching terminology, which often labels reading and listening as the 'passive' skills, and writing and speaking as the 'active'. This certainly relates to a particular, specialist use of the terms 'passive' and 'active' in language learning, a use arguably distinct from the common meanings and connotations of these terms. However, it is also undeniable that the labelling of reading as passive carries echoes of the lay definition: lacking in agency, inert, submissive.

The active-passive dichotomy is a reformation of another dichotomy: while writing is potentially subversive (because it is active, creative, productive, etc.), reading is, by nature, conformist. We read what is on the page, what we have been told to read. Remembering the Puritan focus, reading allows us to receive the word of God, just as the moral lessons embedded within Victorian Canadian reading primers (Graff, 1979) help us to read our way to being obedient members of society. This in turn relates to another dichotomy: reading is divine while writing is earthly (Brandt, 2001).

There are many communities around the world where reading is performed predominantly for religious reasons, in one language and possibly script, while most writing, often concerned with life administration, is done in another language and sometimes script. Maddox (2001) provides the example of north-west Bangladesh, where Bangla 'is the dominant literacy in terms of political and economic life' (p. 139) and Arabic the language of prayer and reading the Qur'an. Reading performed for religious reasons is itself diverse, including reading and listening to holy books and prayers, but also reading funeral cards, such as those of the Nafaanras of north-west Ghana (Herbert and Robinson, 2001), and marriage announcements (Gebre et al., 2009; Ghose, 2007). Of course, in each of these communities people do read for 'earthly' or civil reasons, but the core idea of 'reading' is bound up with reading longer narratives, and for many communities this means religious texts.

There are numerous other examples of reading for religious purposes, often in the same language and scripts as are used for 'earthly' life: for example, people read newsletters from their religious communities (Tusting, 2000). Perhaps the most fascinating example, though, is the 'burden box', a literacy practice of an American Protestant church. If a member of the church has a grave worry, they write it down on a small piece of paper, read it themselves and then deposit it in a box where no one else, apart from God,will ever read it (Brandt, 2001). Though individuals have to write their worries before they can be read, it is the personal reading of the worry, combined with handing it over to God, which is key.

Seeing reading and writing as separate practices serving different life functions can therefore be valuable, allowing us to get closer to thinking about the purposes behind the practices. Could examining how reading and writing are undeniably linked be equally fruitful? The most obvious way in which reading and writing are united is as two sides of one process of written communication. When asked what reading is, many adult literacy learners emphasized this communicative aspect of reading:

'I'm reading something someone else has wrote.'
'It's like speaking, but because I can't be with that person. It is like us speaking but now it is in reading and writing.'

Reading and writing are firmly linked, therefore, as communication. They are also linked by inspiration. Reading someone else's words, whether the words of someone known or unknown, can inspire writing. One of the members of the main research case-study discussed how reading a novel made her want to write a book of her own:

> When I read it's interesting, so I'm interested and I say like ok I can write my story and somebody can read it, so it's interesting for them. It's an interesting life story, the place I was born, the fighting that happened, the war, when I came here. Things like that.

Brandt's participant Martha Day agrees that reading can inspire writing. Talking of why she was drawn to write in her high-school days, she explains: 'I got the feeling of emotions coming through words on paper ... I think reading makes people want to write'(Brandt, 2001, p. 32). Similarly, the novelist Philip Roth explains how reading is part of his workday writing routine:

> I read all the time when I'm working [writing], usually at night. It's a way of keeping the circuits open. It's a way of thinking about my line of work while getting a little rest from the work at hand. It helps inasmuch as it fuels the overall obsession (Editors of the *Paris Review*, 1984).

Reading and writing are separate practices and yet are joined as communication and inspiration; reading can inspire writing, as writing inspires readers.

Reading Aloud and Reading Silently

Between 2005 and 2009, I spoke to around a hundred different adult literacy learners about what reading is or involves for them. Every single person discussed reading silently *and* reading aloud. They identified reading aloud as both a specific type of reading, performed for a particular reason (for example, reading to children) and as a *method* of improving their reading (for example, listening to others reading aloud to gain confidence in decoding). Yet, most used the word 'reading' to signify reading silently and 'reading aloud' to specify non-silent reading. The status of reading aloud therefore presents a paradox. Reading aloud is a common practice and yet, for these learners, as for many of us today, it is the marked form, the unusual form, the form that needs specifying. The unmarked – the 'normal' – is silent reading.

According to many scholars, this has only recently been the case. Pugh argues:

> Silent reading was not a common activity in schools or elsewhere before the middle of the nineteenth century. It was almost unknown to the scholars of the classical and medieval worlds (1978, p. 12).

Others support this idea of a shift in reading practices over time. Parkes stresses that 'in antiquity the emphasis had been on oral delivery of a text' (1999, p. 92). Manguel (1996) writes of Augustine's shock at finding Ambrose engaged in such a strange activity as silent reading and argues that until the late Middle Ages all writers assumed that their texts would be read aloud. Taylor agrees, though pushes back the timeline, writing that silent reading only 'became common among clerics in the twelfth century and gradually spread to the laity' (1996, p. 43). Importantly, however, Cavallo and Chartier (1999) point out that people did in fact read silently in the ancient world, just as people do read aloud today. In other words, over time there has been a shift in which form is more common, but reading aloud and reading silently have always coexisted.

Pugh goes on to offer an explanation for the rise to dominance of reading aloud: 'as the number of readers increased so there was a relative decrease in the number of potential listeners for a text read aloud' (1978, p. 12). While useful in highlighting the relationship between increased literacy levels and increased silent reading, this explanation makes three questionable assumptions: it assumes that reading is only about gathering information or understanding a narrative (a narrow definition of reading); it assumes that this gaining of information is always more important than saying or hearing words; and it assumes that if you can read, you have no need or desire to be read to. Pugh's explanation also ignores the intermediate form (or forms) of 'reading in a low voice' or 'murmured reading' (Hamesse, 1999, p. 104).

In order to examine these assumptions, I would like to look at how, why and what people read aloud, and then how, why and what people read silently. I am dividing reading aloud into four groups of practices: reading aloud as performance, reading aloud to those who *cannot* read, reading aloud to those who *can* read, and reading aloud to oneself.

Reading aloud as performance

When asked to draw a picture summing up what reading is to her, One adult literacy learner drew this (figure 2).

She explained that this is a picture of her, reading aloud to an audience. Words are flowing from her mouth to the audience. Reading, for this woman, as for many others, is a performance. Reading as performance is about more than imparting information orally; rather, the act of reading, the use of voice and body, provides an experience in itself. This is the essence of performance. In Ancient Greek, Roman and Ancient Jewish cultures reading as performance was common (Boyarin, 1993; Cavallo and Chartier, 1999; Svenbro, 1999), as it was in eighteenth-century coffee houses, where jostling audiences waited to hear the latest novel or political scandal read in a theatrical manner (Altick, 1957).

An excellent example of reading as performance is provided by Charles Dickens's world-famous reading tours. Dickens toured England, Scotland, Ireland, the United States and France, giving more than four hundred public readings of his novels to packed and often raucous audiences, acting the part of each of his characters and almost giving himself a heart attack doing the Bill Sikes and Nancy murder scene in *Oliver Twist* (Small, 1996). Following this lead, the English Department of the University of Edinburgh read aloud the entire text of *Paradise Lost* to an audience of students and staff over approximately twelve hours in the mid-1990s. The enduring popularity of reading aloud as performance is further evident in the popularity of

Figure 2   An image of reading.

books read on the radio, audio books spoken by famous actors and readings given by writers to their fans in bookshops across the globe. The vast majority of audience members for each of these examples are people who can and do read themselves, but who have chosen to experience someone else performing a text.

Reading aloud to those who *cannot* read

People also read aloud as a service to help those who cannot read, whether for cognitive, physical or circumstantial reasons. In the eighteenth century it was common throughout Europe for those who had never learnt to read to pay a small fee to have news or letters read to them in public squares (Houston, 2002). This service is immortalized by Isabel Allende's fictional heroine Belisa Crepusculario, a woman 'born into a family so poor they did not even have names to give their children'. Faced with a choice between prostitution, servitude and starvation, Belisa happened upon a sheet of newspaper crumpled on the ground. Upon being told that 'the fly tracks scattered across the page' were words and that 'words make their way in the world without a master', she pays a priest to teach her how to read and write, and thereafter makes her living 'selling words': reading and writing letters and speeches for those who cannot read and write (Allende, 1996). This service is still offered in public spaces around the world, and performed in private by children reading for their parents, parents for children, friends for friends.

However, not being able to read does not necessarily mean that someone does not know how to read, or has never been able to read. When I was a student, I had a job reading post and newspaper articles to a blind professor. He had been able to read for most of his life until becoming blind in his seventies. Many people read to blind friends, colleagues or relatives. For instance, an elderly South African was motivated to learn to read herself so that she could read to her blind husband every evening (McKay, 2007); and a newly blind member of a British reading circle asked a friend to record their reading of books on to a tape for her so that she could continue this important aspect of her life (Hartley, 2002). Further, not being able to read is often temporary or circumstantial. We read to others in churches and restaurants when they have forgotten or lost their glasses. We read to those who cannot read at a particular time because they are busy working: for example, the enduring Cuban cigar factory 'lector' tradition, where a reader is employed to read (usually novels and newspapers) to rows of employees whose hands are busy rolling cigars (Tinajero, 2010).

Reading aloud to those who *can* read

We also read to those who can read but would simply like someone to read to them. In late medieval England there was a rage for 'chamber reading', where intimate groups would gather in bedchambers to listen to one person read aloud, everyone huddling around the book to see the illustrations (Taylor, 1996). The 'intimacy' of this arrangement comes from the sound of the voice, the feel of the book, the small group, the candlelight and the chamber location. The reading routines of Samuel Richardson's family represent another form of reading-aloud-intimacy. Mrs. Richardson read the Psalms to the family in the morning and, after a day of exertions, in the evening the family gathered to read sermons to one another as they worked (Tadmore, 1996). Finally, Boyarin (1993) analyses another type of reading intimacy, in the form of the erotic tête-à-tête reading scene of Paolo and Francesca in Dante's Inferno (Canto V), where the couple read of Lancelot, kiss and then read no more.

In London and New York professional readers can be hired to read aloud to guests in hotels (Barr, 2009), and anecdotal evidence suggests husbands read to wives, wives to husbands, partners to partners, friends to friends. A Somali woman explained to me that she cannot understand poetry (in any language) when she reads it herself, but she can when her husband reads it to her. When he reads and she listens, she explained, all meanings become clear.

Reading aloud to ourselves

What is probably most often forgotten, though, is the amount of reading aloud we do to ourselves. Monks read aloud to themselves to aid their copying work in medieval scriptoriums, but from the early modern period onwards, the assumed norm for individual, private reading has been silence. Yet this assumption demands to be questioned. Many people read dense or complicated text (such as academic writing or flatpack furniture instructions) aloud to aid understanding. An adult literacy learner explained to me that she prefers to read aloud when she is alone because 'it helps you when you try to position your mouth to how the letters are written'. She was describing an incredibly common, if rarely talked about, phenomenon. People often read aloud to *hear* the sounds of words, when reading difficult text, practising another language, or reading poetry and heartfelt letters.

The above represents a small selection of the many possible practices involving reading aloud. Few of these are simply about transferring written information to those who cannot get this information in any other way.

They are to do with performance, the intimacy of sharing words and the pleasures of the ear. In her introduction to *The Best American Short Stories 1989*, Margaret Atwood explores the idea of how she could possibly judge the worth of a short story, to 'tell the best from the merely better' (Atwood, 1989, p. 69). In doing so, she discusses the importance of the *sound* of a short story: 'I'm not arguing for the abolition of the eye, merely for the reinstatement of the voice, and for an appreciation of the way it carries the listener along with it' (p. 71).

Silent reading

The unmarked form of reading in the present-day Anglophone world is undoubtedly silent reading. How long this has been the case is hard to say: scholars' answers vary from the medieval period to Pugh's nineteenth century. However, whether by many or few, silent reading has been done for as long as people have been reading at all. The reasons why silent reading became dominant are difficult to pinpoint. Silent reading has been linked to the desire to skip around in a text to find specific pieces of information, rather than reading word for word from beginning to end as is more common when reading aloud. This fits with claims that gaps between words, punctuation marks, paragraph divisions and section headings were all introduced to facilitate silent reading; silent reading allows the reader to navigate texts for study purposes more easily (Clanchy, 2009; Manguel, 1996; Petrucci, 1999). Another argument stresses that reading silently not only prevents the reader from disturbing neighbours with his or her reading, but also keeps what he or she is reading secret, undisclosed to those around. The silent reader can read in privacy. We read silently when completely alone to alleviate our loneliness, and yet we also read silently when in very large groups or busy places (such as crowded public transport or argument-filled homes) in order to be alone when we are not really alone. Reading silently can bring an aloneness, a profound privacy, in the company of seen and unseen others. Finally, approaching the idea of privacy from another angle, Saint Isaac of Syria argued in the sixth century that it is simply easier to concentrate on what you are reading when you are reading silently (Manguel, 1996).

These may all be reasons to read silently: to concentrate, to study, to skip around and for privacy. Yet there is another, more common type and purpose of silent reading. We read silently to deal with all the texts that come at us in twenty-first century life: shop signs, adverts, road signs, posters, transport information. We read most of this silently, often without registering that we have read it. We may sometimes choose to read bits aloud ('"The Dog and Duck", I didn't know that was still open'), but only after having read a great deal more silently and then choosing what we want to share aloud. Imagine if we could *only* read aloud, and were still drawn to reading all the text that comes our way. For those of us living in town and cities, it would take hours to get to work, and we would arrive with a sore throat.

With silent reading potentially offering so many practical advantages – speed, ease, filtering, concentration, private spaces, secrecy – it would be tempting to return to Pugh's idea and conclude that we read silently simply because we *can*, that reading aloud was merely a stage in our individual and societal development of silent reading competence. But what of the pleasures of sound, sharing and community? What, Margaret Atwood must be gasping, of the ear?

Reading, Civil Rights and Illiteracy

Learning how to read, as the next chapter will describe, was the basis for acquiring socially sanctioned moral behaviour, religious or otherwise. Yet, as much as reading has been linked to morality, reading has never been seen as an intrinsically moral act. Indeed, certain texts have been labelled as most definitely immoral. From the early Christian censorship of 'pagan' (classical and Muslim) texts to Henry Miller's *Tropic of Cancer*, the most common reason for text censorship is the claim of immorality. Further, a moral spotlight on reading identifies not only inappropriate texts, but also inappropriate readers. Early modern scholars feared what teaching the poor to read could unleash (Houston, 2002). For similar reasons, there was a ban on teaching a slave or freed Black person to read in the United States before (and at a certain stage after) the Civil War (Salvino, 1989). In the face of this ban, Black Americans risked their lives to read. Conversely, young Native American high-school students on reservations have refused to read English in order to fight the imposition of Anglo-Saxon American culture (Sarris, 1993). Reading practices have been encouraged, enforced and banned by states and individuals for moral reasons, making reading a practice of social conformity or resistance as well as a choice, need or desire.

If, over the past five hundred years, the discourse linking reading and religion has been replaced with (or, in some contexts, joined by) a discourse linking reading and morality, then over the past hundred years this may well have been replaced with a discourse linking reading with democratic participation. Being able to read, the twentieth century proclaimed, means being able to participate in the democratic process. Reading, importantly, became a citizen's right. It became, as Brandt (2001) stresses, the responsibility of a democracy to equip its citizens with the tools for participation – chief among these was learning to read. This discourse provided a powerful argument for governments to supply the means for both adults and children to learn to read. It also, however, contributed to rising expectations of literacy and put in motion a dangerous slide, from literacy as every citizen's democratic right to literacy as an obligation, and illiteracy as a form of social irresponsibility (Brandt, 2001) – or even criminality.

Freire remembers talking with a Brazilian peasant about the difference between two hunters, an 'Indian' and a peasant:

> 'Between these two hunters,' he asserted, 'only the second can be illiterate. The first is not.' 'Why?' I asked him. [...] He answered, 'One cannot say that the Indian is illiterate because he lives in a culture that does not recognize letters. To be illiterate you need to live where there are letters and you don't know them' (Freire, 1985, p. 4).

The label of illiteracy comes with a literate society, and as expectations of literacy rise, so does the stigma of the 'illiterate'. The cycle of increased expectations wrongly assumes that if you teach everyone to read, then everyone will learn to read. It makes a deficit of those for whom reading does not come easily. Rising expectations of literacy can also become, as Brandt (2001) warns, a way to divide the population: the literate get more literate as the rich get richer. The role of reading in adult life has never been less than supremely political.

Chapter Summary

We have read from stone, wood, animal skin, our own skin and paper. Our languages, writing systems, textual artefacts, text types and associated reading practices have been passed around the globe with the best and worst products of the human imagination: stories, war, trade, dreams, religion and ideology. Our reading practices have been influenced by invention: paper, reading glasses, the printing press and libraries, inspiring and inspired by writing practices. We have read aloud and silently, alone and in groups, enacting and creating shifting notions of public and private. Our reading has been linked to our rights and obligations as members of religious communities and as national citizens, and our reading has reaped reward, punishment and judgement. The crucial point is that we read for different reasons and in different ways. This is the background against which we need to understand the development of reading pedagogies in the next chapter, as well as this book's wider examination of reading development, adult education and reading circles.

Suggested Reading

Allende, I. (1996), 'Two words' (M. Sayers Peden, trans.). In K. Figes (ed.), *The Penguin Book of International Women's Stories* (pp. 212–219). London: Penguin.
Allende's short story about literacy, illiteracy, love and selling words.

Brandt, D. (2001), *Literacy in American Lives*. Cambridge: Cambridge University Press.
Insightful and influential study of the role of reading and writing in American lives between 1895 and 1985.

Cavallo, G., & Chartier, R. (eds) (1999), *A History of Reading in the West*. (L. Cochrane, trans.). Cambridge: Polity.
As the title suggests, this is a detailed and wide-reaching collection of articles on the history of reading.

Davidson, C. N. (ed.) (1989), *Reading in America: Literature and Social History*. Baltimore, ML: The Johns Hopkins University Press.
A diverse collection of articles on literacy and literature in the United States, includes E. Jennifer Monaghan on colonial literacy instruction, Dana Nelson Salvino on race and literacy and Barbara Sicherman on what reading meant to late Victorian American women.

Eliot, S., & Rose, J. (eds) (2009), *A Companion to the History of the Book*. Oxford: Wiley-Blackwell.
Like Cavallo & Chartier above, a thorough reader of 'the history of the book': forty articles covering all corners of the ancient and modern worlds.

Gebre, A. H., Rogers, A., Street, B., & Openjuru, G. (2009), *Everyday Literacies in Africa: Ethnographic Studies in Literacy and Numeracy Practices in Ethiopia*. Kampala, Uganda: Fountain Publishing.
This ethnographic study examines present-day literacy and numeracy practices in Ethiopia and what these mean for the teaching of literacy and numeracy.

Graff, H. J. (1979), *The Literacy Myth: Literacy and Social Structure in the Nineteenth-Century City*. New York City, NY: Academic Press.
Graff's study of literacy practices, expectations and teaching in the new nineteenth-century cities of Canada and the United States includes a comparison of the literacies of various immigrant populations.

Manguel, A. (1996), *A History of Reading*. New York, NY: Viking.
Manguel's history of reading should be read cover-to-cover by every literacy teacher.

Chapter 3

How We Learnt to Read

The previous chapters have unearthed many assumptions we have to be wary of making: that only those who could write could read (or those who could read could write), that participating in a literate culture always means being able to read (rather than being read to), or even that there is a common understanding of what 'reading' or 'knowing how to read' means. There is also a danger of making assumptions about the relationship between what we do now and what was done in the past, of assuming that we have a clear understanding of past practices and pedagogies, or that our present dilemmas and debates are startlingly original and very different from those of the past. For this reason I feel it is important, particularly for literacy teachers, to go back and try to find out how things were done.

Historical studies often present a different assumption: that those learning to read are children. It is unclear whether this means that only children learnt to read (unlikely) or that the teaching of children was simply more documented than the teaching of adults, as it is today. The aim of this chapter is to trace how adults have learnt and been taught to read from the Roman and medieval worlds to the late twentieth-century Anglophone adult literacy campaigns. Yet, for the reason indicated above, this will include work on how children, as well as adults, have learnt and been taught to read.

A Historical Overview

The history of how people have been taught to read in Western Europe is surprisingly familiar. In Ancient Greek and Roman times the 'alphabetic', or 'ABC' method (later called the 'old Roman' or 'Latin' method) dominated: those learning to read were first taught the *names* of the letters of the alphabet and then taught to *say the names* of the letters of each word before 'reading' the word itself ('cee ay tee is cat'). Learners were also taught to chant how letters combined into syllables ('cee ay is ca', 'bee ay is ba', etc.), syllables into words and words into sentences (Huey, 1908/1968; Manguel, 1996). Three things strike me about this approach. First of all, it builds from letters to syllables in a way that indicates a relatively straightforward relationship between phonemes and graphemes (a shallow orthography). This seems to have been the case with the writing systems of Ancient Greece and Rome. Second, it demonstrates an emphasis on chanting and memorization, in keeping with the oral tradition of both cultures (Cavallo and Chartier, 1999; Houston, 2002). Finally, remembering our present-day reading wars, this method is actually a *type* of phonic approach, one based not on identifying individual phonemes, but rather on building syllables into words.

Today, phonics (the explicit teaching of phoneme-grapheme correspondence) is often classified in three ways: synthetic, analytic and onset-rime. *Synthetic phonics* usually refers to approaches that build up from individual phonemes, 'sounding out' words one phoneme at a time (cccccc, aaaaaa, tttttt is cat). *Analytic phonics* usually refers to approaches where teachers look at groups of words of a similar pattern and use these words to analyse phoneme-grapheme relationships (cat, car, cab, can). *Onset-rime phonics* usually refers to breaking down words into their initial consonant sounds (the onset) and the rest of the syllable (the rime) to observe patterns of phoneme-grapheme correspondence (cat, bat, hat, mat, sat). Unfortunately, these terms are defined slightly differently in different publications, and the distinction between analytic phonics and onset-rime phonics is particularly problematic, as arguably onset-rime phonics is a sub-type of analytic phonics. More significantly, though, policies which make so much of the distinction seem to be forgetting that in reality, in any one classroom, it would be very difficult to use one approach and not the other three; the logic of good teaching would mean that all three approaches are constantly blended. However, using these terms, the Roman and Greek alphabetic approach, with its syllabic step, could be seen as a form of analytic phonics because it involves looking at patterns of sounds in syllables and how these are realized in words. This contradicts a present-day English assumption that synthetic phonics is the more 'traditional' or 'old-fashioned' form and analytic phonics is a modern aberration (David Cameron, for example, spoke of 'good old-fashioned synthetic phonics' in the televised British pre-election debates of 2010).

There were various strategies for developing this letter-to-syllable-to-word process, including an Ancient Greek who bought twenty-four slaves, one to represent each letter of their alphabet, and instructed them to move into different combinations to teach his son to read (Huey, 1908/1968). The Athenian poet Callias wrote and performed the *Grammatical Play* or *Alphabet Show* around 500 BC. Twenty-four women representing the letters of the Greek alphabet were the chorus, and sang a syllabic chant ('Beta alpha ba, Beta epsilon be', etc..) (Svenbro, 1999, pp. 60–61). The Romans used ivory letter tiles to teach each letter of their alphabet and then combined these into syllables and then into words (Cavallo, 1999; Huey, 1908/1968).

The alphabetic method dominated European formal education until at least the fifteenth century (Altick, 1957), suggesting that after the fall of the Roman Empire it remained as the dominant method of teaching reading, regardless of whether Latin, or forms of Latin, continued to be used. In the British Isles, for example, after the Romans withdrew, the use of Latin fell into a sharp decline (Ostler, 2005). Celtic languages dominated instead. Yet the Celts began to use the Roman alphabet to write their own languages, as did the Anglo-Saxons on their conquest of southern/central England in the fifth century (Freeborn, 1998; Ostler, 2005), and may have maintained the use of the alphabetic method for teaching reading. However, Britain's and Ireland's conversion to Christianity (in the seventh and fifth centuries, respectively) may have simply reintroduced the alphabetic method of teaching reading along with its reintroduction of Latin as the language of Western Christianity (Clanchy, 1984).

In this early Christian period, reading instruction was for and by the Church. Reading was primarily taught by older monks to novice monks as part of their training. This meant that even in the British Isles, where Old English, Old Irish (a Celtic language) and other Celtic and Germanic languages were used by both the common people and the kings, the vast majority of the reading, and reading instruction, was done in and for Latin *by* men and *to* men or boys in monasteries (Clanchy, 1984, 2009). However, this may not be the full story. Brown (2009) argues that nuns and female lay-scribes played a significant role in British and Irish text production before 1100; it likely that these women were also involved in the teaching of reading. Brown further notes that the reading and writing done by and for the Church was not, in fact, all in Latin; Old English and Old Irish were also used, suggesting that some people were taught to read both Latin and Old English/Old Irish both within and outside of the monasteries.

From the eleventh to thirteenth centuries, it became more common for aristocratic children to learn to read, whether destined for the Church or not (Clanchy, 2009; Manguel, 1996). However, reading (in this Christian world) was still primarily an education in learning to pray and confess. From at least the fourteenth century primers were used to teach reading.

Primers were basic prayer books which started with the alphabet, followed by syllables, the Our Father, the Hail Mary and the Creed – the three key texts of medieval Christianity (Clanchy, 2009). Primers in both Latin and vernacular languages became the dominant resource of reading instruction throughout Western Europe.

Medieval Jewish society presented a similar integration of reading pedagogy and religious practice:

> On the Feast of Shavout, when Moses received the Torah from the hands of God, the boy about to be initiated was wrapped in a prayer shawl and taken by his father to the teacher. The teacher sat the boy on his lap and showed him a slate on which were written the Hebrew alphabet, a passage from the Scriptures and the words 'May the Torah be your occupation'. The teacher read out every word and the child repeated it. Then the slate was covered with honey and the child licked it, thereby bodily assimilating the holy words. (Manguel, 1996, p. 71)

This shares with the alphabetic method the starting-point of the alphabet and the end-point of reading holy words, as well as an emphasis on repetition and recitation. It is also similar to the medieval and early modern European 'gingerbread method' of learning the alphabet, where a child received the letters of the alphabet baked as individual pieces of gingerbread and was allowed to eat a letter only after it was 'learnt', usually for breakfast on study days. The 'gingerbread method' continued to be used in eighteenth-century Europe, leading one schoolmaster to declare 'it is not necessary for any child to eat the alphabet for more than three weeks' (Huey, 1908/1968, p. 241).

In England, from the fifteenth and sixteenth centuries, it became more common for children to be taught to read English in village schools, while 'song schools' taught choirboys to read Latin and 'classical schools' taught boys to read both Latin and Greek (Altick, 1957). Clanchy (1984) reports that by the fifteenth century about half of the British population could read (though it is unclear what 'knowing how to read' meant, and equally unclear whether this means half the male population, half the Christian population or half the entire population), most having been taught to read Latin the 'old Roman way' (the alphabetic method followed by chanting the Scriptures), and both Latin and English using primers or hornbooks (wooden boards containing the alphabet, syllables and the 'Our Father' prayer). There is evidence of a gender and social-class divide in educational provision, with increasing numbers of boys and some girls being taught to read

English, while wealthier boys were taught to read and write Latin, alongside a wider education which included mathematics (Houston, 2002).

Other factors influenced the teaching of reading in this early modern period (1500–1800): the Reformation not only made reading a more significant part of religious worship for the new Protestant populations, but both the Reformation and Counter-Reformation generated a renewed interest in the control and content of education for all Christian groups. Additionally, throughout Europe the power of the state was growing, which brought new levels of administrative jobs requiring a higher standard of literacy. This expanded what would now be called secondary and higher education, which in turn influenced primary schooling. At the other end of the educational spectrum, a sharp increase in the numbers of the rural and urban 'poor' in Europe produced a more divided society, particularly in urban areas. In the sixteenth century, 'poor hospitals' and 'work schools', including boarding houses for orphans or street children, were created to keep 'the poor' of all ages off the streets while providing an education in societal expectations. At the core of this education was being taught how to read, usually the vernacular, as part of both religious indoctrination and as training in practical work-skills. This aspect of educational provision as social containment increased with the Industrial Revolution (Houston, 2002).

The seventeenth century brought changes to how and where reading was taught in Europe. Calvinism and Puritanism emphasized reading as an essential part of religious worship, placing importance on personal Bible reading. This had a profound influence on the teaching of reading in many European countries. In Scotland, for example, John Knox's *Book of Discipline*, central to the Scottish Protestant Reformation, Stressed the importance of everyone being taught to read, and in 1616 the Scottish Parliament ruled that 'every parish was to have a school and a teacher whose salary was to be paid by the local landowners in rural areas, and by the town council in urban communities' (Houston, 2002, p. 44). Similarly, in the new Puritan communities of Colonial North America, reading was the basis for religious and social life. In 1642 Massachusetts passed a law stating that every child had to be taught to read; Connecticut followed in 1650 (Monaghan, 2005). As described in the previous chapter, such was the emphasis on reading as part of religious worship that in 1663 John Eliot and the Native American translators John Sassoman, Job Nesutan and James Printer produced a Bible in the Massachusett language (using the Roman alphabet) (Monaghan, 1989, 2005; Ostler, 2005; Wyss, 2000). This Bible was an instrument of conversion, and the precursor to numerous primers in the Massachusett language designed to teach Massachusett speakers to read English and Massachusett (both using the Roman alphabet) (Monaghan, 1989). However, despite this interest in converting Native Americans to Christianity, the laws on teaching children to read covered the White settlers only, not the indigenous or slave populations.

As in Ancient Rome, reading was taught separately from writing. However, in contrast to the Romans, for the Puritans reading came first, as the first of three consecutive steps in education: reading, writing and arithmetic. Most boys were expected to complete all three steps, while girls were required to learn to read and then to concentrate on sewing and other home-making crafts. There was a gender division in teaching as well: reading was an 'everyday' skill, ideally suiting women, and teaching could be done in the home. By contrast, writing was perceived as a specialist skill requiring a male teacher and a professional teaching location (a school rather than a home) (Monaghan, 1989).

The reading curriculum was imported from England: the hornbook, a primer, the Psalter [the psalms] and the Bible. Another common teaching resource, particularly popular in North America, was the 'spelling book', which provides evidence of the continued dominance of the alphabetic method. The spelling book was testament to the idea that 'spelling' was the key to learning to read: 'After mastering the letters of the alphabet, the novice reader's next task was to spell out, orally, syllables and words (broken into syllables) from the printed page' (Monaghan, 2005, p. 57). While primers presented the alphabet followed by syllables and prayers, spelling books featured lists of words of similar spelling patterns followed by (often bizarre) texts specially created to feature these words. In direct opposition to its present-day association with writing, 'spelling' was primarily associated with reading, with the oral 'spelling out' of words. This spelling book culture reveals itself in the oral 'spelling bees' still popular in the United States and Canada today, and, to a lesser extent, in Australia, New Zealand and India.

The seventeenth century also saw a breaking of the dominance of the alphabetic method, as 'whole-word' methods became popular. 'Orbis pictus' books of words and pictures were used to teach whole-word recognition in Nuremburg (Huey, 1908/1968) and soon the rest of Western Europe. The popularity of the whole-word trend was reinforced by Frenchman Nicolas Adam's influential eighteenth-century 'trustworthy method', calling for teachers to '"hide ... all the ABCs" and instead "entertain them with whole words which they can understand"' (Manguel, 1996, p. 79). In Colonial North America, horn-books and primers were joined by 'battledores' (fold-up cardboard pieces displaying letters, words and pictures), which were used to teach reading with both alphabetic and whole-word methods (Monaghan, 2005; Monaghan and Barry, 1999).

This period also brought an interest in (synthetic) phonic methods: teaching reading starting from individual phoneme-grapheme correspondences. From the eighteenth century onwards, therefore, three conventions dominated the teaching of reading in English: the alphabetic method, the whole-word method and the (synthetic) phonic method, with the phonic and whole-word methods becoming more popular as the alphabetic became less so (Huey, 1908/1968; Monaghan and Barry, 1999).

In the young United States a free – and reading-focused – public schooling system was developing at this time, though it excluded most of the Black and Native American populations (Sticht, 2002). Meanwhile, in the newer English-speaking colonies of Australia and New Zealand schools were set up for white settlers, largely following the English curriculum for the teaching of reading (which by now was a mixture of alphabetic, whole-word and phonic methods) combined with a 'scholastic' method involving reading summaries or commentaries of longer academic texts. In England, Mary Astell and Mary Wollstonecraft led a feminist movement questioning the circular thinking that argued women have inferior brains and therefore should receive less education. Educational opportunities (including literacy) for girls and women developed (Houston, 2002), despite grave fears that if girls learn to read too competently or confidently they may read unsuitable texts, and if they learnt to write they would write love letters to unsuitable men (Manguel, 1996).

In the United States the nineteenth century saw a move away from the overtly religious focus of reading instruction and towards secularity and debates on the importance of 'meaning' in teaching reading. Texts had to be meaningful (as primers became secular, prayers had been replaced by nonsense rhymes). By the end of the nineteenth century, a focus on sentence, story and the use of literature became popular (Monaghan and Barry, 1999). Throughout Europe, North America, Australia and New Zealand 'chapbooks', or cheap booklets containing fiction (a shorter precursor to pulp fiction), and political articles came into use for formal and informal reading instruction (Neuburg, 1989).

In Canada, amid the boom of the city populations in the nineteenth century, reading instruction consisted of 'lesson books' containing lists of words followed by a short text (similar to the American 'spelling books'). The choice of the words indicates a mixture of alphabetic and whole-word methods, and the texts were usually moral tales. The moral philosophy of

North American education at this time was clear: 'Proper education ... revolved around the nature of man, for man was a moral being ... Morality, therefore, formed the only safe basis for popular education' (Graff, 1979, p. 39). By the 1870s and 1890s, though, the emphasis in Canadian reading instruction, like American, was firmly on comprehension, and what an 1871 governmental report called 'intelligent reading': that is, reading aloud in a 'natural' manner which was taken to indicate comprehension (Graff, 1979, p. 288).

Contemporary educationalists quickly saw the error in judging comprehension from only the 'naturalness' of reading aloud, and so looked instead to silent reading, and a link between silent reading and comprehension. This new interest in silent reading was also the product of two movements: the silent reading of literature was becoming increasingly popular (in and out of educational contexts) and, at the same time, reading researchers were using experimental evidence to argue that children understand more of what they read when they read silently (Monaghan and Barry, 1999). In 1908, Huey influentially argued that silent reading is 'simpler' and 'faster' for most readers (Huey, 1908/1968, p. 120). Though Huey does not seem to have been arguing that beginner reading could be *taught* silently, the overall interest in silent reading, and arguments that it had previously been neglected in the teaching of reading, contributed to the final notable shift in reading pedagogy: the early twentieth-century American movement of initial silent reading instruction. Controversially, teachers tried to teach reading as a silent process from the beginning, sometimes using a series of written instructions which children had to read and act upon, thus demonstrating their understanding of the written code. In Britain, the spotlight on silent reading meant that teachers began to develop reading skills using individual silent reading followed by comprehension activities (Brooks, 1984; Pugh, 1978).

Learning to Read Formally and Informally

With the exception of the initial silent reading method, these methods – developed over hundreds, if not thousands, of years – continue to dominate debates on teaching reading today: use of story, use of sentences, synthetic and analytic phonic approaches and whole-word recognition, along with the corresponding discussions on the meaningfulness of texts and whether to start from the letter and work 'up' to the text, or from the text and work 'down' to the letter (Moss, 2005; Purcell-Gates, 1997). However, this is how reading was taught in relatively formal educational settings. It does not tell us about how reading was taught outside of these settings, how many people learnt as adults (as opposed to as children), or indeed how many people – children or adults – taught themselves.

The dominant images of 'learning to read' in Anglo-Saxon culture are probably the iconic images of St Anne instructing the Virgin (her daughter) to read, and the Virgin and Child absorbed in a prayer book. These images represent the medieval importance of reading instruction by mothers as part of Christian religious practice (Clanchy, 1984). They suggest that at least some women could read, while the medieval focus of formal education around training for the (male only) clergy indicates that it is unlikely that these mothers learnt to read in formal educational settings. This in turn suggests that a significant amount of learning to read happened informally. Vincent (1989) notes that in England, by the end of the eighteenth century, even parents who read little themselves 'could manage to teach a child its letters' (p. 14), therefore supporting the idea that learning to read outside of formal educational settings was common. Joseph Mayett, for example, was one of ten children of a farm labourer and had to 'spend his childhood making lace rather than attending school', but he remembers being taught to read at the age of four by his grandmother who read picture books to him (p. 1). It is very likely that children (and adults) learnt to read informally as much as, or more than, they learnt to read in formal educational situations.

Adult Reading Provision and Pedagogy

Much literature assumes that people either learnt to read as children or not at all. Yet work on adult education in the seventeenth, eighteenth and nineteenth centuries indicates that people did indeed learn to read, and devote themselves to improving their existing reading skills, as adults. Rose (2010) stresses the link between adult reading, adult education and workers' political movements, citing examples from the Reformation (and associated movements for universal access to holy texts) to workers united by their reading of the national press. He notes that adult education in the eighteenth and nineteenth centuries had two strands: a strong autodidactic culture on the one hand, and the development of educational provision – specifically for working people (usually working men) – on the other.

I will start with the first of these: autodidactism. The self-education movement developed from (at least) the Industrial Revolution onwards, gathering momentum with the self-improvement focus of the political Chartist movement of the mid-nineteenth century and other mutual improvement societies (Altick, 1957; Jonathan Rose, 2002; Thompson, 1964; Vincent, 1989). The autodidact tradition, or more often the tradition of *collective* autodidactism (Houston, 2002), is well documented in Europe and North America as a way that people learnt literacy and other skills from friends and family. Much of this evidence takes the form of isolated cases preserved in diaries which happen to have survived. Examples include 'the seventeenth-century Puritan Englishman Adam Martindale who took his first steps in literacy with a primer and the help of a young man who came to court his sister' and the French and German women-only spinning circles 'where unmarried girls ... met to spin, talk, knit [and] practice reading and to learn other practical skills' (Houston, 2002, pp. 103–104). These are further explored in Chapter 5.

It is worth stressing that collective or individual autodidactism was the only educational option for many. For periods both before and after the Civil War, Black people (slaves and free) in the young United States were not legally allowed to be taught to read. Instead, they taught themselves how to read by watching the teaching of children in their charge, by teaching each other or by tricking white 'street urchins' into teaching them (Salvino, 1989). There was, however, a strong autodidact tradition in all parts and all periods of American society, from Colonial days, where subscription libraries involved popular discussion groups, to the Lyceum movement, more than three thousand local study groups connected in a national network by 1835 (Sticht, 2002). In Canada, where working men protested against paying taxes towards a university system which was still too expensive for their own children to attend, the 'working-class press' encouraged self-education in reading, with the *Ontario Workman*, for example, proclaiming that learning to read was '"the Open Sesame which admits us to the realms of enchantment"' (Graff, 1979, p. 299).

Alongside this widespread collective autodidactisim, however, was educational provision organized specifically for adults. An organization in Bala, Merionethshire, started teaching 'adult poor' to read in 1811, and by 1850 was teaching three and a half thousand adults to read (James, 1973). Similarly, in 1812 Bristol, the Quakers introduced provision to teach adults to read. Soon more schools were established in London and the Midlands, until, by 1832, more than twelve thousand men and women were attending. By the mid-nineteenth century, however, an economic slump meant that many adult learners had more pressing problems to deal with, and schools were forced to close. Interestingly, though, by the end of the nineteenth-century evening elementary schools for adolescents and adults grew in popularity again to serve the needs of the tens of thousands who had left the newly funded elementary day schools without having learnt to read (Altick, 1957). The expectations and results of compulsory schooling became (and remain) key to adult literacy policy and practice.

The first Mechanics' Institutes, later Polytechnics, devoted themselves to educating working men (James, 1973). They offered classes in a range of subjects, held meetings, had libraries, circulated grammar books and dictionaries, and included literacy development alongside a wider, and often political, education. This blend of adult reading and writing instruction, adult education and political/cultural consciousness-raising was also common in North America. The United States Government first devoted its resources to adult education when teaching the troops of the Continental Army to read and write during and after the War of Independence. Later, in the Civil War, the Union Army hired teachers and chaplains to teach the Black soldiers to read. After the Civil War, the Freedmen's Bureau taught newly freed slaves to read (in the periods when this was legal). Throughout the nineteenth century, voluntary organizations, such as the Young Men's Christian Association, the Young Women's Christian Association, the American Library Association and the General Federation of Women's Clubs promoted and provided literacy education for young people and adults. There was also specifically focused adult education, such as the Hull House provision designed to help new immigrants 'assimilate' into American life (Sticht, 2002).

Also in the United States, the Chautauqua Movement emerged in 1874 from the initial idea of running short courses to train Sunday school teachers. It developed into a national touring adult education organization, including reading programmes, Hebrew lessons, swimming instruction and 'library sciences'. The inclusive educational philosophy of Chautauqua (what Gould calls 'our continuing American revolution') influenced the creation of Chicago University in the late nineteenth century (Gould, 1961). Similarly, O'Leary (1991) situates Canadian adult literacy provision in broader adult education movements of the early twentieth century, including 'the Farm Forum', 'the Workers' Educational Association' and the 'Frontier College' (p. 4).

How adults were taught to read in the eighteenth and nineteenth centuries is less clear, whether the methods (mainly phonic and whole-word) that were common in schools at the time were used or whether distinct adult pedagogies were developed, perhaps centred upon the newspapers, periodicals, novels, political or religious texts that were so popular at the time (James, 1973; Jonathan Rose, 2010). Throughout Western Europe, correspondence courses following the alphabetic method combined with political reading matter were popular (Houston, 2002). Moving into the twentieth century, Sticht (2004) identifies three key movements in early to mid-twentieth-century American adult literacy education: the 'Moonlight Schools' for adult 'illiterates' in 1911 (so named because of the lack of public lighting in rural Kentucky: classes could only take place on moonlit nights); the 'Write-Your-Name Crusade' to teach adults to write their names in order to vote and take part in other civic activities in 1922–23 South Carolina; and the Highlander Folk School in Tennessee, which led to the Citizenship School for 'adult African Americans' in South Carolina 1957–1962. What these movements shared was the starting-point of writing one's name, an emphasis on literacy for social inclusion (particularly voting) and the use of kinesthetic teaching approaches, such as carving letters or words into thick paper and tracing them with one's fingers (Sticht, 2004).

Cora Wilson Stewarts' Moonlight Schools were also influential in their use of resources; they created and adapted materials for adults learning to read, including their own local newspaper, and, for use in the Armed Forces literacy classes, a 'Soldier's First Book' (Sticht, 2002). Taking a similarly practical approach, the Works Progress Administration (WPA) was formed during the Depression to solve two problems simultaneously – high levels of unemployed teachers and high levels of adults who could not read – by training teachers to teach adults. They developed practical materials using content of significance to adult lives, such as health, safety, work and family (Sticht, 2002). In Britain, during and after the Second World War, formal literacy programmes were developed in the army to support the many recruits who could not manage the reading and writing required for increasingly mechanized warfare (Haviland, 1973; Jones and Marriott, 1995). For this purpose, in 1945 'some appropriate methods' for teaching adult literacy were identified, like those of the Moonlight Schools or Works Progress Affair, 'stressing the need to use non-school resources such as football and racing results and reports, comic strips, and to provide typewriters and printing sets'(Jones and Marriott, 1995, p. 339). A specifically *adult* reading pedagogy was emerging, focused on citizenship and the use of texts important to adult lives.

The Late Twentieth-Century Anglophone Adult Literacy Campaigns

The late twentieth century brought national adult literacy campaigns to Canada, England and Wales, the United States, Australia, New Zealand,

South Africa, Ireland, Scotland and Northern Ireland. These were not as high-profile as the campaigns in Nicaragua, Tanzania and Brazil, and their political and social contexts were quite different, but they were nevertheless part of the same global zeitgeist linking literacy with liberation (Derrick, 2010). The word 'campaign' for the adult literacy work in most of the Anglophone world is also misleading as in each case it was less one single drive and more a complex series of movements and policy shifts, involving a continuous creation or rebranding of voluntary, governmental and semi-governmental organizations. To summarize even one of these, let alone each, would be a daunting task, and one that is outside the scope of this book. However, I will try to outline some key similarities and differences of these late twentieth-century Anglophone adult literacy movements in order to explore what they meant for how adult reading was and is developed.

Each of the above-mentioned campaigns has incorporated a transition from more 'grassroots' community-organized provision to a larger, higher-profile, national system. In most cases, this was not one shift, or even a one-way shift, but rather the product of a series of initiatives. For Canada, Ireland, New Zealand, England, Wales and Northern Ireland, the introduction of high-profile central government initiatives was the direct result of the International Adult Literacy Surveys (IALS) published by the Organization for Economic Co-operation and Development (OECD) in the 1990s, indicating 'poor' national literacy levels and therefore both denting national pride and producing fears of disadvantaged international economic competitiveness. For my entire original list of Anglophone nations, the dominant discourse of their early twenty-first-century national adult literacy policies has featured some sense of the importance of international competitiveness in a 'global market' (Bailey, 2006; Crowther et al., 2006; Johnson Cain and Benseman, 2005; McKay, 2007; Moser, 1999; Shohet, 2001; Sticht, 2002; Wickert et al., 2007).

Second, for each nation the shifts in adult literacy policy have involved adult literacy provision being at times located within larger adult education structures, and at other times separate. For example, in Ireland, between 1969 and the mid-1970s, adult literacy provision moved from being a relatively small and often-forgotten part of a broader adult education provision operated by the National Association of Adult Education (AONTAS) to being driven by separate initiatives, such the Dublin Literacy Scheme set up by the Archdiocese of Dublin, and the Cork literacy and anti-poverty initiative. By the late 1980s, the National Adult Literacy Agency (NALA) was set up as an organization separate from AONTAS and devoted to coordinating adult literacy work in Ireland. From the late 1990s, adult literacy provision, still nationally coordinated by NALA, was partially integrated back into larger adult education initiatives around vocational education and training (Bailey, 2006). These shifts into – and out of – other adult education provision have implications not only for the underlying philosophy of the literacy provision (is it part of a wider adult education offer to meet a range of adult needs in the tradition of the Mechanics' Institutes? Is it something organized to 'solve' a deficit or social problem in the tradition of the sixteenth-century poor schools?), but also for its public profile, organization, funding, assessment and accreditation.

A third similarity lies in the nature of its workforce. In each case, the workforce of adult literacy teachers has always been predominantly part-time, containing a mixture of paid and voluntary teachers. Despite the raising of the profile of adult literacy work in the late twentieth century, and its resulting expansion, this overall situation has not changed. There remain very few full-time, paid, adult literacy teachers in the Anglophone world. At the same time, there has been, in most cases, a shift towards a government-driven professionalization of adult literacy teachers, with increased opportunities – and in some cases requirements – for teachers to undertake specific qualifications. This transition was probably at its most extreme in England, where the Skills for Life initiative of the first few years of the twenty-first century (driven by national embarrassment at an IALS report and the subsequent 'Moser Report' [Moser, 1999] identifying a significant national 'problem' with adult literacy and proposing a nationally standardized solution) brought a requirement that teachers were qualified not only as adult educators, but also as adult literacy specialists. This transition, though rarely to the same extent, has occurred throughout the Anglophone world, and with it questions arise of how we define literacy, what the training for adult literacy teachers should involve, how to monitor standards of provision and, of course, how much public money should be spent in this area.

Finally, the adult literacy campaigns and provision of these nations all link adult literacy provision with other national concerns. Recently, this has included a near-universal emphasis on 'employability' and family literacy. However, it also includes issues which are very particular to each nation. For example, in South Africa adult literacy provision is often integrated with HIV/AIDS education (McKay, 2007), and in Northern Ireland with education for peace between the Protestant and Catholic communities (Crowther et al., 2006).

There are also significant differences between these adult literacy campaigns. The first relates to differences in the organization of each nation.

For example, in the United States and Canada the federal government has limited influence over the educational decisions made at state or province level. This means that a national organization can coordinate and advise but not manage or enforce (unlike in Ireland, Scotland or England). Other differences relate to forms of control over adult literacy teaching, such as curricula, assessment of programmes and accreditation of learning. The United States and Scotland have curricula ('Equipped for the Future' and the 'Curriculum Wheel', respectively) which map out literacy as a series of practices in present-day adult life. These prescribe a vision, or definition, of literacy rather than how literacy should be taught. The Scottish 'Curriculum Wheel' is enforced, but does not prescribe teaching or dictate accreditation. Similarly, the Irish model of working from learners' needs is enforced nationally (i.e. adult literacy provision in Ireland must follow this model), but by nature it is not prescriptive (teachers must take their lead from learners' needs) or accredited. In contrast, England's Adult Literacy Core Curriculum breaks literacy down into a series of skills at word, sentence and text level. This curriculum can therefore be seen as prescriptive and exerting control over how teachers teach and how courses are accredited.

Finally, differences in geography and population patterns influence each national adult literacy programme. Online learning, for example, is a far bigger part of adult literacy provision in Canada and Australia, with their huge land masses and scattered populations (and resulting traditions of distance learning), and in Scotland and Ireland with their sparse rural populations, than in England, with its denser population. Each nation also has other native, common or official languages, in addition to English, which influence its literacy provision. In Canada, for example, 'Northwest Territories have eleven official languages: English, French, and nine Native languages' (Shohet, 2001, p. 5). In Scotland there are many native Scots and Scottish Gaelic speakers, just as there are Irish Gaelic speakers in Ireland, speakers of Welsh in Wales, Cornish in parts of Cornwall (England), and speakers of indigenous languages in the United States, Australia, New Zealand and South Africa. The status, politics and histories of these additional languages vary from nation to nation, and this has implications for the relationship between adult literacy provision and English language provision for speakers of other languages. It also means there may be a need for adult literacy classes dealing with literacy in languages other than English, with ramifications for the organization and funding of adult literacy provision.

But what does all this mean for how reading is taught to adult learners? How does pedagogy relate to policy, politics and teacher training? What actually drives what teachers do with learners? What goes on in a teaching situation is rarely documented: tacit pedagogic knowledge is often passed from teacher to teacher, making it invisible in policy or even teacher-training documentation. However, I will try to approach an answer by using England as a case-study.

The adult literacy provision run by the Cambridge House Settlement in England in the late 1960s was largely one-to-one provision; adults would come to see a tutor with a particular literacy need, such as a letter to be read or written, and the tutor would help (Hamilton, 1996; Haviland, 1973; Jones and Marriott, 1995). There were few published materials specifically for adults, and training opportunities for the mainly voluntary pool of tutors were minimal. Tutors predominantly worked from the real-life texts that learners brought with them, including extracts from the national and local press (Mace, 1979). Writing of her own experience as a volunteer literacy tutor with Cambridge House at this time, Mace stresses that while some tutors worked hard to develop innovative and effective adult-focused pedagogies such as language experience (scribing a learner's oral storytelling and using this as the basis for reading or writing work), other tutors used materials designed for schoolchildren, sometimes inappropriately or (without the benefit of school teachers' training) incorrectly.

The 1970s saw significant changes in the organization of English adult literacy provision, which Hamilton and Hillier (2006, p. 8) classify as the first of 'four key policy phases'. The first, from the mid-1970s, starts with the British Association of Settlements' 'Right to Read: Action for a Literate Britain' report (Harrison, 1974), leading to a literacy campaign in partnership with the BBC. The second, in the 1980s, was one of increasingly settled Adult Basic Education provision run by Local Education Authorities and voluntary organizations; while the third, from 1989 to 1998, saw a 'reduction of LEA [Local Education Authority] funding and control' and 'a more formalized further education (FE) system, dependent on funding through a national funding body'(Hamilton and Hillier, 2006, p. 12). Their final phase is the development of the already mentioned Skills for Life era. Throughout each policy phase, a specifically *adult* literacy pedagogy was developing.

Haviland (1973) argues that the majority of materials used in adult literacy classes in the 1970s were created for children, and Moss (2005) recalls that adult literacy teaching in the early 1970s was 'heavily influenced' by the phonic approach fashionable in primary schools at the time. Moss goes on to note, however, that 'early guidance for adult literacy teachers (such as the BBC teacher's book *On the Move* in 1974)' recommended a 'mixed approach' using 'both whole-word ... and phonic approaches' (p. 23). Freire's (1978) call that literacy education should challenge existing political power structures was also a key influence on a developing adult literacy pedagogy: texts used to teach reading must be meaningful and empowering, questioning dominant and potentially oppressive practices (Moss, 2005).

These influences together contributed to the dominance of a text-focused approach to teaching reading, the popularity of the language experience approach, and the association of both with a learner-centred educational philosophy – a powerful sense that the curriculum comes from the learners. These influences also relate to the popularity, in the 1970s and 1980s, of teaching reading using texts written by other adult literacy learners (Hamilton and Hillier, 2006; Lindsay and Gawn, 2005; Mace, 1992; Moss, 2005; Woodin, 2008): for example, the Gatehouse series and compilations of student work such as *Write First Time* (1976–1986), *If It Wasn't for this 2nd Chance* (Mace, Smith and Aylett, 1990) and *Yes I Like It* (1984). The often overtly political, anti-establishment learner publishing movements in the 1970s and 1980s stressed the importance of 'seeing yourself in others' and engaging in 'complex and philosophical notions' (Woodin, 2008, pp. 227–231) as a part of literacy learning.

Hamilton and Hillier's fourth policy phase could be characterized by its departure from this learner-centred pedagogy with the creation of a national Adult Literacy Core Curriculum (Good et al., 2001). This Core Curriculum, complete with suggested activities, directs teachers to ways of teaching reading (including phonic, whole-word and text-focused approaches), often based around daily life 'functions', such as using a washing machine or looking something up in the Yellow Pages. Moss (2005) argues that this embodies a deficit model because it implies that 'adult literacy learners ... are unable to choose the right washing cycle [or] make a meal', while 'in fact many learners ... may also be interested in, and motivated by, reading about lives they can relate to, in fiction and poetry, and in discussion and writing about new ideas' (p. 27). The newer online curriculum (Excellence Gateway, 2008) is similar in its 'functional' approach. Both are curricula imposed 'from above', based on externally assessed notions of deficit and therefore a dramatic contrast to the learner-focused, self-liberating philosophies of the earlier phases. This fourth phase can also be characterized pedagogically by more whole group and less individual provision (Hamilton, 2005). Teaching was increasingly led by external accreditation requirements, focused on the utilitarian rather than expressive or philosophical aspects of literacy (Duncan, 2006), and a preoccupation with literacy for 'employability', which potentially marginalizes older learners and others whose motivation is unrelated to employment (Meadows, 2008).

Whether English adult literacy teachers in 2011 are still in Hamilton and Hillier's fourth policy phase or in a new one is debatable: it is unclear what will follow the now-crumbling Skills for Life initiative. Certainly, we are now enjoying an unprecedented amount of research on a specifically adult literacy pedagogy, produced (directly or indirectly) by the Skills for Life initiative, which may well merit the conceptualization of a fifth phase. For example, in England, from 2002 to 2008, the National Research and Development Centre for Adult Literacy and Numeracy (NRDC) received government funding to research adult literacy, language, numeracy and ICT practices and pedagogies. A number of studies on teaching adult reading came out of this funding, such as Besser et al. (2004), and Brooks, Burton et al. (2007). Burton (2007a, 2007b; Burton et al., 2008) extended these research findings into teaching guides on developing adult emergent reading (including oral reading fluency) through reciprocal reading, language experience, explicit teaching of comprehension strategies and – controversially – a strong focus on phonics. At the same time as this renewed interest in phonics, the 'Voices on the Page' adult learner creative writing campaign (Duncan, 2006; Duncan and Mallows, 2007; Woodin, 2008) saw a renewed 'official' emphasis on using learner writing to develop adult literacy.

However, it is important to remember that the debates for and against phonic approaches, and for and against text-based approaches, are not new and, crucially, that these are not necessarily opposing approaches. Throughout the medieval period, remember, the alphabetic method involved a syllable-based phonic approach (what we would now call analytic phonics) in combination with the key religious texts meaningful to most adults at the time. Yet with phonics today associated with primary school pedagogy – and teacher authority – and a whole-text approach associated with the student publishing movements, a learner-centred philosophy and Freirean ideology, it is easy to see how these approaches came to be seen as political opposites, or emotionally charged reactions to one another, rather than complementary pedagogies. We have to use history to remind ourselves that all of these approaches – alphabetic/phonic, whole-word and text-focused – have been used to teach both children and adults to read for centuries, and therefore there is no reason to associate phonics, rather than any other approach, with child-focused pedagogy. Likewise, debates about the meaningfulness and appropriacy of texts used to teach reading have taken place in school education as much as in the adult context.

Adult Literacy Pedagogy Today

There is one last shift in pedagogy and practice worth exploring. Today, the Anglophone adult literacy world is sharing teaching materials, ideas for good practice and research findings more than ever before, at least partly because of the internet. For example, the United States government-funded 'Applying Research in Reading Instruction for Adults' (McShane, 2005), with its guidelines for the teaching of alphabetics, fluency, comprehension and vocabulary development, has been hugely influential in England and Scotland. Likewise, in the reading chapter of *Teaching Adult Literacy: Principle and Practice* (Hughes and Schwab, 2010) – arguably the first ever English textbook of adult literacy pedagogy – Schwab (2010) uses the Australian framework of Freebody and Luke's(1999) 'four resources model' (code-breaking, meaning-making, text-user and text-analyser) to present a range of approaches, from synthetic phonics to critical questioning, and from schema activation to pre-teaching vocabulary, to develop learners' reading skills in these four areas. Taking a similarly inclusive and internationally looking approach, the Scottish government commissioned a series of workshops leading to the publication of *Teaching Reading to Adults: A Pack of Resources and Ideas for Literacies Tutors* (Gawn et al., 2009). This pack built on research from throughout the Anglophone world, along with action research by Scottish literacies tutors, to present a range of approaches for developing adult reading, including language experience, whole-word recognition, phonic approaches and book clubs.

These examples represent not only a more internationally minded, but also a more settled and less reaction-based adult reading pedagogy. They demonstrate phonic, whole-word and text-based approaches to be complementary rather than in opposition, and look less towards a life-dysfunction deficit model and more towards the uses and pleasures of literacy. Sharing pedagogies across nations and contexts not only potentially frees pedagogy from particular local or national policy preoccupations, but also – in the transfer of ideas and resources across the internet – makes the work of adult literacy teachers visible as never before.

Chapter Summary

I ended the last chapter by emphasizing that we read for different purposes and in different ways: our reading practices are truly diverse. Yet charting the ways that reading has been formally taught reveals a great deal of homogeneity. For hundreds (if not thousands) of years we have shared common preoccupations of pedagogy, debating the merits of alphabetic, whole-world and phonic approaches, exploring whether to start from the word, the sentence or the text, and, if text, we have debated which texts to use: which are meaningful or appropriate? The importance of understanding the historical nature of these debates is one of the key arguments of this book. Yet the debates of formal reading pedagogy are only part of the picture of how people have learnt to read. This chapter examined informal learning as both a necessity (the only educational option open to many) and as a preference. Autonomously organized informal adult learning is one of the two traditions of adult education emerging from the eighteenth and nineteenth centuries (the other is the Mechanics' Institute model of provision organized for working men) which fed into the particular adult literacy pedagogy further developed through the adult literacy campaigns of the late twentieth-century Anglophone worlds. The following two chapters will develop these ideas: first, in Chapter 4, examining the role of literature in formal literacy provision and pedagogy, and then, in Chapter 5, analysing the reading circle tradition and its relationship with traditions of informal adult education.

Suggested Reading

Huey, E. B. (1908/1968), *The Psychology and Pedagogy of Reading.* Cambridge, MA: M.I.T. Press.
Chapter 13, 'The history of reading methods and texts', is a useful and accessible historical account of reading pedagogies.

Hughes, N., & Schwab, I. (2010), *Teaching Adult Literacy: Principles and Practice.* London: Open University Press.
This is one of the very few books about how to teach literacy to adults, highly practical.

McShane, S. (2005), *Applying Research in Reading Instruction for Adults: First Steps for Teachers.* Washington DC: National Institute for Literacy, The Partnership for Reading and National Center for Family Literacy.

This provides detailed guidance on the teaching of reading to adults, including an excellent section on 'alphabetics', with classroom suggestions and useful definitions.

Sticht, T. (2002), 'The rise of adult education and literacy system in the United States: 1600–2000'. In NCSALL (ed.), *Review of Adult Learning and Literacy* (Vol. 3, online edition).
This article provides an invaluable, detailed account of the history of adult literacy, and, more broadly, adult education provision in the United States.

Chapter 4

Literature and Literacy Development

What place does literature hold in the literacy pedagogy outlined in the previous chapter? Starting out as an adult literacy teacher, I was surprised to come across so little reference to poems, novels, plays, stories or songs in the official documentation of English and Scottish adult literacy teaching. Yet it may have been equally logical for me to ask myself different questions: why has literature been associated with the development of literacy skills in schools for so long? What is the link, really, between literature and literacy development? The aim of this chapter is to examine the historical relationship between literature and literacy development, before analysing how and why literature, and the novel in particular, could be useful in the development of literacy skills.

Starting Definitions

By *fiction*, I mean writing that is primarily concerned with beauty or insight: what McRae, working from Jakobson (1960/1988), calls the 'representational' rather than 'referential' function of language (McRae, 1991, pp. 2–7). Eagleton's definition offers another vital perspective: fiction 'means something like "a story (either true or false) treated in such a way as to make it clear that it has a significance beyond itself"'(2005, p. 13). By a *novel*, I mean an extended, book-length piece of prose fiction. Burgess puts it like this: 'The term novel has, in fact, come to mean any imaginative prose composition long enough to be stitched rather than stapled' (1967, p. 16). Finally, by *literature*, I mean written fiction: novels, short stories, plays and screenplays, and, perhaps controversially, poetry. This is not a definition hinging on a value judgement in terms of high versus mass culture, on a canon or on personal taste. Any novel, in my definition, is literature, regardless of whether it is pulp fiction or a canonical nineteenth-century novel; some novels may be good literature and others bad literature, but all are literature.

These are the definitions that inform this book, and probably the dominant ways *fiction*, the *novel* and *literature* are understood today. However,
these terms and their definitions have been far from static. The English
word 'novel' is derived from the Italian 'novella' and Spanish 'novela', and
was used in the sixteenth, seventeenth and eighteenth centuries to refer to
collections of short stories about the novelties of contemporary, everyday
life. The label 'novel' was used in contrast to another type of prose fiction,
the 'romance'. It was only in the nineteenth century, Cuddon (1991)
argues, that the term *novel* takes on its present-day meaning: that 'hold-all
and Gladstone bag of literature' – extended prose fiction (Cuddon, 1991,
p. 600).

Convention places the birth of the English-language novel in the
eighteenth century with Defoe and Richardson (Eagleton, 2005; Mullan,
2006; Watt, 2000), though it is equally commonplace to talk of the nineteenth
century as the century of the great European novel, with Britain and North
America particularly preoccupied with Scott, Austen, Dickens, Trollope,
Thackeray, the Brontës, Hardy, Tolstoy, Dostoevsky, Stendhal and Manzoni.
However, Cuddon (1991) argues that the Egyptians wrote novels in the
Middle Kingdom (1200 BC), that *Daphuis and Chloe* in the second century
AD is an example of a classical novel, and that medieval Japan produced
romantic and military novels, such as *The Tale of the Genji* (1000). Others
take a more ideological approach to defining the novel. Watt (2000) sees
the novel as born of modern realism, the product of a very particular point
in British and European philosophy and culture, and therefore only in existence from the eighteenth century onwards. For Lukacs, the novel is of a
particular nineteenth-century cultural predicament: 'The novel is the epic
of a world that has been abandoned by God' (1978, p. 88). Eagleton (2005)
further complicates our classification system by considering Pushkin's
Eugene Onegin a novel in verse.

Despite the earlier ideas around 'representational' language with
'significance', fiction is often characterized more simply as imaginative or
creative work. Yet the classification 'fiction' does not always, or indeed
often, include poetry and drama, though these are imaginative forms.
However, before we conclude that fiction therefore refers to prose, the
term is also often applied to film, particularly to emphasize the distinction
between fiction and documentary film. This resonates a cruder, but no
simpler, way of defining fiction: in opposition to its school-library-twin
non-fiction. Non-fiction means something 'true', and therefore fiction
must mean 'not true'. The complexities of this definition, the potential
confusion for those unfamiliar with literary conventions and the way that

fiction does indeed address truth, are discussed as part of the main case-study findings in Chapter 7.

However, the most shifting term is probably literature itself. Present-day understandings of the term literature or of 'literariness' (that which makes a work 'literary' (Jakobson, 1960/1988)) fall into five categories. The first category consists of what I am calling 'definitions of contrast': that literature is about writing which is fiction and *not* fact, or that it is concerned with 'artistic' and *not* 'historical' truths (Eagleton, 1996, p. 1). The second category is less about contrasting the content of a work and more about classifying its genesis. Literature is creative; it is the product of the imagination. Literature is playful: it 'play[s] with the boundaries between fact and fiction' (Thomson, 2010, p. 7). The third approach could be called formalist, both in terms of its association with Russian Formalism and in the simpler sense (and the origin of the term Formalism) that it identifies literariness as a particular *form* of text. Literature, here, is distinguished by its specific language, or use of language (the much contested notion of 'literary language' as opposed to 'ordinary language'). In Jakobson's frequently repeated phrase, literature is 'organized violence committed on ordinary speech'. Fourth, the literariness of a work rests on the manner in which it is read'; that is, through interpretive, exploratory reading. In this view, it is not that the literary text has a different relationship to reality, or uses different language, but the reader approaches a literary text differently, producing a distinctive type of reading, using a greater number of acts of interpretation to produce different kinds of truths. The fifth and final way that literature can be classified concerns personal or societal value judgements: literariness is an assessment of artistic or cultural worth. In this view, all novels are fiction, but only some are important or valued enough to be considered 'literary'. These five categories of definition each echo – if somewhat quietly – whenever the word 'literature' appears.

Yet, like the novel, the term 'literature' has been used differently in the past. In the eighteenth century it referred to 'the whole body of valued writing in society: philosophy, history, essays and letters as well as poems' (Eagleton, 1996, p. 15). The body of work labelled 'literature', Eagleton argues, played a significant role in establishing a social order, common values, and bringing the growing middle classes into line with the ideas and ideals of the aristocracy. Our present-day emphasis on the literary as creative and imaginative, he goes on to argue, was born with the Romantics in the late eighteenth and early nineteenth centuries, as their revolutionary mission strove to reintroduce the 'creative values' that had been 'expunged ... by industrial capitalism ... Literature had become a whole alternative ideology, and the "imagination" itself ... becomes a political force' (1996, p. 17).

Our present-day use of 'literature' seems to be equally the product of the earlier eighteenth-century sense of valued writing as it is the more recent nineteenth-century radical emphasis on creativity and imagination as socially transformative forces. Our use incorporates both of these potentially contrasting notions of the literary, along with resonances of key cultural debates of the twentieth century. For example, Walter Benjamin's idea of the 'aura' of an original work of art as opposed to a mechanical reproduction (1936/1969) refers to fine art, but this notion of art as 'original' to its time and place has been, I would argue, influential in our thinking about 'great' literature as representing an 'aura' of authenticity of time and place, or an 'originality'. Related to this, the argument that there are two opposing forms of culture – namely, high culture, and its manufactured parody, mass culture, or 'masscult' (Macdonald, 1961) – has been extremely influential in conceptualizations of literature as original, elite, exclusive and in opposition to mechanized, formulaic products of mass popular culture.

The Historical Relationship between Literature and Literacy Development

Literature and literacy in schools

What literature means or includes is complex and contested: placed alongside the equally slippery and power-saturated notion of literacy, it is even more so.

Chapter 3 told a story of how in Western Europe, the British Isles and then the Anglophone worlds reading was taught using primarily religious texts until the eighteenth and nineteenth centuries, when literature (stories, poems and novels) began to take their place. Whether religious texts can be classified as literature is a discussion for another time and place; either way, it is clear that literature has been used to teach children and adults to read for either hundreds or thousands of years. Yet imagining that literary texts replaced religious texts as a vehicle for the teaching of reading obscures the complexity of what was being taught and why. Accessing religious texts was, for many people and for many centuries, the single purpose behind learning to read. Learning to read was not a means to master what we would now call a 'transferable skill', but a means to worship. The introduction of other texts to teach reading was therefore more than a shift in teaching materials: it was a symptom of a shift in the very purpose behind learning to read.

The use of English literature in the teaching of reading can therefore be interpreted in two ways. To be able to read was increasingly seen as being an end it itself, and therefore the choice of texts for teaching became a pedagogic issue. For example, short rhymes were created and used to teach children how to read words of a particular spelling pattern (*tall, ball, hall, wall, all,* etc.), or popular stories or poems were seen as meaningful and motivating. A slightly different interpretation is that the use of literature to teach reading (whether specifically created stories with moral messages or the use of an existing literary canon) was part of literature's expanding role as a source of cultural values. Children and adults absorbed dominant values as they learnt how to read: there were thus two learning processes happening side by side.

Significantly, elite education (predominantly for boys) in all regions of the Anglophone world continued to involve the teaching of Ancient Greek and Latin well into the twentieth century, and in some cases the twenty-first. This involved the reading of the classical canon, but these texts were not read simply in order for boys to be able to develop literacy in Latin and Greek. Rather, literacy in Latin and Greek was part of an education in analysis and rhetoric, and an induction into a world of values and capabilities which would allow pupils to access a certain level or sphere of work or social standing. Once again, the development of literacy is more than learning to read and write: it is an initiation into a culture, which includes familiarity with a core group of texts.

The development of formal primary, or elementary, schooling began, as the seventeenth-century legislation of Scotland and Puritan America demonstrates, with a primary focus on learning to read. Present-day primary schooling differs in its organization across the Anglophone world, but the core focus is universal: to teach children to read and write. Literary texts may often be the means for this literacy education, but not, in elementary education, the principal end. Nevertheless, Applebee (1974) argues that our elementary school English/literacy practices and resources do indeed follow what he calls the 'ethical tradition' of reading instruction, evolved from a time when children learnt to read using primers containing explicit religious or moral messages. We cannot, therefore, see the use of literature in present-day primary reading instruction as entirely divorced from an element of cultural indoctrination.

The use of literature in the development of literacy in secondary (or post-elementary) school education is, however, even more complex. Secondary schooling by definition follows elementary schooling, and therefore does not, on the whole, include the teaching of beginner reading as part of its curriculum. Nevertheless, secondary schools throughout the Anglophone worlds feature the subject of English, a nebulous and contested subject shaped by primary-school literacy at one end, and the university study of English at the other. While English in elementary schooling follows the early-primer 'ethical tradition', secondary schooling follows the 'classical model' (Applebee, 1974), where literacy skills are developed alongside literary study, grammatical analysis and a development of 'critical and analytical ability', 'social skills', 'the use of the imagination' and the development of 'liberal, ethical, humanitarian attitudes' (Burke and Brumfit, 1986, pp. 171–172) or 'personal growth', 'cultural heritage' and 'cultural analysis' (Goodwyn, 2005, p. 10).

The present-day secondary school study of English retains the tensions inherent in the breadth of what the subject includes, as well as tensions between its literary and cultural education aspect and its literacy development aspect, tensions concerning what that literary or cultural education should include (whose culture? whose canon?) and issues concerning teacher training. Most secondary school English teachers (particularly in the British Isles) have university degrees in English literature, yet literary study is only a small part of the secondary school English curriculum, thus leaving many teachers unsure about how to teach the rest (Goodwyn, 2005).

Literature and literacy at university

The relationship between literary and literacy study at secondary school level cannot, therefore, be contemplated in isolation from how literature and literacy are studied at universities. I would like to examine three stories of the study of English at university level. Eagleton's (1996) tale starts in the nineteenth-century English Mechanics' Institutes and other working men's colleges where English literature was offered as a 'poor man's classics'. It was the ideal subject for study by women and less manly men because it was 'untaxing' and associated with 'finer feelings' (p. 24). English literature as a subject for serious study filled, to a certain extent, a vacuum left by a weakened Church, while also celebrating and perpetuating a Victorian preoccupation with 'Englishness'. Yet it was not an entirely respectable subject for higher study until the early twentieth century, when it 'rode into power on the back of wartime nationalism'. By the 1920s English literature was taught at Oxford, Cambridge and Edinburgh universities, and by the 1930s it was firmly established as the subject to study for serious engagement with 'the most fundamental questions of human existence' (p. 27).

Irvine tells a slightly different, or perhaps fuller, story in his chapter 'English Literary Studies: Origins and Nature' (2010). He starts by observing that one could not take a degree entitled 'English literature' in Britain or Ireland until the twentieth century, despite the fact that literary criticism is 'as old as European literature itself' (p. 16). Irvine notes that the academic discipline we now think of as English literature was first taught at universities in Scotland in the 1760s, when Adam Smith and Hugh Blair gave a popular lecture series at Glasgow University called 'Rhetoric and Belles Letters'. Law and Divinity students attended these lectures motivated by their interests in speech-making and the art of persuasive writing. The students attending also included speakers of the Scots dialect wishing to refine their use of a 'higher-class' variety of English.

Irvine explains that literature was also being taught in England at this time, but not at the two universities – rather by organizations of 'Dissenters', Protestants who could not enter Oxford or Cambridge because of their rejection of the Church of England. Those teaching at Dissenting organizations (where they also taught natural science, another subject banned by Oxford and Cambridge) were often Presbyterians who had studied in Scotland. When University College London was founded in 1828 as a university for Dissenters and others who did not belong to the Church of England, it included a 'Professor of English Language and Literature'. Other universities followed: King's College London (when it was founded) in 1835, Glasgow University in 1862, and Trinity College Dublin in 1867. Cambridge University introduced 'Medieval and Modern Languages' in 1878, including English, and a professorship in English literature in 1911, while Oxford had introduced a professorship in English language and literature in 1885. The subject studied was different, though, from that studied in the eighteenth century, with a greater emphasis on establishing a canon of English literature, and defining literature as poems and plays rather than valued non-fiction. It looked to the literary past for ideas of Englishness and a way of glorifying a national identity (Irvine, 2010). This is a story, then, not only of class and curriculum, but also of religion and nationalism.

By contrast, the study of English emerged in American universities in the second half of the nineteenth century under the influence of a German approach to philological scholarship. Literature and culture were studied only as part of a 'scientific study' of language (Applebee, 1974). English therefore meant the study of Old German, Old and Middle English, and

Old French alongside the study of English literature. At the beginning of the twentieth century this approach was joined by an interest in the study of 'world literature as part of the "total heritage" of the American student' (1974, p. 208), and so literary and cultural study became an aim in itself.

Today, the graduate study of English at many American universities involves the study of both language and literature, and often the demonstration of reading ability in at least one additional language (the study of literature still legitimized by the rigour of language studies), while at most British universities English literature and English language are separate undergraduate degree programmes, with the notable exception of Oxford, where English literature can only be studied in conjunction with classics, English language, a modern language or with history. However, by far the most significant factor for our purposes is that however English literature and English language are aligned as academic disciplines, *neither* is closely related to the university development of (academic) literacy skills offered by university centres of academic literacy or introductory level undergraduate writing or composition courses. The development of literacy at university level, though deemed necessary by nearly all universities, is linked neither to the study of literature nor to the study of the English language.

Literature and English as a Foreign Language

If the delineation, definition and purpose of English studies at university level have been less than explicit, the same cannot be said for the work of EFL (English as a foreign language), which is both an international industry and one of the most carefully researched and debated areas in education. Its research includes studies of the shifting use of literature in language teaching, a much-debated topic. Paran (2006b) sums up one possible story:

> The received wisdom is that literature, once the mainstay of language teaching, being both its purpose and one of its main tools, was relegated to a marginal role with the advent of communicative language teaching in the 1970s. (p. 1)

The popularity of the communicative approach signalled the dominance of learning languages to communicate in real-life situations, rather than to access the important texts of another culture, and this necessarily pushed literary study to the sidelines. Paran also introduces the possibility of a slightly different story: that literature never actually disappeared from the EFL classroom, but rather maintained a dominant role as a language-teaching resource in EFL classrooms around the world. What changed was the degree to which literature was used explicitly to teach language points (Gilroy and Parkinson, 1996; Maley, 1989), rather than studied as an end in itself. Once again, literature, or literary study, has been both purpose and vehicle for language teaching.

Present-day arguments against the use of literature in second-language teaching often focus on how it is used, rather than the fact it is used: for example, that 'linguistic elements [are] underplayed' (Hall, 2005, p. 47) or that the study of literary texts is not sufficiently integrated into wider aspects of language study. Other common criticisms are centred on the suitability of literature itself: for example, that literary texts may be too difficult for most second-language learners or that literary language is not 'typical', authentic or useful language. Hall (2005) and Paran (2006a, 2008) disagree with – and provide excellent summaries of – these arguments.

The counter arguments are more convincing. Short and Candlin (1986) summarize a range of reasons why literature and language teaching should be integrated: literary language and non-literary language are not actually different; learners will usually recognize literature as a part of language; literary texts often contain a range of varieties of English which can be use-ful for language teaching; and, very simply, 'many students enjoy reading literature' (p. 91). Hall (2005) divides the arguments into the affective (that reading literature is 'pleasurable, motivating, personalizing'), the cultural (that literature develops the cultural awareness which is part of learning a language), the psycholinguistic (the development of inference, for exam-ple) and the miscellaneous, including that the use of literature can develop reading fluency, expand vocabulary and help learners remember language structures. Literature is used and has always been used in EFL teaching simply because it is an authentic and popular use of language. Each of these arguments would apply equally to the use of literature in adult literacy teaching, though they are seldom made.

Literature and adult literacy teaching

As noted in the introduction to this chapter, as a new literacy teacher in Scotland and then England, I was surprised at the lack of mention of litera-ture in the official documentation of my early training, for precisely the reasons noted above with regard to EFL: literature is a popular and stimu-lating literacy practice. The 2001 English adult literacy core curriculum mentions literature only twice: reading 'a short story to a child' and (if we interpret magazine stories as potentially including fiction) knowing 'the different purposes of texts encountered in daily life, e.g. ... magazine stories' (Good et al., 2001). 'Equipped for the Future' in the United States and the 'Curriculum Wheel' in Scotland are less detailed, but references to literature are still hard to find. I wondered why such a widely used literacy practice was being ignored.

The dominant discourse of adult literacy teaching across the Anglophone world today is what is often referred to 'functional', focused on the literacy required for the daily organization and administration of adult life: shopping, dealing with healthcare and schools, applying for and keeping jobs, voting. This is a deliberate focus on adult needs, away from the traditions of school literacy teaching. This, surely, is sensible. Yet, given that the literary texts (songs, poems, stories, novels, etc.) are indeed an authentic and common adult literacy practice, the extent of literature's absence is still noteworthy and needs explaining. Literature has been seen as elitist (and therefore inappropriate to the inclusive nature of adult literacy education), passive (to do with reading the work of a few 'great' writers occupying a different cultural position from the readers) and value-laden (associated with a Victorian/colonial canon) (Barton, 2007). Literature is also, echoing the EFL research, often damned with the charge of being 'too difficult' and not representing 'real life'.

The opposing arguments are plentiful and easy to make, but they are largely unpublished and therefore have had less impact. Whether or not literature is elitist depends on one's definition of literature: stories, folk tales and songs are clearly not elitist. Reading literature, whether alone or in a group, is rarely passive (see Chapters 5 and 7) and readers are often prompted by their reading to write themselves. Literary texts, like any texts, most certainly are 'value-laden', but to claim that they represent one value system is to ignore both the history of literature and of contemporary literary production. The charge of difficulty is an interesting one. The potential for increased difficulty in terms of structure, vocabulary, syntax and cultural references is genuine and therefore both a reason *not* to use certain literary texts in certain teaching situations and, at times, precisely why one would want to use those texts. Difficulty in terms of intellectual/philosophical context is a more treacherous claim: are we assuming that adult literacy learners cannot handle the same intellectual and philosophical concepts as a person confident in literacy? Do we literacy teachers, deep down, not actually believe our often-repeated mantra, 'a beginner reader is not a beginner thinker'?.

Finally, the idea that literature is removed from 'real life' or somehow not 'authentic' in the way that post office forms are authentic seems to be both itself an elitist judgement about which members of society have literature in their lives (i.e. not adult literacy learners) and, again, a misunderstanding of what literature means or includes. There is, however, one very strong tradition within adult literacy teaching throughout the Anglophone world which recognizes and celebrates the authenticity of literature: learner publishing movements. The popularity of stories, poetry, songs and autobiographical pieces written by adult learners for adult learners declares loud and clear that the reading and writing of literature is an active and authentic part of adult life, for all adults, regardless of educational background.

Perhaps the more important point is that anecdotal evidence suggests that literature is indeed being used in adult literacy teaching, despite its seeming absence from official documentation. This, then, is the real answer to my initial question. Literature has always been used as part of adult literacy development (to a greater or lesser extent), but what goes on in adult literacy teaching sessions was, and often still is, largely invisible to the outside world. Over the past 5 years, initiatives such as the UK Quick Reads (Quick Reads, accessed 2010) (an initiative whereby high-profile writers write short novels and non-fiction pieces especially for adult literacy learners) and web resource libraries (such as the Canadian NALD Library [National Adult Literacy Database, accessed 2010] containing hundreds of literary pieces) have increased the profile of literature in adult literacy teaching.

Literature has been linked to the development of children's literacy in schools for centuries. The study of literature at university level is separate from an explicit development of literacy, though is often linked to the wider study of language. Literature has been a much-debated, but undeniable, part of EFL teaching over the past 40 years. Finally, contrary to the impression given by its 'official' documentation, literature is used in adult literacy provision, as both a vehicle for the development of particular reading and writing skills and as an authentic literacy practice around writing for an audience and reading others' work. A final question remains: why? *What is it about literature?*

What is it About Literature?

Could there be something about literature itself that makes it particularly suited to the development of literacy skills? Carter (1986, 1997) and Hall

(2005) discuss the prevalent idea that there may be something particular about 'literary language', a 'literariness', which marks it as different from 'ordinary language' and is especially suited to the development of literacy skills. Monaghan and Barry (1999) suggest another answer, linking a late nineteenth-century call for the use of 'more meaningful' texts in reading instruction with 'the literature movement' (p. 31): *meaningful* (in this newly secular context) meant literary. I would like to look at the use of literature in literacy development in these two ways: is literary language different from 'ordinary language', and could literature be 'more meaningful'?.

Poetics: is 'literary language' different?

> Does literature have a language of its own, perhaps unrepresentative of, or rather different from, ordinary language? ... The simple answer to this question is no ... but ....(Hall, 2005, p. 9).

As Hall indicates, it would be hard to argue that literary language is always or necessarily different from 'ordinary language'. However, two continuations of Hall's 'but' seem particularly applicable here. Halliday and Hasan (1989) write of literary language containing referencing chains with in-built ambiguity for the reader to 'solve', while Carter (1997) points out that literary language is a speech act referring to what is not real, making the references 'more real' than what is referred to. He also emphasizes the frequency of polysemy in literary language, meaning that literature demands that its readers perform more acts of interpretation. However, Brumfit and Carter (1986) argue, 'we believe there is no such thing as literary language' (p.6), as any traits of 'literary language' that can be identified (such as alliteration or ambiguity) can also be found in non-literary uses of language, in other texts. In this view, there is simply no such thing as 'literary language'.

Yet there may be some generalizations to be made about the novel. As discussed in Chapter 1, reception theorists and narrative poetics theorists (Culler, 1975; Iser, 1972; Perry, 1979; Rimmon-Kenan, 1989) present a highly 'active' novel-reading process where, as the reader reads, he or she interprets and reinterprets to 'build' and constantly revise 'frames' of meaning. Iser discusses how the literary writer deliberately creates 'intentional sentence correlatives' (1972, p. 215) – or gaps between and within sentences – to be filled in by the reader. In this sense, the literary writer does try to create a different kind of written language from 'ordinary' language: the writer creates more 'gaps' to be filled, more ambiguities to be interpreted.

That other texts may contain similar ambiguities, or that other writers may also deliberately leave such gaps for interpretation, is undeniable, but the key difference is that these gaps are part of what defines a novel and what the novel reader craves.

Further, there is another, more obvious, peculiarity about how written language is used in a novel: length. The novel is a written text of a certain length. This means, very simply, that it is composed of *more* language – more words, more sentences, more paragraphs, more chapters. Returning to Carter's idea of literary language referring to (or rather creating) what is 'not real', the 'not real' woven by the novel's language is more developed, sustained over two hundred or so pages. This means that the reader's acts of interpretation, adaptation and revision are played out over a longer reading process, involving a greater use of memory and exercise of judgement. In this way, I would argue that the novel's language is significantly different from 'ordinary language' because it encourages, or even necessitates, a different reading process. As noted earlier, the 'literary' can also be located in the act of reading itself: the literary as a *way* of reading. Reading literature could therefore be seen as a kind of training in a particular type of highly interpretive reading, including knowing what is left for the reader to interpret and on what basis to make that interpretation. This is an important part of literacy development, making literature an important tool for reading development.

Hermeneutics: is literature 'more meaningful'?

Significantly, Monaghan and Barry (1999) link the call for the use of more 'meaningful' texts with 'the literature movement' in American reading pedagogy, suggesting that literature is, or can be seen as, 'more meaningful'. Meek (1988, 1991) writes passionately of the place of literature in a child's literacy development: 'To learn to read a book, as distinct from simply recognizing the words on the page, a young reader has to become both the teller (picking up the author's view and voice) and the told (the recipient of the story, the interpreter)'(1988, p. 10). She argues that emergent readers must 'enter the reading network through the multiple meanings of polysemic texts' as opposed to 'the reductive features of words written to be "sounded out" or "recognized"'(p. 24). Meek links this wrestling with 'multiple meanings' with the development of moral value systems, 'both life and text have to be interrogated about "the way things might be"' (p. 29). Her emphasis is on the power of literature, including children's literature, to make the reader explore the world and literacy's place within that world: 'The reading of stories makes skilful, powerful readers who come to understand not only the meaning but also the force of texts' (p. 40).

Rose (2010) makes a remarkably similar argument from the perspective of social history, tracing the use of literature in the working-class autodidact tradition of the nineteenth and early twentieth centuries. Rose warns against arguments that the literary canon is elitist or not of relevance to working people, and argues that this kind of thinking is both patronizing (in making decisions on behalf of working people) and an act of withholding. He argues that 'the "great books" [do indeed] embody universal moral values, psychological insights, and aesthetic standards'(p. 4). 'Again and again we find classic literature embraced by working people who thoroughly lacked literary education' (p. 5) precisely because it relates to the personal and political struggles of their daily lives.

Both Rose and Meek argue that literature has been used for literacy development in the past (and should continue to be used in the future) for the same reason that literature has been read in the past and will continue to be read in the future: it *means* something to its readers. Arguing for the use of literature in EFL teaching, Paran (2008) makes this point more simply: 'Literary texts are suitable because language is learnt by human beings, and the interest and love of literature for its various qualities is a human characteristic'(p. 469).

Chapter Summary

Just as all reading practices change, so too does our understanding or classification of reading practices. Literature, fiction and the novel are all terms which have denoted reading (and listening) practices, but the meanings of these terms, the nature of the practices they represent, have changed: from literature as any writing valued by a society to literature as written fiction, or from the novel as a collection of tales about modern life to a book-length piece of fictional prose. How, where and (crucially) why literature has been studied has also changed, along with its relationship to literacy development. Literature has been both purpose and tool for literacy development, including adult literacy development. If literary language is not necessarily different from 'ordinary language', it nevertheless offers a distinctive reading process, with, for example, more work on inference. If literature is not always or necessarily 'more meaningful' than other texts, it is undeniable that many literary texts have been powerfully meaningful to many people on many occasions. For these two reasons, literature offers specific potential for literacy development. This is important to remember when moving on to the next chapter's exploration of reading circles – informal learning situations that usually (though not always) involve reading and discussing novels.

Suggested Reading

Applebee, A. N. (1974), *Tradition and Reform in the Teaching of English: A History*. Urbana, IL: National Council of Teachers of English.
Unusual and interesting examination of English as a school and university subject, with a focus on the United States.

Brumfit, C., & Carter, R. (eds) (1986), *Literature and Language Teaching*. Oxford: Oxford University Press.
Classic collection on the role of literature in language teaching.

Cavanagh, D., Gillis, A., Keown, M., Loxley, J., & Stevenson, R. (eds) (2010), *The Edinburgh Introduction to Studying English Literature*. Edinburgh: Edinburgh University Press.
This is a rare and stimulating guide to the university study of English literature. It examines often taken-for-granted assumptions of literary study. Section 1, 'What is Literature? English Literary Studies: Origins and Nature and Kinds of Literature', is particularly useful for thinking about what literature is and why it is studied.

Eagleton, T. (1996), *Literary Theory: An Introduction*. Oxford: Blackwell.
Seminal, hard to ignore, and well-worth-reading introduction to literary theory.

Eagleton, T. (2005), *The English Novel: An Introduction*. Oxford: Blackwell.
See Chapter 1: 'What is a Novel?'

Forster, E. M. (1927/1962), *Aspects of the Novel*. Harmondsworth: Penguin Books.
An entertaining and thought-provoking exploration of the novel by one of England's greatest novelists, based on lectures delivered at Trinity College, Cambridge in 1927.

Paran, A. (ed.) (2006), *Literature in Language Teaching and Learning*. Alexandria, VA: Teachers of English to Speakers of Other Languages.
Provides an important update on the debates around the use of literature in language teaching.

Chapter 5

Reading Circles

We read novels for many different reasons. We also read them in many different ways. Novel reading may often, or even usually, be done alone: in bed, on a bus, in a quiet corner of a public library or on a sofa behind tightly drawn curtains. Yet, novel reading is done not only in the company of others, but also *with* others in reading circles. This chapter provides an overview of educational, historical and ethnographic research into reading circles in order to gain a better understanding of when, how and why they are formed.

The terms used for communal reading and discussion groups are numerous, including reading clubs, reading groups, book clubs, book groups, literature circles and reading circles. These terms are all used to describe peer-led groups concerned with reading and discussion, what I am calling *reading circles*. Reading circles are a communal form of what is often thought of as an intensely individual process – novel reading. Why do so many people want to read together? I will start by examining educational research into the use of reading circles in formal educational situations, before turning to historical and ethnographic research into the reading circles set up informally by adults in various times and places. This chapter also explores two larger-scale contemporary studies of reading circles (one American and one British), examples of reading circles in 2011 and, finally, two fictional reading circles.

Educational Research

Most educational research into reading circles falls into two categories: the use of reading circles in English classes in schools, and their use in English as a Foreign Langauge [EFL] teaching. Research in primary and secondary schools in Australia and the United States has overwhelmingly found reading circles to be an effective method of developing comprehension strategies, confidence and of encouraging both the enjoyment of reading and greater learner autonomy (Burns, 1998; Chinn, Anderson & Waggoner, 2001; Day & Ainley, 2008; English, Robinson, Mathews & Gill, 2006; Hunter, 2003; Katz, Kuby & Hobgood, 1997; Lloyd, 2004; Sutherland, 2003). Additionally, King (2001) studied the use of reading circles in English schools, arguing that the transfer (from teacher to pupils) of control over, and responsibility for, reading circle discussion is an excellent way to develop interpretive skills: linking control, autonomy and decision-making in the workings of the reading circle with the control, autonomy and decision-making of literary interpretation.

Research has also highlighted key challenges of this transfer of control. Malchow Lloyd (2006) notes the danger that 'some groups displayed more hierarchical interactions than would be permitted in a teacher-led discussion' (p. 55). However, she argues for the importance of pupils choosing their own texts, and produces evidence for reading circles as effective training in critical reading. Once again, a link is made (if implicitly) between social/organizational skills and reading skills, this time between criticality in choosing which text to read and, when reading, a critical analysis of the choices that the author has made in producing the text.

Cumming-Potvin (2007) examines one Australian elementary school pupil's experience of a reading circle, concluding, like King, that reading circles provide the scaffolding, or 'guided participation' (p. 502), of challenging aspects of literacy development, such as decoding and reading comprehension. Similarly, Day's (2003) research in Australian elementary schools argues for the benefits of the peer support offered by literature circles. Daniels (2006) surveyed the use of literature circles in (mainly American) schools, emphasizing that they 'work' because of member engagement, choice and responsibility. Daniels also reviews conclusions from other reading circle research, which include arguments that reading circles develop critical reading and comprehension skills, 'reading attitude' and a sense of gender equality (pp. 11–12). Anderson and Corbett (2008) note that literature circles are not often used by 'special education' teachers, while arguing that the collaborative nature of literature circles and their potential for peer support and development of social as well as literacy skills make them particularly helpful when working with pupils with global and specific learning disabilities. Reading circles, according to this body of research, develop the reading skills that are required to choose, decode, understand, interpret and critically engage with a text, in parallel with the social/organizational skills that are required to work in a group situation.

Interestingly, reading circles are also noted for bringing more authentic reading practices into the classroom. Gordon writes that 'setting up reading clubs in a class or school is about having children read as adults read' (1999, p. i). He argues that adults choose what they want to read, choose how to read it and respond to their reading with discussion, and therefore this is what teachers should be encouraging children to do in schools. Discussing 'ways of making [adult ELF] reading lessons less of a tedious task', Paran offers a similar argument (though for the EFL context) that 'reading in the classroom' should be closer to 'reading outside of the classroom' (2003, p. 26), which means (among other things) readers choosing the texts they read and following their reading with discussion. Reading pedagogies, Gordon and Paran agree, should follow the patterns of reading practices, and reading circles manage to be both an authentic practice and a well-researched pedagogy.

Research in ELF has also found that reading circles are an effective way of developing speaking and listening skills, active and passive vocabulary and greater proficiency and confidence in reading and writing (Kim, 2004; Yang, 2001; Ying Lao & Krashen, 2000). Zakaluk (1991) used a ten-week programme of reading circles as part of a language project for immigrant women and their children, finding that the women's reading comprehension improved along with their confidence when reading to their children. This link between confidence and comprehension echoes the school reading circle research and warrants further attention. It seems to be about more than two separate areas of development, confidence and comprehension. Rather, these two areas are interrelated: comprehension (whether on the level of individual words or sentences, paragraphs or whole texts) is always interpretive, and interpretation requires confidence in one's abilities. One simply cannot interpret without trusting in one's own decoding and judgement-making abilities, meaning that comprehension both requires and builds confidence.

Four years later Zakaluk & Wynes (1995) reported on a continuation of Zakaluk's programme, finding that the women's language and literacy were improving along with their confidence not only in reading to their children, but also in taking a more active part in their new communities. Similarly, Clarke (2008b) writes of 'a monthly reading group' for English for speakers of other languages (hereafter ESOL) learners in Lewisham, London, meeting in a local library. The participants reported benefits including developed vocabulary and improved speaking skills, as well as renewed social confidence, which allowed them to enjoy this semi-public engagement in that most authentic of authentic communicative purposes, 'shar[ing] our feelings and opinions' (p. 15). Making a more pragmatic point, Rado & Foster (1995) investigated 'strategies for expanding learning opportunities for NESB [non-English speaking background]' learners in Melbourne. They argue that 'current contact hours are inadequate' and that reading circles could be used as a way to extend learning time (without a teacher needing to be present), while both developing and 'draw[ing] on the adult's capacity for independent learning and the bilingualism of the learners' (p. 59). Research therefore firmly supports the idea that reading circles in the formal (or semi-formal) educational settings of ELF, school and community education offer significant pedagogic advantages.

There may be very little research on the use of reading circles in provision specifically for adult literacy learners, but we are moving in that direction. The UK government-funded Reading Agency's 2008 'Six Book Challenge', aimed to develop the reading habits of less confident adult readers (Clarke, 2008a). The Reading Agency worked with library services, colleges, community organizations and the Costa Book Awards to promote their challenge for adult literacy learners to read six books. Their report identifies five key outcomes for the majority of participants: achieving the goal of reading six books, enjoying reading and discussing books, improved literacy skills, increased confidence and inspiration 'to do something different' (Grylls, 2009, p. 2). In November 2009, The Reading Agency took this work further and launched 'Chatabout: a unique new national network to support the growing number of reading groups for adults with literacy needs' (The Reading Agency, 2009). Chatabout offers a database of adult reading groups and opportunities for librarians, teachers and adults wanting to join a reading group to share information and ideas online. Like the Six Book Challenge, Chatabout promises to be a useful resource in linking formal adult literacy provision with informal adult reading groups.

Historical and Ethnographic Research

In addition to the above studies of reading circles in educational settings, there is a significant amount of research on reading circles from a historical or sociological/ethnographic perspective. Though reading circles could quite rightly be seen as a trend of the late 1990s and early twenty-first century (particularly in the Anglophone world), we could also do worse than take our lead from Hartley (2002), who (sounding a little like Cole Porter on love) declares that 'reading in groups has been around for as long as there has been reading ... The Romans did it, emigrants on board ship to Australia did it, Schubert and his friends meeting to read and discuss the poems of Heine were doing it' (p. 1). Yet, however true this may be, for a closer look at reading circles as a chosen reading practice, it is important to differenti-ate between other kinds of communal reading (such as those outlined in Chapter 2) and formations we could classify as *reading circles*. In reading circles, as in the Knights of the Round Table, it is the *circle* that is key; the circle both symbolizes and creates the equality among members, the lack of a hierarchy which creates a community capable of a certain type of discus-sion. Jonathan Boyarin (1993) examines the reading practices in Jewish culture. He is interested in the importance of the community produced by communal study.

> One day our Bible teacher, expounding on the multiplicity of valid under-standings, cited Rabi Akiba Eger's version of the messianic age, when all the righteous will sit and study together in a circle. The point of the image is the equidistance and equal view of one another: I can see your truth and you can see my truth. (p. 230)

Although not intending to, this passage both defines a reading circle and explains its appeal. Dickens reading to a fascinated audience is communal reading, but not a reading circle. A wife reading to her husband, and a husband to his wife, is communal; but two is not a circle, while three just about is. A Cuban cigar factory reader employed to read while workers listen is not a reading circle. By contrast, members of the 'medieval textual communities' in Christianized Anglo-Saxon England would get together to read and interpret texts communally, sharing and building one another's truths. 'In a culture unaccustomed to the written text, the act of reading would have seemed remarkably like solving a riddle ... The squiggles must be made to speak' (Howe, 1993, p. 62). This sort of interpretation required the collective effort of a circle. Similarly, the medieval European monastic tradition of reading in a group was often in circle formation, with individu-als taking turns to read aloud and then discuss what they had read for the sake of teaching and religious worship. Reading circles also existed in the medieval lay-world. Taylor's (1996) study of 'reading and privacy in late medieval England' examines the reading circle of Elizabeth de Vere, Count-ess of Oxford. Elizabeth died in 1537, leaving behind her 'Devotional Manual' which indicates her range of reading practices, including reading 'with an inner circle of relatives and dependents' (p. 61). This reading cir-cle was conducted in private rooms, for private spiritual/religious purposes, but as a small group – a reading circle – sharing reading and discussion.

Around a hundred years later, in the seventeenth century, the formal education that schools were providing for part of the population, for part of the time, was still secondary to the more prevalent networks of informal education. These frequently operated as reading circles, with people reading to and learning from one another. Reading circles were often organized among trade groups or combined with housework, such as in the previously mentioned German *Spinnstube* or French *veilleé*, where unmarried girls gathered to 'spin, knit and talk' while reading to and with one another (Houston, 2002, p. 103). Reading circles also occurred within families: in the eighteenth century, as suggested in Chapter 2, Samuel Richardson's family formed themselves into a reading circle for daily reading sessions which were both 'sociable and part of a religious and moral discipline' (Tadmore, 1996, p. 171).

The dominant eighteenth-century presumption was that readers read socially, in a group, with either one reader reading to an assembled audience, or with readers taking turns, in a reading circle formation. This convention continued throughout the nineteenth century: for example, 'When Thomas Hardy and John Thelwall structured the early Corresponding Societies they made it a rule that all participants took turns to read and speak regardless of education, status or fame' (Cowan, 2010a). Similarly, the Hamilton family of late nineteenth-century Indiana formed themselves into what younger sister Agnes described as 'a sort of reading club' (Sicherman, 1989, p. 206) and 'every Saturday in Aunt Marge's room, we read Henry Esmond and while one reads the rest of us do our mending or other sewing' (p. 221). Yet more than a pleasant way to pass the time together while they did their chores, the Hamilton sisters described how reading novels allowed them to 'try out different identities' beyond what their class and gender had dictated for them, and therefore to enjoy 'a world more satisfying than the one originally inhabited' (p. 208) – a *larger* world. Their reading circle (like the reading of the Brontë sisters) was a private schooling in the public worlds they could not access. This was also, crucially, their only educational option, a common situation for women in the nineteenth century, and an education which offered the advantage of encouraging more 'self invention' than the formal educational systems that women were later allowed to enter (p. 217).

Victorian reading circles where participants gathered to read and discuss novels, and only novels, were commonplace (Altick, 1957), and yet the most common form of nineteenth-century reading circles were better known as 'mutual improvement societies', organizations presenting an alternative to Mechanics' Institutes. Mechanics' Institutes can be seen as the product of the eighteenth-century notion of education as a debt that society owes its citizens, and so the education of adult workers becomes the logical extension of the establishment of charity schools to educate needy children. Seen in this way, the development of Mechanics' Institutes was the product of 'the growth of philanthropic and humanitarian sentiment', so that 'adult education takes its place alongside the anti-slavery movement, the movements for factory reform, for the abolition of climbing boys and the like' (Kelly, 1952, pp. 17–18).

Mutual improvement societies, by marked contrast, 'were *of* the people not *for* the people' (Radcliffe, 1997, p. 141) (my italics). Radcliffe argues that mutual improvement societies were a little-documented, but dominant form of working-class education in Britain from 1780 to 1900, and outlines five reasons for their dominance. The first relates directly to the Mechanics' Institutes: in the 1830s, places at Mechanics' Institutes began to be almost exclusively taken up by the middle classes and, shortly after, political and religious debate was banned within the Institutes. This meant that the working classes needed to find their educational and discussion opportunities elsewhere. Second, Radcliffe considers mutual improvement societies to be a reaction to the Industrial Revolution by a working class striving to maintain 'moral, physical and intellectual' health (p. 144). He also notes greatly reduced formal educational provision for all age groups, leading to sharply reduced levels of literacy, and from 1835, many Sunday schools banned literacy teaching on Sundays. Finally, women were not allowed to enter most Mechanics' Institutes until the middle of the nineteenth century, while they were welcome at some mutual improvement societies, and indeed, all-female societies were common. Additionally, in his earlier work on mutual improvement societies in nineteenth-century Yorkshire, Radcliffe argues that mutual improvement societies (in this particular region) had a predominantly working-class membership, driven by the low literacy rates among (formerly rural) working people who moved to the newly industrial towns (Radcliffe, 1986). All of these factors contributed to the growing popularity of mutual improvement societies as an educational option for working people.

Mutual improvement societies met in members' homes or public houses, where group reading and discussion was interspersed by 'elementary subjects ... taught on a one-to-one basis by the members themselves' (Radcliffe, 1997, p. 147). This included reading and writing. These were peer-learning and discussion groups, what Radcliffe calls 'co-operative self-instruction', located within 'a tri-partite and interlocked, self-generated collective effort to increase the intellectual powers, financial (and hence physical) well-being, and the political status of the masses' (1997, p. 144).

The dominance of mutual improvement societies can also be seen as part of a wider nineteenth-century cultural craze for 'self-help' following Samuel Smiles's 1859 publication, *Self-Help*, which 'codified the supremacy of aspiration over occupation as a marker of identity for thousands of readers on the ill-defined boundary of the lower-middle and upper-working classes' (Rodrick, 2001, p. 39). This interest in self-help, with a particular emphasis on the importance of an intellectual life for all, reached all sectors of society. There were, therefore, mutual improvement societies among all social groups – even those, such as the middle and upper classes, who had other educational options available to them.

The theme of the relationship between mutual improvement societies and Mechanics' Institutes (or other educational opportunities for working people) recurs in Dakin's (1991) work on New Zealand. Dakin argues that New Zealand imported the British traditions of both Mechanics' Institutes and mutual improvement societies, and yet mutual improvement societies only really took off in New Zealand when Mechanics' Institutes went into decline (largely to do with funding) in the 1870s. Between 1870 and 1915, these self-run societies 'constituted the most significant development in adult education' (p. 243) in New Zealand. Their popularity was also compounded by the predominantly rural, sparsely populated nature of New Zealand, making a trip to a town large enough to have formal educational provision difficult for many. By contrast, mutual improvement societies, as in Britain, met at members' homes or in village halls, making them an educational, and social, opportunity available to most people. As in Britain, mutual improvement societies seem to have gone into decline from World War I onwards, potentially because of new educational and work opportunities opening up, the role of the radio, or other factors in a dramatically changing society. However, as Dakin warns, because mutual improvement societies (like other reading circles) met informally and usually received no public funding, they were (and are) by nature obscured, making it harder to chart their existence.

One mutual improvement society that was well-documented is the Kalamazoo Ladies' Library Association, a reading circle founded in 1852 with the aim of furthering women's 'mental development and self-improvement' (Jackson, 1999, p. 14). The women of Kalamazoo, Michigan, gathered together on a regular basis to read and discuss their reading, electing a weekly chairwoman and group note-taker. The existence of the chairwoman and note-taker (and official library location) meant that regular records were taken of the group's activities, which were carefully filed away in the library. The Kalamazoo Ladies' Library Association still exists, except now to provide women from the Kalamazoo area with scholarships for accessing higher education. Graff (1979) describes similar, though perhaps less well-organized, reading circles within late nineteenth- and early twentieth-century Canadian 'workingmen's reading rooms', forums where workers got to know one another over reading, study and discussion. In Southwold, Suffolk, England, there remains a Sailors' Reading Room, purpose-built in 1864 as a 'Room of Rest and Recreation' – and reading – for sailors and fishermen. It is now both a museum and a social club for local fisherman, life boatmen and coastguards, and still the site of regular reading and discussion (Southwold Museum, 2010).

Providing an insight into reading circles formed of religious, rather than occupational, groupings, Baker (1993) explores contemporary reading practices in Kalaodi, a village in eastern Indonesia, during Ramadan:

> Every evening neighbours (men and women) gather at someone's house and sit around a cluster of tables on which are laid several copies of the Koran ... Taking turns and correcting each other when mistakes are made, they read each evening ... so that in thirty days they will have completed their task of reading the Koran twice (pp. 105–106).

These are reading circles formed for a very specific religious purpose, and yet, as Baker stresses, these circles are also about enjoying the company of friends and neighbours. After each evening's reading is finished, they serve one another refreshments and talk into the night. The reminiscences groups written about by Mace (1995) (discussed briefly in Chapter 1) are also examples of reading circles, as members met on a weekly basis to talk, write and read, learning from one another.

Finally, sociologist Joan Swann and colleagues (Swann, 2009; Swann & Allington, 2009) studied sixteen reading circles across Britain, including all-male, all-female and mixed-gender groups, groups meeting in private homes, in a library, shops, bars, village halls, a school, a workplace and a prison. She found that groups were differently organized (some had 'facilitators' elected each week to balance the discussions, others did not) but shared key features. For example, each group combined a discussion of a book (usually a novel) with more personal discussions. Swann found members enjoyed the discussions, developed a greater understanding of the book, expanded their vocabularies, and relished the intellectual challenge and the chance to talk about the books' use of language (a completely new experience to most) along with the opportunity to discuss their own lives. The members also valued making interpretations individually and as a group. To further pursue what reading circle members get out of their circles, I'd like to turn to two larger-scale, contemporary studies of reading circles: the work of Elizabeth Long and the work of Jenny Hartley.

Elizabeth Long

The American scholar Elizabeth Long has made two invaluable contributions to reading circle research. The first, 'Textual Interpretation as Collective Action', was published in *The Ethnography of Reading* in 1993. Here, Long argues that the culturally dominant idea of the lone reader is a misleading myth which obscures both the 'social infrastructure' and the 'socially framed' nature of reading: 'social isolation depresses readership, and social involvement encourages it. Most readers need the support of talk with other readers' (Long, 1993, pp. 190–191). She goes on to argue that the myth of the lone reader also obscures the history of reading circles, such the sixteenth-century French village gatherings, where groups read romances, and 'perhaps more radically, from the vernacular Bible' (p. 193). Long also describes 'secret Protestant' reading groups and late nineteenth-century women's literary societies and study groups, where middle-class women met to read literature as well as to organize themselves in local and national politics. These circles were formed for concrete political, educational and social purposes.

Long then turns to the *why* of the reading circles formed without such overt or obvious political purposes, arguing that reading in groups 'not only offers occasions for explicitly collective textual interpretations, but … nurtures new ideas that are developed in conversation with other people as well as with the books'. Reading circles are a way of forging a 'social identity' through conversation (p. 194). Finally, she turns to her own research on contemporary reading circles: male, female and mixed-gender groups, groups meeting in cafés, libraries, bookshops and, most frequently, participants' homes. These groups are 'the territory of middle- and upper-class literary culture in Houston' (p. 196) and, for housewives with children, are often a much-needed 'lifeline out of their housebound existence into a world of adult sociability and intellectual conversation' (p. 198). The conversation of these groups was often 'transformative' for individuals: indeed, people joined circles for this very challenge to their own thinking and life decisions. Reading circles, Long stresses, represent reading at its most active; they are both 'products and producers of culture' (p. 205).

This work is expanded in a book-length study published in 2003: *Book Clubs: Women and the Uses of Reading in Everyday Life*. This too combines a historical examination of reading circles with primary research into contemporary groups. While recognizing that reading circles are difficult to study because of their invisibility to official or documented culture, Long's primary interest remains: why do so many women talk of their reading circles as a 'salvation, life raft, saving grace' (Long, 2003, p. ix)? Looking to the past, she notes that in the United States, women's book clubs 'spread from the urban centres of the Northeast across the American continent to the West almost as fast as did the frontier' (p. 34) precisely because, as Sicherman (1989) has also suggested, at a time of limited educational opportunities for women, women's reading circles fulfilled the function of the more formal education that many young men received.

However, this argument does not explain the enduring, and perhaps even increasing, popularity of women's reading circles. Long researched well over a hundred different reading groups in Houston and Harris County, before focusing on one particular subsection: groups of White women. Numerous commonalities emerged. Books were selected through group negotiation and/or members taking turns to make selections. Most circles read novels and spent at least an hour of each meeting discussing the book they had all been assigned to read at home, followed by more general/personal discussion. In all cases, the group interaction was in the form of an extended conversation, with most groups preferring to explore and research ideas themselves rather than invite visiting experts into the circles. Many groups observed how their discussions of character and character motivation blurred the boundaries between themselves and their fictional 'others'. Reading circles offered these women a chance to try on another identity while experiencing a relief from their own. In the words of one member, 'It's a kind of therapy' (p. 147).

Long makes three points that are crucial to understanding the appeal of contemporary reading circles. At a time where women in the United States have (most would argue) the same educational opportunities as men (and therefore reading circles are not a stand-in for formal educational opportunities), the rise of all-female groups may be the result of a decreasing number of other all-female social spaces. Because of (not despite) a greater number of choices in most women's lives, women need a place to meet other women and articulate the complexities of these choices. Second, reading circles are places of potential, if temporary, loss of self (in identification with action and characters) and, simultaneously, places for exploration of personal and social identity. Finally, and integrally, members do not come to their circles simply to express their already formulated conclusions about the book (or about life): members come in order to formulate ideas communally. The *communal* thinking processes and formulation of ideas is key.

Jenny Hartley

Jenny Hartley's *The Reading Groups Book* (2002) is – superficially – quite different from Long's work. It is less academic in style, locating itself for a different market – less for academics and more for adult reading circle members themselves. A quarter of the book consists of tables and appendices, including charts analysing the characteristics of three hundred and fifty UK groups, the types/genres of books read, popular authors, bestsellers lists and reading lists from individual groups. It also begins with a foreword by the novelist Margaret Forster, whose novels are particularly popular with reading circles. In her foreword, Forster discusses the recent 'explosion' of reading circles and writes that, as someone who would not consider reading in a circle, preferring to read alone, she longed for someone or something to explain their appeal. This, she notes, is exactly what Hartley's book does. This is also, despite the superficial differences, what Long's book does. *The Reading Groups Book* was also researched, written and published in the same time-period as Long's: both writers reacting to the *zeitgeist* of reading circle popularity.

The preface to Hartley's 2002–2003 edition explains that when her research began in 1998, 'we got a few blank looks: "What *is* a reading group?"' (p. xi), while 'now', (in 2002):

> Reading groups are hard to avoid. In the first years of the twenty-first century they have featured in *Simpson*'s cartoons and episodes of *The Sopranos*; and in the UK they have achieved their own TV show, Channel 4's surprise hit comedy, *The Book Group* ... more people are joining one, sometimes more than one ... People have always read in groups of course, but the late 1990s saw an increase in their popularity and a corresponding flurry of media interest ... No one knows how many they are. Estimates run as high as 50,000 in Britain and 500,000 in America. (p. ix)

Heeding numerous warnings that reading circles rarely leave a trace, and so a seeming increase in numbers may simply really be an increase in visibility, it nevertheless seems that there has indeed been what Forster called an 'explosion' in reading circles. While Hartley does not really answer the question of why so many and why at this point in time, she uses data from discussions with more than three hundred and fifty British reading circles – and additional international examples – to examine how groups work and what members get out of them.

Most groups met monthly, with some meeting weekly and some only three or four times a year. Many groups also met for social occasions, such as Christmas parties. Eighty per cent meet in members' homes, 6 per cent in libraries and 14 per cent elsewhere (including bars and cafés). The majority of groups contain members from the same neighbourhood, with people joining through word of mouth. Groups are urban and rural, male, female and mixed, though all-female groups are the majority. Many groups are of approximate age bands, with members in their twenties, or thirties, or over-sixties and so on. Most groups have a clear sense of the right number of members, which is, on average, between six and twelve. Twenty-one per cent of groups have been meeting for more than ten years, while the Bristol Friendly Reading Society has been meeting since October 1799. Many groups serve food and drinks – some just drinks, and lots of them.

Most groups have difficulty choosing their books. Some use selections offered by magazines or online book clubs, some take turns to choose, some vote on suggestions and others have incredibly complicated methods of making selections, involving lists and ranks. Members often feel responsible for their choices, guilty or angry if others do not like their choices, and sometimes resentful if their choices/ideas are not used. Whatever the turmoil of book selection, Hartley reports the passion and energy of the discussions. Some groups have rules to keep discussions of members' personal lives separate from discussions of the book, while others see these as one and the same. It is the discussion which these reading circle members value above all – the opportunity to exchange ideas, what members described as sharing a 'common culture', the 'cross fertilisation' of 'spirited chat' (pp. 128–129) with a loyal, supportive group of people who are (crucially) neither work colleagues nor family.

Reading Circles in 2010/2011

When I was starting to write this chapter, I decided to contact some contemporary reading circles to see what they could tell me about what they did and why they did it. Between January 2010 and January 2011 I followed leads from friends, colleagues, neighbours and libraries, pursued email trails and word-of-mouth recommendations. I spoke to members of fifteen different reading circles, based in the United Kingdom, Ireland, France, Canada and the United States, and exchanged emails with an additional forty-seven, from these same countries and also Sweden, Switzerland and Japan. This was a very informal process, following leads as and when they appeared, but given the often hidden nature of reading circles, it seemed one way of getting a sense of the contemporary, and international, picture.

The vast majority of these circles meet in members' homes, with a few meeting in local libraries and one meeting in a café. Echoing Long and Hartley's findings, more than 80 per cent are women-only groups, with one group for only young men (meeting in a London library), another of older men, and the rest mixed. Most, but not all, read novels. My investigation process told me two things. On one hand, circle members were extraordinarily generous with their time: they were more than happy to talk about their groups and many invited me to visit. The world of reading circles seemed open and visible: once I opened my eyes, reading circles were everywhere. Yet the process of finding circles to talk to was startlingly random: which groups I found was the product of chance, influenced by my own network of contacts, by the chaos of personal memory, by which libraries responded to me or by who checked their email regularly or listened to their voicemail. It is therefore possible that there are many more all-male circles out there, or groups reading only history and never novels. For this reason alone, I will resist the temptation to try to identify majority/minority trends, but rather present isolated examples of how certain reading circles worked – case-studies of the possible.

An all-female Japanese group meet fortnightly and aimed to get through a novel every two months. They set a number of pages or chapters to read between sessions, start each session with a drink and spend one hour taking turns reading aloud from what they have already read at home, before eating dinner together. After dinner, over sweets and tea, they discuss the novel, including predicting what might happen next. They have been following this pattern for five years. The predictive discussion is the highlight of their time together. A member of the mixed-gender Irish circle was particularly interested in talking about how discussions of the book and discussions of their personal lives merged. She explained that they decide on the books to read a year in advance, meet monthly, read one book a month and spend all their meeting time in discussion, 'but we are really talking about ourselves'. Similarly focused was the French woman who echoed Long's idea about the need for all-female gatherings: 'we talk about the books, of course, but we do it to get away from our husbands or boyfriends. There are few times to be just women. There are more for men: they can play football or have "business meetings"'. This, she felt, explained why there are so few all-male reading circles: 'They have other things to do.'

By contrast, an American woman told me that a friend of hers recently joined a reading circle specifically for couples: 'they rotate houses and discuss books over dinner ... She just started going this year and really enjoys it'. At this group, members enjoy socializing with their partners while also talking about books. As if extending this train of thought, a member of an American all-female circle listed the varying motivations of her fellow members, from 'very serious, well-read people to people that hardly read. Some are looking for more intellectual stimulation; others socializing'. She personally likes the supportive aspect of the group: 'We have come to support members in need, i.e. someone is sick or spouse is sick.'

Another woman explained that she has been member of one circle since retiring nineteen years ago, and was in a second for four years. She was very clear on what works and what does not:

Sam, there needs to be a facilitator to avoid 'all jumping in' which sometimes becomes chaos and/or allows for one or two people monopolizing the conversation. Frankly, I don't enjoy most paid facilitators [paid by club dues]. I feel that it is good for us to experience leading and some facilitators are deadly. Once there was an author ... facilitating and I managed to get a good nap.

She further explains why reading circle members should take turns to act as 'facilitator': 'Giving attention to different methods of facilitating makes us alert .... The hostess of each meeting should facilitate.'

An all-female Canadian reading circle of ten members does just this. Each member chooses a novel that she has already read and feels confident that the group will love. She then leads the session where that novel is discussed. One member thought it was 'crazy' for a group to choose books that no one had read: 'What if it turned out to be a waste of time?' The important thing, she explained, is sharing 'wonderful experiences'. The all-older-male rural English circle operates similarly, taking turns to recommend books and then leading the discussions of their own recommendations. Another reading circle (or perhaps more accurately, a mutual improvement society) consists entirely of Ecuadorians living in London. They meet once a month in someone's house for an afternoon. Each month it is one member's turn to present and discuss a book, either fiction or non-fiction. Unlike the other circles I spoke to, only the presenter has read the book being presented. He or she (this was one of the few mixed-gender groups) describes the book, including details of the author's background and historical context, and the others ask questions. After the meeting, the presenter emails a summary of the presentation to the others so they can decide whether or not to read it themselves. However, in the next session, they do not discuss this book further: instead, it is the turn of a different member to present another book. The aim, they explained, is to 'educate each other about different specialisations', and because most members are busy, they like to hear about a book before committing to reading it. One member told me that the group is primarily political: 'The real reason we meet is to talk about politics.'

Similarly driven is the science group that I visited in a café in central London. This group has been running for more than ten years and consists of four women and one man, a science teacher who supplies the desired scientific expertise. In the session I sat in on, however, the science expert did not talk any more than any of the other group members. The women asked the science-related questions that had been bothering them ('Why do your fingers get pruney when you've been in water for too long?' or 'What is the difference between force and energy?') and the science teacher took the lead on the explanation. Significantly, though, the explanation is in the form of a conversation, with each member asking and answering in equal measure. This is unlike the other circles in that books are not central to the meetings (it is a mutual improvement society rather than a reading circle), and yet in every other respect (centrality of discussion, development of relationships, communal formulation of ideas, enjoyment of each others' company) it is remarkably similar.

Though some of these groups used the internet to research information about books and authors, none mentioned using any of the published guides created for reading circles, though these are available. *The Book Club Bible* (2007), for example, consists of novel recommendations, including reviews written by other reading circles. Likewise, the *Bloomsbury 21* series includes 'reading club guides' at the back of each novel, containing information about the book and author, questions for discussion, suggested further reading and a list of the author's favourite books. There are, of course, many TV book clubs, including *Oprah* and *Richard and Judy*, some of which are little more than outlets for selling books, while others involve in-depth discussion. However, none of the reading circle members that I spoke to mentioned watching these, or equivalents in other countries.

The Jane Austen Book Club and *The Guernsey Literary and Potato Peel Pie Society*

I will not here trace the presence of reading circles in the media, though there are, as Hartley (2002) indicated, numerous examples in sitcoms, TV and radio dramas and in films. Usually, these provide a plot device or a flavour of the times, fulfilling the same function as scenes showing characters attending yoga classes or using laptops. However, one example stands out because it really is *about* the what, how and why of reading circles. Karen Joy Fowler's *The Jane Austen Book Club* was first published in 2004, and was followed by Robin Swicord's film of the same name in 2007. The novel includes a 'Reader's Guide' and tongue-in-cheek, self-referential 'questions for discussion' at the end. It is in the 'suggested reading' at the end of this chapter. However, here I would like to examine the film (Swicord, 2007) because in the condensing/refocusing act that any novel-to-film adaptation necessarily makes, the film *The Jane Austen Book Club* is even more startlingly 'about' reading circles, from its first shot to its last.

The film opens with a quotation from *Pride and Prejudice*: 'Is not general incivility the very essence of love?' This is followed by a frenetic soundtrack and then establishing shots locating us in present-day urban California. This is modern life at its most routinely and mundanely stressful and frustrating – not tragic or painful, but absolutely *uncivil*. People struggle to communicate with each other on mobile phones, trying to talk without being able to see each other's faces, machines of all kinds malfunction in the most unhelpful ways. A machine does not hold the parking ticket out far enough for a young woman to reach it. The ticket falls and she has to crawl under her car to retrieve it, watched but not helped by other people whose faces she cannot see. We see another woman forced to take off layers of outdoor clothing and bags as quickly as possible to go through a security scanning machine just to get into her place of work, where she is rushed but not greeted. One woman's beloved dog dies (leading her friends to observe that 'we all need connection, conversation, sex, companionship'), and almost simultaneously another woman weeps, tears of disappointment about her marriage mixing with equally hot tears of disappointment about a new Jane Austen film adaptation. The 'all-Jane-Austen-all-the-time' book club is thus born. Jane Austen is 'the perfect antidote ... to what? ... to life', and so six members (five women and one young man) set about reading six Austen novels in six months.

Jane Austen's words and worlds become a lens through which to view their real-life pains and a foil with which to discuss them: 'Reading

Jane Austen is a battlefield.' As they discuss the novels, they are discussing their lives and vice versa: the novels give them a language to talk about the relationship between their inner and outer lives. As dramas evolve between individual members of the circle, these are played out (as in Austen's novels) in group situations. What is a debate about the book for four of the members is a lovers' quarrel for two; what is a discussion of a passage is also (at times) a dramatization of that passage in the context of their modern lives. Over their six months and six novels, they analyse their own lives, try on new ones, mourn lost loves and plot new ones, act civilly and uncivilly, reach out and shrink back, and develop their understanding of the novels of Jane Austen. And, like Mary Poppins when the wind changes, by the time the six novels are finished their lives are healed. Their reading circle was their civility and their community.

The second fictional reading circle that I would like to discuss is very different: *The Guernsey Literary and Potato Peel Pie Society* (Shaffer & Barrows, 2009). Compared to *The Jane Austen Book Club*, this novel seems, at first reading, to be much less 'about' reading circles and far more about the World War II and postwar experiences of the Guernsey Islanders. Yet in a number of ways it echoes and adds to the ideas on reading circles already presented in this chapter. What seems to be an introduction to the novel (or may be the beginning of the novel) explains that its main author, Mary Ann Shaffer, was encouraged to write it by the members of her writing group. I have not discussed writing groups, or their relationship with reading groups, but writing groups are surely another of our present-day versions of mutual improvement societies, and also, in their efforts to develop one another's writing, these groups usually involve a great deal of reading. Furthermore, the same introductory passage informs us that Mary Ann Shaffer became seriously ill towards the end of writing this book and asked her niece, Annie Barrows, to finish it. This novel is therefore not only about communal reading, but also the product of communal writing and discussion.

The novel's protagonist, a writer called Juliet, is originally motivated to get to know members of the Guernsey Literary and Potato Peel Pie Society by a journalistic assignment to write something on the philosophical importance of reading. We, as readers, never get to read this article, but we are told that her letters from the reading circle members about the role their reading circle has played in their lives formed its basis. We also learn that the reading circle (which operates in a similar way as the Ecuadorian group described earlier in this chapter) originally formed through grave necessity; under the German occupation, a group of friends were caught out after curfew (illegal), having having illegally roasted an illegally possessed pig in the middle of the night. When confronted, they invented the excuse of the reading circle, an idea so respectable or appealing or amusing to the soldiers such that they were let off with a warning. To guard against being found out (if checked upon), they decide that it would be safest to actually start meeting as a reading circle. Born, therefore, of one necessity, the reading circle continues to meet because of another necessity: the need to gather and entertain one another, to take their minds off the occupation, to rediscover other lives unrelated to the rules, restrictions and talk of camps. This pattern of forming a reading circle to meet a pressing necessity and yet continuing it to meet another (equally important but less urgent) necessity echoes the reading circle in *Reading Lolita in Tehran* (Nafisi, 2004), and, perhaps, women's reading circles more broadly, formed as the only educational option for many women, and continued for all the important reasons explored in this chapter.

Finally, the novel's introduction and 'afterword' stress that this is a fiction designed to teach us about the rarely told occupation and post-war experiences of the islanders: it is a gathering of truths (this is worth remembering in the discussions of truth and fiction in Chapter 7). Annie Barrow's 'afterword' also describes how this fictitious reading circle is reborn whenever one reader talks to another reader about the novel. These conversations create the novel (Iser's *work*) not only in one reader's mind, but also communally, *between* readers, conjuring, prolonging and maintaining a real reading circle out of a fiction.

Chapter Summary

Reading circle research in the educational contexts of schools and EFL demonstrates that reading circles can develop learners' vocabularies, comprehension and interpretative, organizational and social skills, along with confidence: confidence as readers, as students and as members of groups. Historical and ethnographic research tells us that adults have formed themselves into reading circles (and other mutual improvement societies) for hundreds of years in order to support and develop one another's literacy, to read and listen to one another, to teach and learn from one another and to enjoy human contact. These groups have formed due to a lack of other educational opportunities, but also as a preference. Individuals want and need the support of others: the challenge, motivation, companionship, discipline, messiness, love and civility that sitting and talking in a circle with other people can bring. This is at the heart of my rationale for the main research case study of this book. Educational research tells us that reading circles can help develop reading, writing and discussion skills; history and ethnography tell us that people benefit from forming themselves into circles to learn from and with one another, and to fit intellectual or spiritual contemplation into busy or difficult lives. There is therefore a great need for research into the use of reading circles in adult literacy education.

Suggested Reading

Boyarin, J. (ed.) (1993), *The Ethnography of Reading*. Berkeley, CA: University of California Press.
A diverse collection of articles on 'the ethnography of reading', from Howe's 'The Cultural Construction of Reading in Anglo-Saxon England' to Long's 'Textual Interpretation as Collective Action'.

Fowler, K. J. (2004), *The Jane Austen Book Club*. London: Penguin Books.
A poignant and very funny novel about six lives meeting one novelist in one reading circle.

Hartley, J. (2002), *The Reading Groups Book* (2002–2003 edn). Oxford: Oxford University Press.
Hartley's in-depth study of (mainly UK) reading circles from 1998–2002 investigates why people join reading circles, how groups operate and what they read.

Harvey, S., & Daniels, H. (2009), *Inquiry Circles in Action: Comprehension & Collaboration*. Portsmouth, NH: Heinemann.
This is a very teacher-focused book on how reading circles or 'inquiry circles' can be used for teaching and learning any subject on the school curriculum.

Long, E. (2003), *Book Clubs: Women and the Uses of Reading in Everyday Life*. Chicago, IL: University of Chicago Press.
Long's contemporary study of all-women Texan reading circles examines why members join and why they stay.

Shaffer, M. A., & Barrows, A. (2009), *The Guernsey Literary and Potato Peel Pie Society*. London: Bloomsbury.
A novel about the members of a reading circle in occupied and post-war Guernsey (see discussion earlier in chapter).

Swicord, R. (2007), *The Jane Austen Book Club* (film). USA: Sony Picture Classics.
The film adaptation of Fowler's novel – if there is one film 'about' reading circles, this is it (see discussion earlier in this chapter).

Chapter 6

Researching a Reading Circle: What We Did

The previous chapter established that adults have developed, explored and enjoyed their reading in peer-led mutual improvement societies and reading circles, over centuries and across the globe. Research from the EFL and schools sectors proclaims, loud and clear, that reading circles can be effective in developing reading, writing, speaking and listening skills. Chapter 4 tentatively suggested that the novel – the most popular choice of text for contemporary reading circles – could offer advantages as a tool for developing certain types of reading skills (such as inference). The historical overview of reading pedagogy and provision in Chapter 3 revealed that adults have learnt to read through informal networks of mutual support (what Radcliffe [1997] calls provision '*of* the people'). Further, the adult literacy pedagogy which has developed across the Anglophone world over the last 40 years includes a focus on adult-appropriate resources, a predominantly text-based approach (with word and sentence-level work led by the text) and an interest in peer-work. Finally, while Chapter 1 argued that reading is itself a vast and contested area, Chapter 2 suggested that we do know that adults read novels, silently and aloud, alone and in groups.

For all of these reasons, I decided to try two things: set up a reading circle within an existing adult literacy group in formal adult literacy provision, and then use this circle as a research case-study. In this chapter, I will discuss the transition from adult literacy class to reading circle, as well as the transition from reading circle to research case-study. This will be followed by a more detailed explanation of how the reading circle worked, which may be of interest to those who would like to try something similar. Finally, I will take a closer look at my research process, which may be of value to those interested in research. Those not interested in research may wish to skip these sections.

Adult Literacy Learners to Reading Circle Members

In September 2008, I was starting the academic year with a new group of adult literacy learners at a large London further education college. This group was labelled according to the English Adult Literacy Core Curriculum (Good et al., 2001) at 'Entry Three/Level 1', meaning that the adults in this group had walked into the college, said they wanted to improve their literacy and been given a formal assessment which placed them at this particular literacy 'level'. Learners placed at this level can usually read shorter texts but may not be confident reading texts of more than one or two pages, and may have trouble decoding longer, less common, or less phonically regular words. These adults all came to college because they wanted to improve their literacy: for some, writing was their priority (perhaps improving their spelling, learning how to use punctuation marks, or practising writing a formal letter), while for others reading was a priority.

There were ten people in this particular group: seven women and three men. Their ages ranged from nineteen to sixty-ish. Three had grown up speaking English, while the other seven had learnt English as a second, third or fourth language as children, teenagers or adults. These proportions were typical of formal adult literacy provision in London at this time. The course began in September 2008 and finished in July 2009, meeting for three hours one evening a week. Three of these ten learners dropped out of the course over the winter break due to work and family commitments. This too is statistically regular: learners in adult literacy courses frequently have to drop out (sometimes for a short time, sometimes for a longer time) when their personal circumstances change.

I had been teaching this level for 8 years and over this time had found that most people placed at this level are eager to experiment with reading longer texts, such as novels or biographies. I had also noticed that most groups wanted to read 'together', usually meaning that everyone reads the same text at more or less the same pace, while also doing some reading aloud to one another, some silent reading and some listening to me read aloud. As anticipated, in our first few weeks together – as we were getting to know one another, our needs and goals – the group came up with a list of the types of text they wanted to read. This included novels (as well as letters, reports, emails and poems), and so we started to talk together about the different ways that people read novels and the possible ways we could read a novel. Several spoke of book clubs (mentioning *Oprah* and *Richard and Judy*), reading clubs or circles (seen on television or in films). We discussed whether it would be feasible or desirable to set up our own reading circle (and this led to a discussion of this research project, which is covered in the next section of this chapter).

Most members of the group were busy and unable to devote extra time outside of our weekly three-hour time slot and so proposed using the last forty minutes of our weekly course time for the reading circle. We could, they argued, stop 'our usual class work' and become a reading circle. We discussed how this would work. With an eye on making sure that everyone's views were represented, I handed out a short questionnaire on what they wanted to do in their reading circle time. Learners filled this in, some with assistance from me, and then we used it as the basis for further discussion. They wanted to: read a novel, read it aloud together, read it at home alone, discuss what they had read, learn new words and how to read more words, and talk through their ideas and feelings about what they were reading. Interestingly, reading aloud was not practised by the majority of the reading circles discussed in the previous chapter, and I had not mentioned reading aloud in our discussions. However, it was something that each of the ten learners requested on their individual questionnaires.

Next, we talked of how to choose the novel. We discussed what a novel was, making sure that everyone shared the same idea, more or less, and established criteria for selection. Someone said that it has to be 'interesting', another stipulated 'not too long' (less than two hundred pages), someone else suggested that we should look for something with 'not too many complicated words' and several noted that it had to be 'fun'. It was decided that the following week everyone would bring in something that met these criteria. Five people brought in novels (*The Alchemist, Of Mice and Men, Double Indemnity, The Color Purple* and *Sex and the City*) and I brought in a further two (*Passenger* and *Dr Jekyll and Mr Hyde*). We agreed that we would not reveal who had contributed which book, but would instead lay them all on the table, look at them, read the back covers and talk. After twenty minutes the learners voted. *Passenger* and *Of Mice and Men* shared equal top position, and so we did a revote on these two. *Passenger* received the most votes and so I ordered eleven copies. Two weeks later the books arrived and the reading circle began.

Passenger

Passenger (Cowie, 2008) is a one hundred and eighty-four-page novel about a forty-two-year-old violinist, Milan, who begins to hear a musical 'tapping' coming from inside his body. When he goes to hospital, they find his twin embedded within him ('foetus in fetu'). The twin seems to be the source of the music. Milan names her Roma, develops a method of communicating with her, and begins to introduce her to his world. As he does so, Milan loses one girlfriend, a Japanese flautist called Karen, and gains another, Murri, a special needs teacher.

Reading Circle to Research Case-Study

As soon as this group expressed their interest in becoming a reading circle, I realized that this was the research opportunity I had been looking for. I wanted to research a reading circle within existing adult literacy provision, and I wanted to use one of my own teaching groups for both practical and methodological reasons. I felt a group that already knew me (if only for a few weeks) would be more likely to believe that I was not looking for a 'right' answer when being interviewed, for example. I also believed that only by using a group I knew could I be sure that they really wanted to be a reading circle. It was integral that this motivation preceded any mention of my own interest in this area or research plans. I also felt that embedding a reading circle within existing provision time would be the more practical option (as the learners felt too), given how busy most people are, and I was reluctant to 'take up' another teacher's teaching time.

There were significant ethical issues at play. It was necessary to ensure that learners were happy with their new reading circle being used for research, and I therefore had to explain the nature of my proposed research and its possible audiences transparently. I also had to speak to each learner individually to ensure each had understood what I was requesting. I had to clarify that saying no to being a case-study for research would not mean that they could not become a reading circle, and would not cause me any difficulties. I had to be prepared to wait for another opportunity to do this research if even one member was unsure. Luckily, after much discussion, all ten members of the group consented to being involved in this research.

However, ethically, there was more at stake than the issue of individuals consenting to being involved in a research study. These learners had signed up for three hours of adult literacy provision per week. To use forty minutes of this for a peer-run reading circle was potentially depriving them of their allotted time; I had to be sure that the reading circle would still be providing a form of adult literacy provision. I received permission from my line manager after convincing her that the proposed reading circle had valuable learning outcomes, as well as my research aims. But what of the learners? I had already determined that each member of the group was happy to be in a reading circle and happy to take part in a research study. However, it is impossible to ignore the myriad reasons why learners may agree to something their teacher suggests: to please the teacher, to be seen as 'good students', out of respect, out of kindness or out of curiosity. Therefore I had to be confident myself that regardless of why participants agreed, the reading circle would be of pedagogical benefit immediately as well as over the longer term. This also meant that I had to keep moving from my role as researcher back to that of teacher to make sure that learners were 'getting educational value' out of the circle.

Coincidentally, research ethics feature in *Passenger* too. Murri, Milan's girlfriend of some months, reveals to him that she has published her PhD thesis on 'communicating with isolates', based almost entirely on Roma (Milan's 'fetus in fetu' sister). He also discovers that Professor Conway, the sociologist who first put Milan in touch with Murri for advice on communicating with Roma, is Murri's PhD supervisor. Every reading circle member felt that Murri had 'used' Milan for her research, and agreed that she should have asked for his permission first. Most thought that Murri had started a relationship with Milan only in order to gather her data, taking advantage of him to complete her PhD and further her career. Participants' outrage at this behaviour reminded me that though I had been open and gained permissions, I too was arguably using these learners to 'further my career'. I therefore had a serious moral obligation to make sure that they benefited from the reading circle time as much as – or more than – I did.

The Reading Circle Process

While we were waiting for the books to arrive, we returned to the subject of how we would use our reading circle time every week. I used, as I am using now, the pronoun 'we' so that the group did not feel abandoned or unsupported in the first weeks of the reading circle. However, as will be discussed in the next section, I aimed to be a 'marginal participant'. I sat with them, but tried to say as little as possible and encouraged them to self-run. The group decided to have a rotating chairperson, one member managing the circle each week. They also had a group note-taker to record what they did, for reference in future weeks. We allocated a notebook for this role and I also gave each member a notebook to use for the reading circle in any way they liked. The group reminded themselves of their initial aims for the circle: reading at home and reading aloud together, discussing ideas and learning to read new words.

Like most reading circles, the weekly sessions varied depending on their priorities and the moods on any given week. However, a pattern emerged: the group would decide on a chairperson and note-taker, the chairperson would remind the group of what they had agreed to read at home that week, the group would then talk about what they had read before taking turns to read aloud, usually stopping after each page to discuss 'what was going on' and to clarify particular words. When the chairperson noticed that it was almost the end of our time, he or she would ask the group how much of the novel they wanted to read for next week. The circle continued in this way until the novel was finished – approximately 6 months.

This is how the reading circle members described their sessions:

We read chapters every week and we talked about each chapter and what we thought about it as well, when something happened, that kind of thing. [The process taught me] to read slowly so I can actually see – because [usually] I read too fast and then I miss out what's going on … in the reading circle I read more slowly so I get it.

We were reading *Passenger* together and at home and we were talking about, we explain when we come back in class, what happen and words which we don't know the meaning, and we underline and then we discuss … and we are writing the meaning in the book to learn and for the spelling practice … I read some paragraphs and chapters at home. I didn't finish it all, I didn't understand it all, but when I read in class I understand the story, what it is saying.

We took notes and read and somebody has to let us know which page we read at home. Then someone read and, if some letters, some words we don't understand, then it mean we have to check together. [When I read at home] if I don't understand some, I look in the dictionary and then I know the meaning, write it down and read more. I read it all. I learn a lot because, it makes me think, you know?.

We read together and we discussed about the book and we had a chairman, and we had somebody who take the notes, and we read and we stopped and we discussed what that was all about and we had everyone's opinion about the pages – what's in there, ideas, words – discussed it all. I was actually trying to figure it out, um, Roma and Milan, what is happening between the two of them, and figuring it out. Milan had a life before Roma decided to pop out and what was going on in Milan's head: had he still got a life or has his life been turned upside down or changed? And for Roma – she appears – did she enjoy that or was it difficult? I was thinking of all this in my head.

We read aloud and analysed what we were reading and discussing types of situations to see if we agree on what is going on. We discussed different subjects. It was good, for example, there were some things that didn't come in my mind but other people got different ideas, or a different angle on the same thing, so it was good to discuss. Things came up.

The Research Process

This section will provide a more detailed examination of the research process.

Overview

Before the first reading circle session, I conducted a thirty-minute semi-structured interview with each participant to gather individual conceptualizations of reading and novel reading. When, from November 2008, the last forty minutes of our three-hour adult literacy session became a reading circle, I audio-taped each session and wrote a page of notes after it finished. Additionally, besides the group note-taker, members were also encouraged to take individual notes throughout. When we finished the novel in April 2009, I did thirty to forty-five minute individual semi-structured interviews with each remaining reading circle member to gather final conceptualizations of, and reflections on, novel reading and the reading circle process.

Theoretical perspectives

As Chapter 1 demonstrates, the theoretical perspectives of a field, or a particular researcher within that field, will determine how research is conducted, what is found and what is valued. For this research, my interest was in how participants conceptualize novel-reading processes and practices, what novel reading and reading circles are *for the reader*. An underlying argument of this book is that reading is, among other things, an experience and therefore can be fully understood only by accessing the first-person perspectives of those experiencing: that is, the readers. The core premise of this approach lies in phenomenology, which stresses 'the perceiver's vital and central role in determining meaning' (Cuddon, 1991, p. 705) and invites us to understand 'social phenomena from the actor's own perspectives, describing the world as experienced by the subjects' (Kvale, 1996,

p. 152). This emphasis on the first-person perspective can also be expressed in terms of philosophy of mind. Following Nagel's influential 'What is it like to be a bat?' (1974), I want to know *what it is like to read a novel.* I am concerned with 'the subjective character of experience' (Nagel, 1974, p. 435) and, also following Nagel, believe that one can find out what it is like to read a novel only by speaking to novel readers. As noted in Chapter 1, neuroscience may be able to tell us that a certain part of the brain is active when reading, but it will never be able to tell us what it *feels like* to read. We need readers to do this.

Methodology

There are three aspects to my methodology: this project as a case-study, this project as grounded theory and this project as community action research. A case-study is the attempt to learn something from a very particular and close look at one example, occurrence or 'case'. Two questions present themselves: what defines or delineates the case and what can be learnt from it? A case could be a person's life, or a year, month or week of a person's life. A case could be a group, an organization or an event. For this study, the case is the reading circle, but was it bounded by its place (our classroom), its weekly time-slot (8.20–9.00 p.m. on Tuesday evenings), its duration (November to April) or its membership? Defining my case became defining a reading circle: the members, the meetings, the duration of the novel-reading process, and the chosen novel itself. Case-study research also raises the question of what one case can tell us: does one case tell us about only that particular case, or can we use it to learn something about the wider world? This project can be classified as an 'explanatory' case-study (Yin, 2003) because I used one case to develop a theory about the use of reading circles in adult reading development. It could also be classified as an 'instrumental' case-study (Stake, 1994, 1998) because I aimed to use this one particular case to find out more about something wider: the potential value of reading circles in adult literacy provision.

The second aspect of my methodology is grounded theory. As well as providing a framework for data analysis (see later in this chapter), grounded theory is also a research methodology which aims to use data to build theory (from the 'ground' up) rather than test existing theory or hypotheses (Strauss, 1987; Strauss and Corbin, 1990). I was aiming to use this case to find out about (to build theory on) the use of reading circles in adult literacy provision. Yet it is the third aspect of my methodology that may be of most relevance to adult literacy teachers: the tradition of community-based action research. Stringer's concept of 'community-based action research':

> works on the assumption ... that all stakeholders – those whose lives are affected by the problem under study – should be engaged in the process of investigation. (Stringer, 1999, p. 10)

This project is an example of community-based action research, because I researched my teaching situation (action research), moving between the role of researcher and teacher on a weekly basis. The participants were also engaged in the process of investigation, continuously reflecting on their reading circle experience. The key stakeholders of this investigation of adult emergent reading – adult literacy learners and their teacher – all took part in the research and reflected on ways it can or should change our practice. For this reason, community-based action research is a popular and integral way for adult literacy teachers to conduct research, bridging the worlds of research and practice.

Data collection

I collected data in three ways: semi-structured interviews (including mind-mapping), observation/audio-taping of weekly reading circle sessions and 'field notes'(mine, the weekly note-taker's and members' individual notes). Additionally, I kept the materials used to set up the reading circles: notes of the group discussion, initial questionnaires and voting slips.

The initial and final semi-structured interviews followed an 'interview guide' (Cohen et al., 2007, p. 353) approach to find out as much as possible about what participants thought with minimal 'leading' through fixed questions. The structure of both sets of interviews was predominantly improvised from participant responses. At the end of each final interview, I asked the interviewee to produce a mind-map ('could be images, words, arrows, lines, anything') to sum up their reading circle experience, and then asked them to explain what they had produced. This was to provide a less word-based form of expression, potentially more suited to less confident writers, but also designed to provide a different way to ask interviewees to consolidate their thoughts and a vehicle for that consolidation. My aim was to better access the participants' own final reflections on the reading circle. Kress and Mavers (2005) suggest that different modes of expression can play different representative roles. This potential difference was one of my motivations for using mind-maps; I wanted to exploit 'the *materiality* of mode [to] provide different *affordances*' (p. 172) for interviewees to communicate their overall ideas about the reading circle. The resulting mind-maps are analysed in the next chapter.

The second form of data collection was audio-taping each weekly reading circle session. Audio-taping the sessions (and transcribing them myself each night) allowed me to be both a part of the reading circle group and a completely detached observer (when later listening to the tapes), even able to listen to, and adjust accordingly, my own participation. Cohen et al. (2007) classify case-study observation as either: 'non-participant' (when the observer is sitting at the back of a room taking notes) and 'participant', with 'participant' further divided into 'covert' (researchers joining groups without saying that they are researchers) and 'overt' (where the researcher's dual role is explicit). Robson (2002) divides overt participant observation into 'the participant as observer' and 'the marginal participant'. The role of 'participant as observer' is made explicit to all participants, but she or he nevertheless fully participates in activities. 'The marginal participant' does not participate fully, being instead 'a largely passive, though completely accepted, participant' (Robson, 2002, pp. 316–319).

I aimed for my role in the reading circle to be that of 'the marginal participant', as passive as possible to allow the learners to take ownership of the reading circle and effectively 'self-run'. Listening to and transcribing the tapes each night, I could see that I was veering between being 'the marginal participant' (as planned) and being 'the participant as observer', participating more fully. It was initially extremely challenging to be a member of the reading circle when the participants knew me as their teacher and so were more likely to want to ask me the meaning of a word than to ask one another. Paradoxically, I had to use my teacher role to encourage them to ask and answer one another's questions, not only as autonomous learners in any classroom, but also as self-managing members of a reading circle. Literature on participant observation discusses the problematic nature of the dual role of participant and researcher, just as literature on action research discusses the problematic nature of the dual role of teacher and researcher. Here I was negotiating all three: teacher, researcher and reading circle marginal participant.

Notes were also a significant aspect of the data collection. I kept a notebook of my own. Every night after the session I would write a page of notes recording who was at the session, what stood out – did we mainly read or mainly talk about words? Did anything strange happen? – and initial observations for analysis. This notebook was therefore a part of both data collection and data analysis. The group notebook and participants' individual notebooks were also both data collection and the beginnings of a communal aspect of data analysis, as participants recorded what they found significant, interesting or useful about the novel or reading circle process. These ideas were then developed in their final interviews.

Data analysis

The above methods of data collection yielded initial interview transcripts, taped reading circle sessions, final interview transcripts and notebooks full of notes. I used a five-stage process to analyse this qualitative data. The first stage was immersion in the data, beginning with writing the notes, listening to the tapes and transcribing. Immersion continued as I listened to all the tapes again to check the transcripts and read, and reread, all notes and transcripts. The second stage I am calling 'Becker-style' analysis after Becker's (1984) recommendation that researchers 'get started' with qualitative data analysis by reading and rereading the data before 'sit[ting] down and writ[ing] whatever came into [my] head, as though the study were done, without consulting … field notes' (Becker, 1984, p. 109). This allowed initial ideas and themes to emerge.

The third stage was a coding and categorization process; I used the grounded theory approach of open coding followed by axial coding (Strauss, 1987; Strauss and Corbin, 1990). This produced one hundred and thirty codes organized in eighteen over-arching categories. The fourth stage was the identification of themes emerging from these categories, extracting what these codes and categories could tell me about novel-reading, reading circles and adult reading development. I identified six themes:

1. *Reading as five acts*
2. *Reading identity*
3. *Knowing words*
4. *Building the story*
5. *Fiction, truth and learning*
6. *Reading as a group*

The fifth and final stage of data analysis was a return to the data for elaboration or exploration of these six themes, a return to the complexity or messiness that any systematic coding process necessarily obscures. This final stage of analysis is detailed in the next chapter.

This was a brief overview of just one way of doing qualitative, practitioner research. In the suggested reading section at the end of this chapter there are several research methods books with more ideas, explanations and integral in-depth discussions of the research issues I have skimmed through. I have not, for example, discussed reliability and validity, a key issue for any research: how do you know you are measuring what you think you are measuring? How do you know your research is trustworthy and will stand up to the scrutiny of others? How do you ensure your research will be useful to your field? Whatever our theoretical perspectives and chosen methods of data collection and analysis, action researchers need to pay close attention to two areas related to the dual role of teacher and researcher: ethics and bias. What are the ethical complexities of doing research with our own students or within our own teaching institutions (as discussed briefly earlier in this chapter)? What is the potential for bias: how could my involvement, as both teacher and researcher, affect my results and what can I do about this? See Duncan (2010) for a full discussion of these issues.

Chapter Summary

Over 9 months in 2008–2009, ten adult literacy learners and I took part in two processes. We created an informal, peer-led reading circle within formal adult literacy provision. This reading circle met for forty minutes every week, discussed what had been read at home, read aloud, asked one another about words, reconstructed or constructed plot and analysed characters. Second, we undertook a piece of action research, collecting and analysing data for a research study. I collected data in the form of individual interviews and mind-maps, audio-recordings of our weekly sessions and notes. The reading circle members analysed their data through their interviews, mind-maps and notes, and I used a five-step process to extract six themes from this mass of data. What we found out about novel-reading, reading circles and adult reading development is presented in the next chapter.

Suggested Reading

Becker, H. S. (1984), *Writing for Social Scientists*. Chicago, IL: University of Chicago Press.
Becker's engaging and highly practical guide to writing in the social sciences includes useful ideas on how to get started with qualitative data analysis.

Cohen, L., Manion, L., & Morrison, K. (2007), *Research Methods in Education* (6th edn). London: Routledge.
A popular and much-used research methods textbook – a valuable resource for newer researchers.

Cowie, B. (2008), *Passenger*. London: Old Street Publishing.
The novel we read (see description earlier in chapter).

Robson, C. (2002), *Real World Research*. Oxford: Blackwell.
As Cohen et al. above.

Stringer, E. T. (1999), *Action Research*. London: Sage.
A useful guide to action/practitioner research.

Chapter 7

Researching a Reading Circle: What We Found

This chapter presents the findings of the case study in two ways. It is the fifth and final stage of analysis, an analysis of six themes: reading as five acts; reading identity; knowing words; building the story; fiction, truth and learning; and reading as a group. However, I would like to start with the reading circle members' own final analyses: the mind-maps they drew and described to sum up their reading circle experience.

The Mind-Maps

At the end of their final individual interviews, I asked each reading circle member to put down on paper something (words or images) representing what the reading circle meant to them. Reading circle member Katherine (I am using pseudonyms) drew a picture of a large cake, with arrows around its edges, pointing outwards like sunbeams towards drawings of members of the reading circle. She described what she had produced:

> It's a cake ... Everybody liked it. We all took part in it. And it was like; how can I put it? Complementary. Everybody was complementing, try-ing to understand, trying to understand each other's points. It's kind of the, um, the physical and the visual, because everybody had the physical cake, the book. Everybody could pick it up and eat it whenever they felt like it, and the visual, that's the actual story, what's going on, what the ingredients is. I don't think there's any boundaries. When we was actually reading the book, everybody took part. We had a kind of, um, we had a spokesperson to keep us in order, but there wasn't any boundaries, every-body explored, everybody was free, explored their own ... wasn't afraid to explore. (Katherine final interview)

Katherine emphasized the reading circle as a communal activity, something that everybody was doing together, sharing and exploring.

Paula, by contrast, drew three small pictures on one sheet of paper. One picture is of a person, with a thought-bubble containing a cross and a book/page with the words 'Death of Roma' written on it. The second picture is of a thick book, perhaps a novel, with scribbles indicating lines or sentences, and the words 'new word' written on each page. The final picture is of a hand writing something into a notebook (Figure 3).

> That's the notebook that I took the notes down in, and that's me imagining what's going on, about Roma and things, and then that's me looking up new words in the dictionary, to learn new words. These were the main things that I was doing. (Paula final interview)

In contrast to Katherine, Paula focused on the three things *she* was doing in our reading circle process: taking notes in order, she explained, to help her

FIGURE 3   Paula's mind-map.

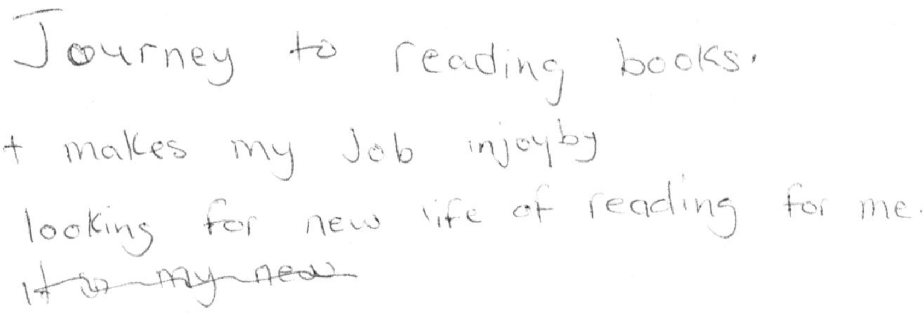

Journey to reading books.
+ makes my Job injoyby
looking for new life of reading for me.
~~it to my new~~

FIGURE 4   Beverley's mind-map.

'remember what's going on', imagining 'what was going on' and learning new words.

Despite being the group member least confident in her literacy, Beverley chose to sum up her experience in words rather than images. She wrote in three lines: 'Journey to reading books. / + makes my job injoyby / looking for new life of reading for me.' (She started to write a fourth line but changed her mind and crossed it out. See Figure 4.)

She elaborated:

> Right, the 'journey to reading books', it means that now I can pick up a novel or a book, knowing that I can read it and I will understand. And 'to make my job enjoyable' – I don't know if that's the way to write it ... because I understand if something is written down I can read it, because they do a lot of writing and if the nurse is not there I just have to pick it up and read what they have done, without them – the care plan – I can do that. And actually I'm looking forward to a new life of reading for myself. (Beverley final interview)

Beverley, too, emphasized her personal experience, and for her this was a journey from feeling unable to pick up a piece of text and read it, to feeling that now she has 'a new life of reading for myself'. She also explicitly linked her reading circle experience to her career as a care worker, indicating that now she feels more confident tackling the reading that is necessary for this role.

Safia did not want to draw or write anything to sum up the reading circle experience. However, she was happy to talk about it:

> I was reflecting on what is going on, what Milan is doing, why he is doing it, who are the others ... Milan was musician and then after he knew his

sister is inside his body, he starts like secret and then when they know, the doctors and then when they told him he started to contact with his sister, and then he was doing what she needs, how he communicated with her … how they were together. (Safia final interview)

Safia continued to talk about the world of the novel: the story and the characters. When asked again about the processes of the reading circle itself, she nevertheless continued to talk about the story.

By contrast, Aisha was eager to draw a representation of her experience (Figure 5), starting to draw as soon as she saw the piece of paper.

She described it:

That's the brain, and the heart, and this is, like, when I start to read and I am happy and I like it. I am happy it goes up and then it goes down because I feel sad about it and then up more and then down more … Most of them [emotions] come from my brain. No, my heart – no, my – both of them – it's your heart, yeah, when she [the reader] is happy. She is reading something happy and she is happy, and she is sad when the things are not right in the story and she feels sad and then it changes as she reads. (Aisha final interview)

Her description examines the interactions between the brain and heart when reading. However, more than providing an insight into how our brains

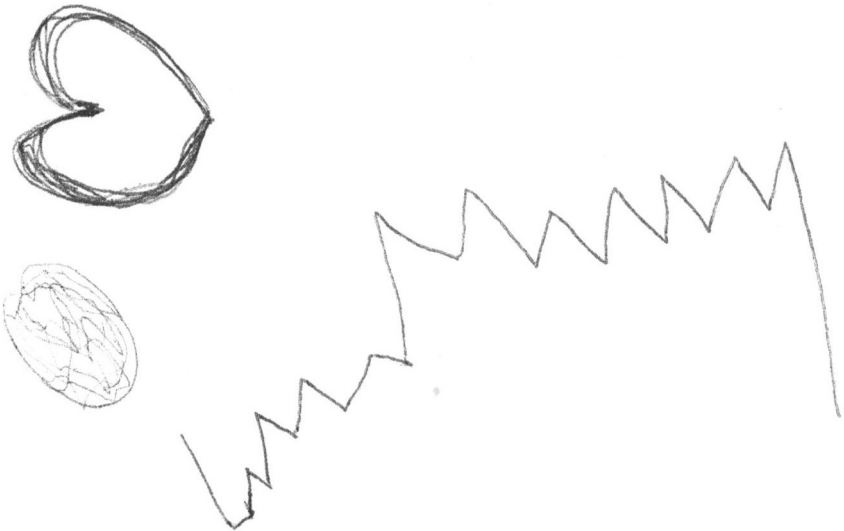

FIGURE 5   Aisha's mind-map.

and hearts work together to produce emotions as we read, Aisha's representation is notable for her absolute surety that this emotional-cognitive process is the most significant aspect of the reading circle experience.

Like Safia, Tania resisted putting anything on paper, but had a clear idea of how she wanted to sum up our reading circle experience:

> Reading *Passenger*, I learnt lots of words that I didn't know it before and we discussed, um, at the room, everybody, in the class, and get their ideas, different ideas ... Develop our language. (Tania final interview)

Tania combines an individual ('*I* learnt lots of words') and a group focus ('*we* discussed ... *everybody*'). In this summing up, as in the rest of her final interview, her focus was on how the reading circle developed her and her classmates' language skills. The discussion on the novel was important because it developed 'our language'.

Luis's mind-map (Figure 6) includes no words. It is a drawing of two people holding hands.

> It's a brother and a sister, with arms joined, a brother and a sister. They could have been like that but they're not ... I was imagining this, how it would have been if she'd been born naturally, how she's his sister, how he would have had some support if she'd been born naturally... I think it's about compassion, all about compassion. His compassion for her and her compassion for him. (Luis final interview)

Luis has identified what he sees as a main theme of *Passenger*, compassion or brotherly support, as also the characteristic feature of his reading circle experience.

Figure 6 Luis's mind-map.

These are the conclusions, or analyses, of the reading circle members themselves. They have identified the reading circle as a process of communal exploration, a group sharing or building, as personal development in following a story, developing vocabulary and expanding their confidence reading. They have described the reading circle as an emotional and intellectual experience, a process of social and linguistic development. Perhaps most importantly, they have characterized the reading circle as both a communal and an individual experience. I will refer back to these ideas in my own analysis of the six themes below.

1. Reading as Five Acts

From the initial interview process onwards, participant responses conceptualized reading as five distinct, though interrelated, acts: an educational act, a cognitive act, a communicative act, an imaginative act and an affective act. These acts are reminiscent of Jakobson's 'six basic functions of verbal communication ... referential, emotive, poetic, phatic, conative and metalingual' (Jakobson, 1960/1988, p. 38), with emotive, poetic and phatic as parallels to affective, imaginative and communicative; and conative, referential and metalingual as corresponding to aspects of the educational or cognitive acts. However, the key difference is that while Jakobson's functions are different reasons *why* we use verbal communication, the participants' five acts of reading are five aspects of *what* we are doing whenever we read.

An educational act

Reading as an educational act includes ideas of reading addressing specific learning goals, such as 'reading improves your language' (Tania initial interview) or reading is a way of 'learning new words to use in your writing' (Tedros initial interview). This idea of reading as a specifically linguistic educational act was evident in members' desires to be part of a reading circle in order to 'learn new words' (initial reading circle discussion), in the way participants asked one another for help decoding or for explanations of meanings of words in every single reading circle session, how the reading circle frequently discussed how they wanted more time to 'talk about words' and how members constantly recorded words and phrases in their notebooks.

This is also an area discussed in their final interviews: 'When you read [a novel] you get the right words – you see them and you know them and you want to write them, so you write' (Aisha final interview) or 'Reading novels could help your reading speed or confidence or teach you new words' (Luis final interview), and was one of the three aspects of the reading circle work that Paula expressed in her mind-map (Figure 3): reading 'new words'.

However, participants spoke even more about reading as a broader learning experience: 'to learn, to find out about everything' (Gregor initial interview), to 'get more knowledge of the world' (Luis initial interview), 'to understand how the world has changed' (Beverley initial interview) and 'to make your life simpler or better' (Tedros initial interview). This is a broader sense of education, the idea of learning from others that was central to the nineteenth-century mutual improvement societies (see Chapter 5): 'I read to get facts, more information, to get someone else's knowledge' (Aisha initial interview).

> When you read, it's like you're finding out something ... challenges that happen in people's lives ... for you to learn from it ... to make sure you don't put yourself in that kind of position. (Tedros initial interview)
>
> I learn a lot because it makes me think, you know? Because before, if I don't read, I don't understand lots – but when I read I realize there's lots happening. (Aisha final interview)
>
> You get knowledge, feeling like you understand or you improve your knowledge, because before you don't have anything, it's blank your mind, but after, you've got some words, some stories. It opens your mind, like you understand some new things. You get some knowledge. (Safia final interview)

This 'knowledge' includes learning specific pieces of information:

> I learnt a lot about the tumour thing. I didn't know about that before, and now I've seen it on TV and everything. Some woman, I think in Afghanistan, had a baby for forty two years and they had to take it out. (Paula final interview)

It also includes learning about other people's points of view:

> It [novel reading]'s educational: it broadens your way of thinking and how to see things ... The way I read the book it's given me a guideline of how I can see things from someone else's head. I can see things better. (Beverley final interview)

This is a conceptualization of reading (particularly novel reading) as a way to learn about and from the lives of others.

A cognitive act

Second, participants construe reading as a cognitive act: an act of 'concentration' (Tedros initial interview); 'understanding' (Katherine initial interview); 'observ[ing] the words' (Jane initial interview); 'associat[ing] sounds with letters' (Paula initial interview); an act which 'makes your brain work better' (Luis initial interview). They described 'concentrating' and 'remembering' (Gregor initial interview) to phonically decode or recognize whole words, assign meanings to words and 'build up' meanings between sentences, paragraphs and chapters. Beverley described the cognitive process of decoding a word:

> I divided it ... If it's something like a 'chair' – I know I'm going to divide it to get 'air' and then the 'ch' [making the sounds and pointing to the letters of the word she's written] and then join them together ... That's what I do all the time. (Beverley final interview)

Luis spoke of recognizing symbols and words to create 'a larger meaning':

> You're looking at the words to recognize the symbols that have a meaning, and then in your mind it's a process of putting them together into a larger meaning. (Luis final interview)

Paula explained how the cognitive processes of memory are significant in reading longer texts:

> If I start reading something again, I remember where I was because it's all stored in my memory. (Paula final interview)

In this conceptualization of reading as five acts, the cognitive act (for example, decoding or remembering above) is distinct from the educational act (learning new words or learning about other people's lives) described above. Reading as an educational act concerns reading as a way to learn new things – about the world, about words, about one another – whereas reading as a cognitive act concerns the processes of mind and brain which are involved in the decoding and interpreting of meaning, such as phonic decoding or remembering what was read in a past chapter in order to interpret an ambiguity in the meaning of a sentence.

A communicative act

Third, reading is a *communicative* act: 'Reading is a form of communication' (Tania initial interview). 'I read to know what other people are thinking' (Jane initial interview). 'Written words and books represent the things we commonly agree on' (Luis final interview). Reading as communication, or social participation, also includes: reading for religious reasons, 'I read the Qur'an out loud' (Aisha initial interview); reading for personal/spiritual reasons, 'we read because we are bored or lonely; it's like a one way conversation' (Luis initial interview); and reading for and with family, 'I read with my Dad; he read a lot, big books' (Paula initial interview), 'I want to read with my grandchildren' (Beverley initial interview).

Significantly, the data also indicate that reading is something we do *with* and *for* others: 'A good reader can read clearly so others can understand, like a news reader' (Luis initial interview), or 'A good reader can explain the story from the beginning to the end for other people to hear. You have to be able to do that' (Paula initial interview). Reading for others requires confidence reading aloud (discussed further in Chapter 9), something the pupil participants in Clark, Osborn & Ackerman's (2008) study of young people's 'reading self-perceptions' agreed was a characteristic of a 'good' reader. This communal, or community, aspect of reading – and how it relates to the reading circle experience – is developed later in this chapter under the theme of 'reading as a group.'

An imaginative act

Reading, for these participants, is also an imaginative act. Reading is 'imagining'. Every single participant used this term in their final interview. Imagination – as an act different from learning, cognitive processing or communication – is as widely used and recognized culturally as it is problematic to define. These participants, however, used this term confidently to express both visualizing what they were reading and the conscious, creative mental activity of conjuring something into existence. This dual use of the term 'imagination' evokes Sadoski and Paivio's (Sadoski, 1998; Sadoski & Paivio, 2001) distinction between *visualization* – or 'spontaneously occurring mental imagery' (Sadoski, 1998) – and *imagination,* the 'individual mind's ability' to 'shape and create' (Sadoski & Paivio, 2001, p. 31). Tomlinson (1998) reviews literature on first- and second-language reading, finding that nearly all readers report visualization in first-language reading while few do so in reading a second language.

Interestingly, both Luis (for whom English is a third language) and Beverley discussed visualizing as part of reading:

> Usually when I read, I get images in my mind, like a short film that I'm watching. I've got this habit – I see the characters. (Luis final interview)
>
> My mind is picturing what I'm reading, and in action, I'm thinking of what's going to happen next. (Beverley final interview)

Tomlinson also argues that visualization is 'functional' (pp. 267–268) in that it helps with the comprehension of, and engagement with, a text. Supporting this argument, Paula connected visualization with 'good readers':

> They ['good' readers] can almost make it like a film, they can see it and act it ... make it like a film ... They can see and express what's happening. (Paula final interview)

Safia emphasized how visualizing helped her decode and understand the words of the novel:

> I saw them [Milan, Karen and Roma], like acting, like pictures, like imagination. Milan is young man and he's acting with his girlfriend, the Japanese, and what they are doing ... to know the story, what happens, then I can understand words and spelling. (Safia final interview)

Katherine links visualization to escapism and learning:

> I'm drifting into the fantasy with a visualization of what was going on ... to visualize and feel the emotion and just get away. I wouldn't say get away from our world but get away into this lovely book, to visualize something new, to learn something new. (Katherine initial interview)

Tania, another speaker of English as a second language, argued that discussing *Passenger* with her peers in the reading circle allowed her to visualize, and therefore better understand, what she was reading:

> When you don't understand many words it is so difficult to go to the dictionary every time ... but when they are talking about what is happening with Milan and his sister, I start to get it. I start to picture him and what is he doing and who he is talking and then it gets easier to read and understand. (Tania final interview)

Interestingly, Tomlinson (1998) stresses the importance of ELT teachers developing the visualization skills of their learners through direct instruction or activities. The discussions of a reading circle may be one such activity.

Luis and Beverley also spoke of imagination in Sadoski and Paivio's second, more creative, sense: forging new ideas, new realities, new possibilities. Luis discussed 'fantasising about the characters and what they're going to do next and why. I imagined it all.' Beverley explained how it was the act of imagining herself in Milan's situation (however unlikely or unusual) that allowed her to 'learn about other people's feelings':

> I think the writer did a good job actually, make your mind work ... He actually put an imagination in your head and you imagine that this is a man and it's impossible for a man to carry a baby. As a woman you know you have your organs and the baby can sit in the right place, but the writer he put it in such a way that it could happen to somebody that a man can actually carry his sister inside and we imagine this man and his sister and how they both feel and we learn about other people's feelings. (Beverley final interview)

This aspect of imagination is instrumental to reading as a broad educational act. Beverley says one only learns from other's lives if one can 'imagine another person's point of view' (Beverley final interview). (Both aspects of imagination are explored further in Chapter 11.)

An affective act

Just as reading as an imaginative act is related to reading as cognitive, educational and communicative acts, it is also related to reading as an affective act. Reading can, as both Long's (2003) and Hartley's (2002) participants noted, make you happy: 'Reading is fun' (Gregor initial interview), 'Reading can be enjoyable' (Luis initial interview).

Each weekly reading circle session included laughter and smiles, as Beverley remembers:

> Everybody enjoyed the book ... the reading and the discussing both, because when we discuss about it, you haven't seen anybody that gone quiet. Everybody actually chipped in and said their way, what they thought about the book and laughed, and a lot of 'awwww's'. (Beverley final interview)

This is related to the concept of reading identity (coming next) – 'reading gives me confidence in myself, in what I'm worth' (Jane initial interview) – and enjoyment of the social interaction of group reading. However, besides the process of reading itself being (potentially) emotional, reading is an affective act because of what one is reading about, what one is learning or imagining: 'You live everything that's in the book: that's why you get the emotions' (Tedros initial interview).

> [Beverley has just read the last paragraph of *Passenger*, where Milan buries his sister].
> Tania: You read a sad part.
> Beverley: Oh yes. Oh God. It's such a sad moment. (29 April 09)

> It's feelings ... if you can imagine it and build it inside you so that you have real feelings. It's like, I'm a mother. It's like parents losing a child and it's very painful and it's like actually somebody died. It's the death of Roma actually, suddenly. I really felt like she should have lived. (Beverley final interview).
>
> When the tumour got taken out of him, that was the most, that was the hardest bit ... 'cause I tried to imagine what it would be like if it was me, and it's not a nice feeling. (Paula final interview)

To sum up her experience of the reading circle (see Figure 5), Aisha charted how a reader's emotions fluctuate when reading, from the experience *of* reading (happiness at being able to read, or pleasure from holding a book) as well as from the experiences she is reading *about* (the events of the story), which imagination allows her to feel as her own. She stresses that this emotional 'rollercoaster' is the product of the interplay between the brain and the heart, thinking and feeling, the cognitive and the affective, with the imaginative, communicative and educational playing their parts.

Interestingly, as suggested in Beverley's quotations above, this interplay also produces the transformative aspect of reading, as emphasized by Long's (2003) reading circle members (see Chapter 5): reading can transform the reader and the reader's relationship with the wider culture precisely because it is at once educational, cognitive, communicative, imaginative and affective.

2. Reading Identity

> I want to pick up a novel like any normal person, but then I run away. (Beverley initial interview)

I think that reading a novel is showing somebody else a part of you, your hobby, or part of your personality: 'I like to read', just like most people say 'I like music'. (Katherine final interview)

The previous theme discussed how reading is a cognitive, educational, communicative, imaginative and affective act, with each of these elements playing a part in what and how people read. This notion of reading identities involves the interplay between these five acts: developing cognitive skill; developing knowledge of words, texts and the world; developing our relationships with others and where reading fits into these relationships; expanding our confidence and desire to make imagination part of reading; and the emotions produced by each of the other acts. The development of each act affects, and is affected by, the development of the others, bound together in an overall 'reading identity'. The psychological notion of identity has three core elements: it refers to a person's 'essential, continuous' self; it can and does change over a person's lifetime (while retaining the above degree of continuality); and it is an 'internal, subjective' self-concept (Reber, 1995, p. 355). These are all key to my notion of reading identity: a personal, shifting yet continuous, self-imposed label. I have chosen to call it 'reading identity' rather than 'read*er* identity' because the reading identities of many people may be those of 'non-readers', a lack of a read*er* identity. Unlike Clark, Osborn & Ackerman's (2008) notion of 'a reader's self-concept', which is that of either a 'reader' or a 'non-reader', I am using 'reading identity' to convey a spectrum of variations.

'Good' readers 'read every day' (Jane initial interview), 'read a book from beginning to end without skipping any of it' (Aisha initial interview), usually 'have a higher education' (Tedros initial interview) and 'are confident reading to friends and family' (Gregor initial interview). Most members contrasted this 'good reader identity' with their own, varied reading identities: 'I have a fear of words and a fear of laughter from other people when I read' (Beverley initial interview); 'the big books really scare me' (Jane initial interview); and 'I'm not really a good reader: I can never remember the whole story to tell someone else' (Tedros initial interview).

The decision to read a novel was therefore a challenge to these reading identities, feeding into the group's initial criteria for choosing a novel: 'not a big one – those scare me' (Jane, initial group discussion to organize reading circle). The initial reading circle sessions were full of surprise as participants' experiences ran contrary to their existing reading identities: 'I understood it, nearly all of it' (Katherine, 9 December 2008); 'I enjoyed reading it actually' (Jane, 2 December 2008). Beverley expressed her happiness at being able to recommend a book to others:

> I got excited because it's my first book ever ... I took it to work, over-whelmed about this first book and reading it, enjoying it at the same time but I wanted my friends to know that I got a book for the first time ever and my friend Jenny decided she wanted to look at it and she highjack it from me and she read it a little bit and ... is going to buy one ... And all my colleagues at work are actually excited – they heard about it ... but I was the first one to take it to work and I'm so proud of that. (Beverley, 16 December 2008)

Though all participants spoke of the relationship between their reading identity and their reading processes and practices, their individual reading identities were of course different, as were the influences the reading circle had on these identities. Beverley started the reading circle thinking of her-self as a non-reader and ended it feeling that she is now someone who 'can pick up a novel or a book'. She reflected on the difference this will make to her work as well as her leisure time:

> Now I can pick up a novel or a book, knowing I can read it and I will understand ... and [this will] make my work enjoyable ... because I understand if something is written down I can read it, because they do a lot of writing and if the nurse is not there I just have to pick it up and read what they have done, without them – the care plan – now I can do that. And actually, I'm looking forward to a new life of reading for myself ... because before I couldn't ... I just shy away and just put it down because I'd think that I'm going to make a fool of myself, but actually it [the read-ing circle] helps me a lot because it made me stronger. Yeah, I have no fear. (Beverley final interview)

Beverley is not claiming that she learnt to read during the reading circle, but rather that she developed a new reading identity as someone who can read and recommend novels, and who can therefore have a go at reading anything that life, including work, throws her way.

Katherine, by contrast, was already a 'fairly confident' reader (Katherine initial interview) at the start of the reading circle process, having joined the literacy class to work on her writing. However, she describes an equally powerful shift of reading identity:

It's quite interesting because I've never come across a reading, a reading, you know, forum like this, in a college or in a university ... I've only seen something like that on an American film of some sort ... While I've never done it before ... I think it's useful because in a college where people are trying to read English and trying to do essays and things like that, it's something different. I think it's a boundary where people don't think they can go to. I – when I'm normally reading a book, I'm normally reading a book with my mother who lives in America, so we kind of – we – she's got the book and I've got the book and we kind of see where each other is in the story ... I've had that kind of relationship before – but not with a group. I suppose you see it as a high-society kind of thing. Something for somebody in Oxford or a higher class. (Katherine final interview)

For Katherine, taking part in a reading circle was taking part in a practice she had previously associated with other social groups, other educational backgrounds, or simply other people.

Aisha also underwent a transition in reading identity: 'I didn't think I could read a whole book like this' (Aisha final interview), but was more interested in a realization that she could write, as well as read, a book:

When I read I realize there's lots happening: I can read, I can write a story about myself. I've got lots of ideas. I can write my story and somebody can read. It's an interesting life story – the place I was born, the fighting that happened, the war, when I came here – things like that. (Aisha final interview)

Aisha's shift in reading identity was part of, or perhaps even a trigger for, a wider shift in her relationship to print culture: she is someone who can read books, but also someone with a story to tell and the ability and authority to write it, for others to read.

3. Knowing Words

'What does it mean to know a word?' (Schmitt, 2000, p. 1)

...the reading, the words and the sounds and the meanings. (Aisha final interview)

Reading words

The issue of what exactly it means to 'know' a word emerges from these data in two ways. The first concerns the distinction between understanding the meaning of a word and being able to vocalize that word (to say that word aloud). This lies in the relationship between the first seven of Nation's (2001) eighteen (receptive and productive) aspects of 'knowing a word':

> 'What does the word sound like? How is the word pronounced? What does the word look like? How is the word written and spelled? What parts are recognizable in this word? What word parts are needed to express the meaning? What meaning does this word signal?' (2001, p. 27)

'Learn[ing] new words' (Safia) and 'learning to read more words' (Jane) were key motivations for taking part in a reading circle, just as the initial interviews identified that reading was largely about 'learning words' (Gregor initial interview). However, when coding the data, I found the phrases 'knowing a word' and 'reading a word' were both used to refer to being able to vocalize a word *and* also to understanding the meaning of a word. In Duncan (2009) I also identified this 'confusion' and related it to the importance of teachers using appropriate meta-language so that learners have the power to say, 'I can phonically decode this word' or 'I can sound out this word', as opposed to (or in addition to), 'I understand the meaning of this word'.

However, looking more closely at the data from the present project, I came to see that rather than participants being 'confused', the error was mine. I was missing the point; these participants saw vocalizing and understanding the meaning of a word as two inseparable aspects of the same process – reading, making the distinction meaningless:

SD: What comes to mind when I say reading?
Beverley: Spelling and the meaning – what the word means.
SD: When you say 'spelling', do you mean how you write words?
Beverley: No, saying the words – how the letters sound – to read them out, to know what they mean. (Beverley final interview)

Beverley is expressing her belief that to be able to vocalize a word and to understand the meaning of a word are two parts of the same process: the ability to decode a meaning from a piece of written code. Of course, some participants were unable to vocalize words despite knowing their meaning, for example the word 'popping' for Paula (10 March 2009) or 'sycamore' for Beverley (29 April 2009). These participants are first-language speakers with large vocabularies but difficulties with phonic decoding and limited whole-word recognition. Other participants, particularly second-language learners who are more confident reading in another alphabetic language, were able to use phonic decoding to vocalize words without knowing their meanings: for example Safia vocalized 'amplifier' (10 March 2009) and Tania vocalized 'thimble' (13 January 2009) without knowing what these words meant (both asked the meaning of these words later in the same session). The difference between these two groups of learners typifies the challenges for teachers of adult literacy classes.

However, the weekly session transcripts reveal the most common pattern: if one knows the meaning of a word, one is *more likely* to be able to vocalize it than if one does not. As participants chose to take turns reading aloud for a portion of every session, their decoding processes were, to an extent, visible in their hesitations, miscues and help offered to others. At times, familiarity with a word, and therefore a degree of knowing its meaning, helped vocalization because the word was part of the participant's active mental lexicon and therefore could be recognized as a whole word or decoded with the familiarity of practice. For example, Beverley read 'abdominal' correctly with no hesitation (10 March 2009), despite needing help with seemingly simpler words such as 'struck' and 'that' in the same session. She had explained earlier that she 'knows the medical words' because of her work as a health-care assistant.

These data also suggest that familiarity with a word helps participants decode words which are not entirely phonically regular due to the morpho-phonemic nature of English (Coulmas, 2003). In these cases, participants started to read the words through the most 'standard' sound/symbol relationships and then self-corrected when they got far enough on in the word to recognize it. For example, reading the word 'patronizing', Aisha first read 'pat' (/æ/), then 'pat' (/æ/) 'ron' and self-corrected to 'patron' (/eɪ/) before getting to 'izing' and self-correcting back to 'patronizing' (with a /æ/ as in the English pronunciation) (24 February 2009). Similarly, Paula reading 'laboriously' first read 'labor' (/eɪ/) then 'i-ously' and then self-corrected to 'oh, laboriously' (with a schwa) (3 March 2009). In both of these examples, participants used their knowledge of standard phoneme/grapheme correspondences to begin to decode these words. When they had decoded enough of the word to recognize it, they self-corrected to the spoken form they knew. Once again, knowing the meaning of a word helps vocalization.

Rather than presenting a distinction between decoding a word and under-standing the meaning of that word, these participants stressed that 'know-ing a word', 'learning a word' or 'reading a word' involves a three-way linking process between a meaning, a spoken form and a written form:

> Words which we don't know, we underline and then we discuss ... and we are writing the meaning in the book to learn and for the spelling ... the reading of the spelling, how I can read each sound ... I improve a lot my writing and my reading ... the words I pick up and the meanings. (Safia final interview)

Phonic decoding and reading aloud are discussed further in Chapter 9.

Knowing meanings

The second aspect of 'what it means to know a word' addresses what *know-ing the meaning* of a word actually involves. What does it really mean to know the meaning of a word, and how do we develop and use this knowledge?

> You're picking up words that you may never have used, and once you've found the meaning and are able to use them yourself, you've used it – and it's part of you. (Katherine final interview)

Without receiving any direction from me, a pattern emerged for how par-ticipants learnt the meanings of new words. Reading at home, when par-ticipants found unfamiliar words they did one of two things: guessed the meaning from the novel's context and moved on, or underlined/circled/highlighted the word. To find the meanings of these words, they asked a friend or colleague, looked them up in a dictionary (monolingual or bilin-gual) and/or brought them to the next reading circle session. If they looked in the dictionary or asked a friend, they wrote down the meaning in a note-book and then double-checked with the context in the novel. If they chose to ask about the word in the next reading circle session, their fellow mem-bers would explain the word to them using the context of their own lives or the novel (as discussed later) and they would then record the meaning of the word. Though faced with a choice of ways to find out the meaning of the word, all participants followed the same three-step process: find mean-ing, check meaning with context and record meaning.

When reading together in the reading circle (one person reading aloud and others following silently), members underlined words as they and others read and then asked one another about these words in the pauses between one person finishing reading and another starting (usually after every page). These discussions about specific words led on to, or from, discussions about 'what was going on'. Participants noted down explanations in their notebooks. Three aspects of this pattern warrant a closer look: the use of peer-learning, *how* participants recorded meanings of words and the use of context in the vocabulary learning process. At first they asked me but then increasingly they asked one another what the words meant, and taught one another words, discussing meanings communally. Here, participants discussed the meaning of the phrase 'back with us':

> Tania: He has been there before. He is returning?
> Safia: No he never been there before, this hospital is in Vienna.
> Tania: But they said, end of page 175, 'You are back with us'?
> Katherine: It means he's come to. He's woken up from the operation –
> Beverley: He's been unconscious and now he's waking up –
> Katherine: That's what they say –
> Beverley: You're back with us. (24 March 2009)

The phrase 'back with us' (meaning 'having regained consciousness') was new to Tania and so Safia, Katherine and Beverley explained it to her. This peer explanation happened, on average, nine times per session.

Reading circle members recorded the meanings of new words in a range of ways: using sentences and notes, English, other languages, and examples from the novel and their own lives. Aisha's personal notebook was entirely devoted to recording lists of new words, recorded in four ways:

1. Words with explanations in English: 'cogitate = means think very carefully.'
2. Words with translations into Somali: 'storm off = isdhipashe.'
3. Words followed by English sentences demonstrating their meaning: 'Apron = I wear an apron when I cook.'
4. Words followed by English sentences demonstrating their meaning using the examples from the novel: 'Mortality = God is never die but what planet will died. Mortal = will die. Roma and Milan are mortal. Roma will die one day and Milan too.'

Finally, participants used the context of the novel in three ways: to guess the meaning of words, to understand the dictionary definition, and to explain items of vocabulary to one another. Participants explained items of vocabulary to one another using the different domains of their own lives and the worlds of the novel. This demonstrates how essential context is for 'learning words' (you cannot identify or explain a meaning without some kind of a context), but it also demonstrates a shift in *which* contexts they used for their explanations. During the reading circle process, participants moved from explaining vocabulary predominantly with reference to their own lives/ domains to using their own lives as well as the world(s) of the novel to, finally, using predominantly the world(s) of the novel. Here are three examples of participants explaining items of vocabulary to one another, the first using mainly the context/experience of their own lives, the second a mixture and the third using the (now shared) experience/context of the novel.

Paula: there's something about the orchestra she was going to.
Jane: It's a rough music or something.
Katherine: No, he says its wholesome, that's the word he used –
Safia: What does it mean 'wholesome'?
Tedros: He explained it –
Beverley: Healthy, like brown bread. I eat brown bread because it's wholesome –
Katherine: It means 'good for you', so kind of 'goody-goody'.
(9 December 2008)

Tania: What's a thimble?
Beverley: You put it on your finger to stop you –
Katherine: From pricking yourself. For sewing.
Safia: Oh I know what that is.
Tania: I didn't know that was a thimble. I have some, but not metal, plastic.
Paula: Oh, to protect your finger –
Beverley: I'll bring my thimble next week. It's not metal but I'll bring it.
Paula: He gets the thimble and has some metal on his belt, to tap –
Katherine: To communicate with his sister. (13 January 2009)

Aisha: 'Accompaniment'? What's that?
Beverley: Where is that?
Katherine: 156, here, here, there you go.
Paula: Maxim is playing something on the piano and Milan is playing the accompaniment –
Aisha: Like company –
Katherine: Maxim's playing the main bit of music and Milan is playing something that goes along –

Paula: Not the main piece but it goes with it –

Beverley: Goes along with it.

Katherine: In the orchestra some instruments are playing the main tune and the others, maybe Daphne, are playing the accompaniments.

Tania: Roma is Milan's accompaniment!

Beverley: Yes!

Katherine: Or is Milan Roma's accompaniment? (17 March 2009)

This shift emphasizes the role of context in learning and using vocabulary, but more than this, it reflects the way in which novel reading involves 'building' a new world, a shared world full of contexts which can be used for explaining and understanding new vocabulary. This world, or bank of experience, comes not from participants' lives but from their reading, though through that reading, they have made it part of their lives.

4. Building a Story

The story gets built up as you read. (Luis final interview)

The above transition in the contexts – what could also be called domains or worlds – used to define, discuss and clarify vocabulary (from participants' 'real' worlds to their newly shared world of the novel) relates to what participants identified as a notable feature of novel reading: that reading novels involves a process of 'building up'. The metaphor of 'building' is often used for reading, and particularly for novel reading, but what is really built, out of what and how?

Cognitive psychologists Garnham & Oakhill (1992) and Noordman & Vonk (1992), and literary theorists Iser (1972), Fish (1980), Perry (1979), Culler (1975) and Rimmon-Kenan (1989), each explore how the reader begins by assigning meaning to the words they read and goes on to make connections between what they have already read and what they are reading now. From a philosophical perspective, Sartre (1967) too writes of reading as 're-invention', where the novel 'does not have an end' because 'the reader's will' (pp. 30–38) continues to create it. This is a process of continuously adapting, rejecting and reforming meaning as the reader 'builds' what Iser calls the individually realized *work* as opposed to the written *text*.

Participants presented a similar account, often using the terms 'story' and 'book' where Iser uses *work* (what is built by the reader) and *text* (what is printed on the page).

This *Passenger*, you read the book from the beginning to end, get knowledge from the beginning to end, building, building. How it starting the story, where is going the story, what happened in the end of the story. (Safia final interview)

As the above theorists and participants found, it is hard to present this building process as a set of discrete steps, as any 'steps' seem to be cyclical or even simultaneous. However, these data present key elements of the process: building sentences from words, building sentences up into a story, and then using this story to read subsequent words into sentences, events and characters of that same ever-developing story.

Five (of seven) participants spoke explicitly of 'building' in their final interviews.

You're looking at the words, to recognize the symbols that have a meaning and then in your mind it's a process of putting them together into a larger meaning. (Luis final interview)

Katherine: In my mind I'd have the character ... so it's like meeting a person and then meeting them again – you remember them because you've met them before. You know them a bit, you remember them and then you will go on to know more about them – come back to them ... as you see that characters, what they are doing, you get more information, slowly it gets built up.
SD: How does it get built up?
Katherine: By the information I get, the words. (Katherine final interview)

As with the vocabulary development described earlier in this chapter, this building process happened both individually and communally. Participants read between half a chapter and a chapter per week at home, often taking notes. Paula noted in her initial interview that she found it hard to 'remember what's going on' (Paula initial interview) in a book or story and so 'I used a notebook to keep track' (Paula final interview). This makes her notebook a relatively rare document, evidencing the stages of how Paula was building her *story*.

Chapter 1: It took me a little while to figure out who is who ... Milan seems humorous, making silly comments all the time then Karen having to correct him ... I'm guessing that Milan and Karen plays for the orchestra.

Chapter 2: The thing I am confused about is Milan's occupation. Andreas is either his father or a friend – I think he is a friend because in Chapter 1 Andreas bring croissants to Milan's house.

18/12/08: Whilst Milan is having an X-ray the conversation about his occupation is brought up and he says that he is a violinist so its all clear now.

02/01/09: Milan's back injury seems to be more than a back injury. They find a tumour inside him making him believe that it is a living thing inside of him which soon becomes news of the world – and questions about clicking.

Chapter 4: 9/01/09 Milan is seeing Dr Conway she discusses with Milan the concept of the thing inside him. This makes me think if this was me and I was in this situation that I have no control over, the first thing I have to realize is that despite that I've had this thing inside me for like 40 years ... thank God I'm still breathing, eating and talking. I don't understand the idea of talking to Roma, saying words or how it's meant to work.

Participants brought these individually developed ideas to the group sessions. For example, in early March, Paula read Chapter 9 at home, recording in her notebook:

Chapter 9: Milan finds out that Murri has publish a book about him and Roma. He is quiet upset about it because she never asked 1st. I think that Murri should have at least consult Milan about this first and get his point of view and permission.

In the reading circle on 10 March 2009, participants began discussing Chapter 9 and Paula contributed: 'It's about Murri. She comes back from holiday and, um, she's like ... wrote about Roma and Milan, and Milan doesn't like it, because she never asked ... I think it's a bit sly.' Influenced by Paula's input, the group go on to discuss Murri's actions. Paula's contribution reflects the notes she has written at home, the building work she has already started.

Conversely, the group discussions also influenced subsequent individual reading. On 17 March 2009 the group discussed the music lesson scene in Chapter 13, where Roma corrects a note that Milan's student plays (from sharp to natural), leading to the discovery that Roma's version not only sounds better than the printed version, but is the note Bach originally intended. Paula asked her fellow participants, 'What is Roma doing? I don't understand, what's 'sharp'?' and others clarify:

Katherine: Is she counting the notes?

Beverley: Yes, her mathematical bit – she's counting and listening –

Katherine: The note was too sharp. It means it didn't sound right.

Safia: He made a mistake, Milan and Maxim both mistake,

Aisha: And she found it –

Katherine: It was supposed to be a different note, what they call a 'natural' one, not sharp. It's different types of notes. (17 March 2009)

Paula writes in her notebook two days later:

> Roma was sure that Maxim and Milan were not playing the right note so she gets them to play the right note – F natural instead of F sharp. This is funny because it seems like she is controlling them and like with the alcohol and cigarets – won't give up until she gets her way. (Paula notebook, 19 March 2009)

From the group discussion, Paula now understands the 'F natural/F sharp' mistake and uses this new understanding to reread, and potentially reinterpret, this passage. However, while the group discussion went on to focus on Roma's 'cleverness', Paula interprets this scene as an example of Roma's continued desire to exert her control (something she has commented on earlier in her notebook). Paula's story is clearly the product of the interplay between group and individual interpretation.

Besides reading alone at home, participants volunteered to read aloud in the session, usually reading a page each and stopping after each page to talk. For example, after Aisha read page 87 (where Roma asks Milan to stop having sex with Karen), the group discussed:

Beverley: What's happening is, I think, Roma has begun to know the brother more but when the romance was taking place ... it's like a strange feeling – she wants it to stop and she wants probably an explanation, why is your body shifting around like this.

Tania: I think the thing that is affecting her –

Safia: She would be moving around quite a lot –

Aisha: Sea-sick!

Paula: Karen is angry.

Safia: Karen wouldn't understand what was going on because this is based in what is happening to Milan. She felt furious at him stopping. When Milan confessed that it is Roma who told him to stop, she went mad – 'how dare she?' – 'Call me later', she said –

Paula: Karen's angry because basically he's allowing someone to take control of him, that's not fair on her. (27 January 2009)

Together, they interpreted the text in light of what they already know about Milan, Roma and Karen: Roma feels every movement of Milan's body, Karen does not understand when it comes to Roma, and Milan does exactly what Roma tells him to do.

These discussions were integral to the 'building' of the novel they were reading together: the interpreting of vocabulary (what does 'back with us' mean?) and hypothesizing of character (is Roma the real musician?) which form the developing, rejecting, adapting and adjusting of the story. As explored in Chapters 2 and 10, a novel may usually be read alone, with the 'building' done entirely in the mind of one individual reader. However, in this reading circle, a significant part of the 'building' was done through group discussion. Significantly, these discussions were not merely *about* what they had read (reflections on completed, individual building processes), but rather *part of* a communal reading process. To take two more examples, after Gregor had just read the last page of Chapter 1 aloud, they discuss:

Tedros: And he gets to try green tea.
Jane: Oh yeah, that's right. He said he quite liked it actually –
Gregor: And he lies that he doesn't like tea. Normally tea, he does like it, but he told her that he doesn't?
Jane: He makes a comment that he sometimes twists the truth a bit. Maybe to have –
Katherine: To have more in common with her?
Luis: That's the second time he'd twisted the truth. He said he didn't hear her mistake on the flute, but he did hear it. (11 November 2008)

The group together interpret that Milan lies 'to have more in common with her', to ingratiate himself. Months later they discuss Milan reading a book to Roma:

Katherine: She started to read something. She wants him to read her a book. About love.
Beverley: *The Heart Is a Lonely Hunter.*
Luis: She says 'I love Murri' and he asks her, 'What is love?'
Safia: Milan asks Roma what love is –
Beverley [reading]: 'Love is when you are sad when you cannot talk to someone any more.'

Luis: Roma knows what love is but is confused by what a book is –

Katherine: Maybe because she's, she's, she knows what the outside world is, she kind of knows what death is, and she's got a kind of, she kind of knows what love is, but asking her to think about something that is written in a book –

Beverley: She cannot physically handle it. She didn't know what a book is –

Katherine: Even if you said a box, a box of words, she, I don't know, she wouldn't know –

Luis: She knows the whole world as words, as clicks, how would she know about worlds created only of words?

Beverley: Might be quite difficult for her. (24 March 2009)

Together they filled in gaps to create Roma's experience, to understand her confusion. The participants interpreted *in and through* their discussions. This reading circle was not an opportunity for the communal discussion of individual reading, but an example of genuinely *communal reading*, with aspects of the reading process (the 'building') completed as a group:

Beverley: You, well, we, recap when we read ... link up ...

SD: Can you explain what you mean by 'link up'?

Beverley: I mean join them together ... Paragraph by paragraph, talking about it together, building up. (Beverley final interview)

These participants are a living example of the work of the literary theorists; they have demonstrated that reading a novel is a building process, and this was a communal building process. They built *their Passenger* together. (Reading as a communal process is discussed further in Chapter 10.)

5. Fiction, Truth and Learning

Like 'knowing' and 'reading words', participants' uses of the terms 'fiction', 'real', 'realistic' and 'true' seemed, at first analysis, to indicate some confusion:

I do like fiction but also I like true stories, because it's more realistic ... fiction is not real, and you know I like to read about a girl who's had troubles maybe and sometimes you can relate to that: it's more real, because you can sort of put yourself in that position, you know, instead of a monster chasing another monster – it's not real – but if the girl's had a few problems, that's really life and that's more interesting really. I can learn from it. (Jane initial interview)

I like realistic stories, true stories, not fiction. (Gregor initial interview)

Fiction means it's not true, doesn't it? No, I don't like those kind of stories. I like stories that are true to life, that make me think about my life. (Tedros initial interview)

These quotations demonstrate uncertainty around the terms and concepts of 'fiction', 'science fiction', 'real', and 'realistic'. Additionally, despite early discussions on the meaning of the terms 'novel' and 'fiction', halfway into reading *Passenger*, a member of the reading circle raised the question, 'So is it a true story?' The issue of whether the events represented in *Passenger could* be true (whether it was realistic) was confused with whether or not it was 'a true story'.

This is certainly the result of a lack of familiarity with the conventions of the classifications 'fiction' and 'non-fiction', which are often (as discussed in Chapter 4) defined as 'true' and 'not true', relying on a familiarity with the conventions of what 'true' and 'not true' mean in the context of this kind of written text classification. However, once again, this 'confusion' reveals a useful learning point. What is true, real, untrue or unreal about a piece of fiction such as a novel? Also, following Jane's lead (above), what is the relationship between the classifications of fiction and non-fiction, and what can be *learnt* from a text?

In the earlier discussion of reading as five acts, I argued that the participants spoke of what they learnt from novel reading, including accessing other people's experience and thereby gaining an increased knowledge of the world. In the final interviews, they argued that 'reading novels is educational' (Beverley final interview), and spoke of what they felt they learnt from *Passenger* in particular:

I learnt new things, like the tumour thing. I can now relate to these stories on the news. (Paula final interview)

I learnt about how orchestras practice and travel to other cities, like Vienna. (Luis final interview)

These participants are describing learning 'real' things from a fictional world. Furthermore, participants spoke of what they learnt from the access to other perspectives that fiction provides:

I got an awful lot of information ... some of the things in the novel I can bring into practice – take it to work. It teach me a thing or two ... how I can approach my patients ... Because normally you [health-care assistants] come to them abruptly, without thinking about their feelings, yeah, and in Milan's case, when he's going to see the doctor – how nervous he is ... for me he's like the patient lying in the bed not knowing who's going to come through that door in the morning. (Beverley final interview)

Passenger contains truths from which participants learnt, ranging from learning about the (real-life) condition of 'foetus in fetu' to learning about feelings of disorientation. Participants did not say that Roma was a symbol, or representation, of Milan's transition from emotional isolation to emotional engagement with others: this may have been a huge jump for those new to fiction. However, they spoke of Roma as instrumental in Milan's emotional transition and allowed for the possibility that Milan was 'imagining' her or willing her into existence. Without specialist literary experience or terminology, these participants nevertheless recognized the different levels of truth which fiction provides. In this sense, fiction cannot really be considered 'not true'.

How, then, is fiction untrue? Simply, perhaps, that the events depicted in a novel are not presented to the reader as events that have definitely taken place in the world (though they may be events that could have taken place). Aisha identifies this as fiction's great strength:

There's a big difference [between reading a newspaper and reading a novel]. If it's the news, when you read the news or a newspaper, you just worry, because ... this is happening, this is true? And because you believe the news, this is true and then you are worrying about this ... you worry. But this [pointing to *Passenger*] is just a fun ... you don't believe it is true, so you go on and read, you exercise but you don't worry. (Aisha final interview)

It is this juxtaposition between the self-evident truths of a novel and its declared untruth, or its simultaneous reality and unreality, which defines fiction. Fiction offers truths from which to learn, while announcing its untruth: 'I am not really happening'. For Aisha, the fact that a novel is not (presented as) something 'really happening' means that it does not cause the worry or anguish that a true story, or the news, could cause. Yet the fact that it *could* be true means that the reader is able to relate to it and explore it as a potential (but safe) experience, from which to learn. Aisha argues that this use of the unreal to provide 'safe' exploration of reality is central to the pleasures of fiction:

> You know it's like exercise for the brain. You are reading something and your mind is really thinking about it. Is it true? Could it happening? Maybe or maybe not? And what would I do? (Aisha final interview)

Safia recognizes this as *useful*:

> A novel is a story, an idea of the people ... the people are writing their ideas, suggesting it, and these ideas are useful for the people, the readers, those listening ... you can get knowledge from that ... and you can understand things, new things, from that story. (Safia final interview)

The final aspect of the (un)truth/reality of the novel which emerges from these data could be called 'the tenacity of the story' and 'the disappearance of the author'. The events portrayed may not be real but the story that the readers build certainly is. The reading circle talked the inner and outer lives of Milan, Roma, Karen, Murri and Andreas into existence and then used them to learn items of vocabulary and have wider philosophical discussions. The story, understandably, dominated the weekly reading circle discussions for six months, but what was less predictable was how the story dominated the final interviews. All my questions in the final interviews relating to the reading circle or *Passenger* were about the processes of our reading, not the story itself; I never asked participants to recount the story or discuss the characters. However, participants were clearly eager to do so. For example, when asked about what they liked best about the processes of our reading circle, Safia and Aisha responded similarly:

> I like best when Milan and Roma are going to Germany and she is dead. (Safia final interview)
> I like best when Milan and Roma they are going to Germany and they have some accident and when he wake up he says like, 'Is she dead? Where is my?' Things like that. I liked that. (Aisha final interview)

Similarly, Tania answered a question about her favourite part of the reading circle process with: 'Roma, she's interesting' (Tania final interview). It would be hard to argue that these characters were not real, that this story was not real.

Yet, as much as the story was tenaciously real, the author was absent. In seven months (from the beginning of the reading circle to the end of the final interviews) the author was mentioned – by any of the participants – only twice. The first mention was in February, when Katherine stopped Luis as he was reading:

Katherine: Can I just ask something? You know how it says 'speakers and microphones and wires' – why has he done that? Why didn't he put in a comma?

Beverley: He's showing that there are all these things – by using too many 'and's –

Luis: He's saying that there are lots of things. (24 February 2009)

The author emerged here as a 'he' responsible for the writing and then disappeared again until our penultimate reading circle session's discussion of Milan's operation in Vienna:

Beverley: Why did he kill Roma? He killed her! He actually killed her!

Tania: Who killed her?

Beverley: The writer!

Katherine: He killed her! Just as you're getting to know her, he killed her.

Beverley: Just as we're getting to know her and she's getting to tapping and getting to books and reading, that was encouraging but then – [makes a cutting noise]. (23 March 2009)

This absence can be seen as the product of the tenacity of the story, the simultaneous truth and untruth of the novel and the readers' communal building process. It was *their* story, until 'he' ended it.

6. Reading as a Group

Everybody liked it. We all took part in it ... There wasn't any boundaries, everybody explored, everybody was free ... wasn't afraid to explore. (Katherine final interview)

This is my first book I ever ever read. I never ever picked up a novel and thought of reading it myself. I'd pick up a novel and maybe just look inside quickly and think it's too much for me to read and put it down quickly and forget about it. But this one, because we were doing it in a group, did encourage me to read it, for myself. And sometimes I didn't understand some of the words, and then when I come back in the class and reflect back and talk about what it meant, then I'd get those words. It was very good. (Beverley final interview)

Participants all reported their enjoyment of reading as a *group* and gave five reasons for this: help with learning vocabulary, help with decoding words, group interpretation or 'building' of the story, mutual support and confidence building, and simply enjoying spending time with a group. Reading in a group helped them learn the meaning of new words and use them in conversation. In each and every reading circle session they identified words that they were not sure about and defined words for one another.

> If some words we don't understand, we can check together, read them, talk about them, write them, the meaning. (Aisha final interview)
>
> I want to read it, to tell the story, about the words I pick up and the meanings. I like learning the meanings ... when we are talking the stories – Milan did that, and the other girl live with him. (Safia final interview)
>
> We understand from each other, you know. If I don't understand this, I can understand from my colleagues, from my classmates ... the words that we don't understand. (Tania final interview)

Significantly, after defining words for one another, they used them in their reading circle conversations: 'Roma is Milan's accompaniment!' (17 March 2009)

Second, they argued that reading aloud in a group helped to develop phonic decoding and/or whole-word recognition skill. Reading aloud (and having others listen and correct), or following the text while others read aloud, was seen by the majority of participants as helpful in the development of decoding skills:

> I like when we read together because I can hear somebody's voice, better than me, or somebody like me, because I want to improve and you can hear my voice and correct me if I'm wrong. (Aisha final interview).
>
> I can hear the words [when somebody else is reading] and I am looking at the book and I'm following what they say and what the words look like. (Paula final interview)
>
> I knew that at the end of the reading, nobody's going to look at me like, 'Oh, you didn't read well' – they were all there to support me

and the words that I couldn't read or didn't understand or got stuck – they helped me along, to make the reading enjoyable. (Beverley final interview)

Participants helped one another with decoding an average of sixteen times per session. For example:

- Beverley read 'slyly' and Paula corrected 'slightly'. Beverley repeated 'slightly' and responded 'thank you' (27 January 2009).
- Luis hesitated and read 'd, d, d' and hesitated again and Katherine read 'declines' for him. Luis repeated 'declines' (24 February 2009).
- Aisha read 'pass' and Beverley corrected 'pissing' (3 March 2009).

Reading in a group was appealing because of the opportunity it offered to read to others and listen to others read, all the time clarifying the link between the spoken word and the written word.

The third aspect of their enjoyment of reading as a group relates to the earlier theme of 'building up' the story: reading as a group models and supports the interpretative processes of novel reading. The reading circle encouraged collective interpretation, while also making it clear that everyone has individual interpretations, based on individual experience. The notion that there is not one correct interpretation, and yet interpretation is nevertheless based on 'evidence' in the text, can be particularly challenging to less confident readers (Kendall, 2008). If reading is seen as only an individual, silent act, this would be hard to model. The reading circle formation modelled and supported this potentially challenging aspect of reading:

> The group input was interesting because I think when you are reading the book it's just you and the author, you don't realize what other people are thinking ... I was interested in what other people, from different backgrounds, different nationalities, where they were coming from. (Katherine final interview)
> There were some things that didn't come in my mind but other people got different ideas, or a different angle on the same thing, so it was good to discuss. (Luis final interview)

Reading as a group, to these participants, was also valuable because it provided a supportive and encouraging environment, allowing them to increase their reading confidence (and adjustment of their *reading identities*):

There are certain people that are weak like me, it actually bring them out. One or two students, when they first came in the class, they couldn't speak up, you remember? Eventually, in the end, they were actually reading even louder and speaking openly, giving their opinions, feeling free ... because everybody chipped in and nobody made anybody else feel down. Everybody encourage everybody to read and the beauty of it is that when somebody finish reading, you can't wait to read ... As a first-time reader, it did encourage me ... [Before] there was always a fear of reading a book. The thought of not being able to read in class, or to feel embarrassed ... Am I going to make myself look a fool? But nobody laughed and it did encourage me to read even more. (Beverley final interview)

Similarly, in her mind-map, Katherine drew the reading circle experience as a cake, created and shared by everyone, allowing every participant to feel 'free' and not 'afraid to explore'.

Finally, the social factor: they enjoyed meeting and talking with the same group of people every week.

Paula: I liked the group ... They are just a bunch of nice people.

SD: But we're with this group every week – is there something different about when we are reading *Passenger*?

Paula: We have something to talk about – we are getting together over something ... We are concentrating on something – something to discuss. (Paula final interview)

Well, it's nice to read together, it's nice to read in a group – it's just nice. We get to understand each other more. (Luis final interview)

Like Long's (2003) reading circle members, Paula notes how you can get to know a group of people better with 'something to discuss'. Furthermore, Luis's last point goes beyond the pleasure of being with other people, beyond Paula's stress on meeting others with a focus for the conversation, beyond pedagogical benefits of reading as a group, and even beyond even the realization that reading can be a communal as well as an individual process. It moves towards a link between reading, novels and empathy, which will be developed in Chapter 11.

Chapter Summary

This chapter returned us to the message of Chapter 1: that reading is something slightly different to different groups of 'reading experts', and that those of us involved in adult literacy development need to listen to all of them. One way of doing this is to start from the perspective of individual readers, linking what they say to findings from these diverse disciplines. This chapter presented an analysis of the six themes emerging from the main case-study data, research which aimed to work from the experiences of the reading circle members themselves. Each theme points us in the direction of the fields explored in Chapter 1: cognitive psychology/neuroscience (the scientific studies of reading), literary theory, social history, social practice theory and educational research.

The first theme presents reading as five acts (an educational act, a cognitive act, a communicative act, an imaginative act and an affective act). The second argues that we each have a reading identity, linking our reading practices with our reading skills and confidence. The third presents two aspects of reading words – decoding and understanding meaning – and analyses links between decoding and meaning, meaning and use. The fourth theme concerns how the 'story' is 'built up' through a combination of individual and group cognition, echoing the work of the cognitive psychologists and literary theorists on how meaning is made and constantly adapted. Theme five addresses the relationship between fiction, truth and learning; it asks what fiction is and what can be learnt from it, uniting ideas from social history (on evolving reading practices), literary theory and education. The last theme, the benefits of reading as a group, includes ideas on how vocabulary and word-level decoding can be developed, how groups can support individual confidence development, and the potential social pleasures of reading circles. These six themes therefore not only present ideas about adult reading development, reading circles and the novel (to be further developed in the following chapters), but also function as a reminder that working from the reader's perspective is one way to integrate the work of the often-segregated camps of reading expertise.

Suggested Reading

Iser, W. (1978), *The Act of Reading: A Theory of Aesthetic Response.* Baltimore, MA: The Johns Hopkins University Press.
Iser analyses literary reading as an active, interpretative process.

Rimmon-Kenan, S. (1989), *Narrative Fiction: Contemporary Poetics.* London: Routledge.
A challenging look at how narrative fiction works.

Chapter 8

Reading as Experience

This is the first of four chapters in which the findings of the main case study are placed alongside the reading pedagogies and practices examined in the earlier chapters in order to explore the following discussion points: reading as experience, reading circles as ideal pedagogy, reading as individual versus reading as communal, and the pleasures and politics of novels and reading circles. In Chapter 6, I suggested that reading is, among other things, an experience and, as such, can only be accessed through the first-person perspectives of those doing the experiencing: the readers themselves. I explained that this is why I have chosen to research reading by talking to readers and listening to readers talking to one another.

This idea – that reading is experience – is hardly new: since her seminal original work in 1938, Louise Rosenblatt has conceptualized reading as experience in her analyses of literary reading as 'transaction' between the reader and the text (see Rosenblatt [2005] for an introduction to her work). There is even a 'Reading Experience Database', where readers and researchers can input information and access 'reading experiences' from 1450 to 1945 (The Open University, 2010). Indeed, several of the contemporary reading circle members I spoke to referred to their 'reading experiences'. And yet, experience is a term often used, usually understood, but rarely defined. The most commonly accepted lay definition (and the one I am using) is a dual one. An experience is something lived, an event or activity in time and space that an individual lives or moves through. Here, 'experience' can be a verb or a noun, for example: 'I experienced reading in a group' or 'He enjoyed the experience of meeting with the same group of people every week'. 'Experience' is also a noun referring to the product of a lived event – what remains of that event within the individual: for example, 'Milan's orchestra experience is considerable' or 'Karen has experience with UK and Japanese orchestras'. This usage also has an adjectival form: 'Milan is an experienced violinist'. Which of these, then, applies to reading, or can they all? Can reading be both a lived event or activity, and the product, within the individual or group, of that activity? Reading and rereading the data from the case study, there seems to be much more that could – and should – be said about what identifying reading as experience really means.

This focus on experience is also the argument made by Gordon (2009), writing of the place of poetry in the English secondary school syllabus. Gordon feels that poetry is an experience, that poems are to be understood as lived experience, and that poetry needs to be treated as such, by reading and listening to poems aloud. The instinctive sense of experience as something 'lived' over time, where 'action' and 'consequence' are united to bring meaning or understanding, is theorized by Dewey (1934), who stresses the criticality of 'perception': 'To put one's hand in the fire that consumes it is not necessarily to have an experience. The action and its consequence must be joined in perception'(1934, p. 46).

Gordon, however, adds another dimension to his understanding of poetry as experience, evoking the notion of a 'lifeworld' (Cope & Kalantzis, 2000), 'the voice, history and culture – the *life* – of an individual', stating that 'any poetry encounter is a meeting of two *lifeworlds*, the first that of the listener or reader, the second that newly unconcealed world projected as poem' (J. Gordon, 2009, p. 166). Crucially, this concept of a lifeworld comes from Habermas's (1984) 'theory of communicative action', where he writes of the lifeworld as the 'context-forming horizon'(p. 337) from which we communicate and interpret. Gordon's argument is that literature (poetry in his case) is experience in two ways: literary works exist only as they are experienced, as they are read, seen or listened to – what I am calling 'lived experience' – and reading/listening to literature is an interplay between (at least) two different interpretative lifeworlds of experience: the reader/listener's and the work's. The data from the main case study illustrate both of these two aspects of reading as experience.

As discussed in the previous chapter, the data present reading as five acts (an educational act, a cognitive act, a communicative act, an imaginative act and an affective act). These can be seen as five aspects of the reading circle as lived experience: learning words and ideas, decoding, thinking and remembering, communicating, imagining and feeling. Participants explained what they did every week at home: reading both silently and aloud, looking up words in the dictionary, asking friends, writing notes, thinking, feeling, assessing. They spoke of enjoying holding the books, owning them, smelling them and carrying them around. Together as a circle, participants discussed, read, listened, remembered, reminded one another, argued, made decisions about activities, analysed characters, questioned one another and laughed. This was all part of their communal and individual lived experience of the reading circle.

The data also demonstrate Gordon's second aspect of literature as experience: reading as a meeting of lifeworlds. On 10 March 2009 we read the passage where Murri reveals that she has published her research on communicating with Roma, and that throughout their relationship she had been secretly studying Roma for her PhD. Every circle member agreed that Murri had done something wrong, but opinions varied greatly between whether she was simply 'a bit sly' (as Paula put it) or whether her behaviour was seriously morally reprehensible, a betrayal, as Luis argued:

> She's using him ... that's the worst thing ... She used him badly, if she wanted to use him, she shouldn't have got involved with him – that's bad ... That was bad ... treachery ... It's like 'et tu Brutus'! (Luis 10 March 2009)

He was visibly angry as he was talking, and he remembered this in his final interview:

> When ... the main character slept with this woman who used him or whatever to do her PhD and we had quite a heated discussion about that. She could have done it differently ... If someone knows how important a thing is, then you make different interpretations from the same piece of information that you read ... and that's what happened. I had my experience that made my observations and they had theirs. (Luis final interview)

Luis's lifeworld was different from those of his colleagues, and this, combined with the lifeworld of the novel, produced his 'different interpretation'. Similarly attuned to the workings of this manifestation of reading as experience, Katherine noted how she was drawn into an unfamiliar lifeworld (that of the professional orchestra in *Passenger*) through the use of the familiar experience of personal relationships:

> It's always easier to pull someone in with a friendship, everybody's had a friendship with someone ... so the friendship part was interesting ... the way he meets this girl ... and he was quite funny, and I don't know, because I've never, I've never been or spoken to somebody who's part of an orchestra ... I thought it was apart from my world, but the friendship brought it closer. (Katherine final interview)

Gordon's use of the term 'lifeworld', its evocation of linguistics' 'mindstyle' (the world-view of an individual/literary character as manifested in their use of language [R. Fowler, 1977; Leech & Short, 1981]) and its application to novel reading conjures another way to express the novel as experience: Bakhtin's (1981) notion of the novel as multi-voiced discourse. A novel (unlike *some* poems or short stories) does not represent only one lifeworld, but many – not merely those of each character (in direct speech and 'character zones'), but also those of the various domains the characters inhabit. Very simply, a novel contains many different voices, representing many different worlds. Gordon writes that 'any poetic encounter is a meeting of two lifeworlds' (2009, p. 166). Following Bakhtin, we could rephrase this as 'any *novelistic* encounter is a meeting of *many* lifeworlds: the reader's and the many represented in the novel'. In a reading circle this is further amplified by the interactions of the lifeworlds of its members. Reading a novel as a reading circle is therefore a meeting of *a great many* lifeworlds: the many of the novel and the many of the readers. This meeting of multiple lifeworlds is the basis of the simultaneous 'loss of self' and exploration of personal identity valued by Long's (2003) Texan reading circle members, and one of the reasons why participants of the main case-study felt it was 'nice to read in a group':

> It [reading together] was good because we got different angles; different interpretations based on our different life experiences. (Luis final interview)

However, more than Gordon's *two* aspects of reading as experience, these data evoke the *three*-way classification of art as experience evident in Dewey's (1934) *Art as Experience*. The first is the distilled experience (of the artist or culture) which goes *into* producing a work of art: for example the experiences of Billy Cowie's life which enabled him to write *Passenger*. The second is the lived experience *of* looking at (taking in, consuming) a work of art (or reading a novel, listening to music, watching a play): for example the experience of reading Chapter 1 of *Passenger*. The third is the future experience *produced by* that lived artistic experience: those who have looked at a piece of art, or read a book, will go on to do certain things, to have certain thoughts and therefore experiences as a result. For example, a person may go to buy a CD of classical music after reading about the orchestra rehearsals in *Passenger*.

Yet, Dewey's distinction between the experience *of* looking at a piece of art and the experienced *produced by* looking at a piece of art is more complex for certain art forms than others. Taking in a painting, for example, takes less time than reading a novel – or rather, the premise of its spectatorship does not rely on an extended engagement in the same way that a novel's does (a novel is meant to be read, page by page, if not word by word). It may be possible to experience a painting in an instant, but a novel takes time: it necessitates, and presupposes, a developmental process. Therefore, the experience produced by reading *Passenger* is not only how *finishing* reading the entire novel will affect the future actions of its readers (for example, Aisha deciding to write a novel based on her wartime experiences), but also how each day's (or even each paragraph's) reading changes the reader by slightly altering his or her lifeworld, and this change in turn influences the next lived experience of reading. In short, the experience resulting from reading one page of *Passenger* affects the future experience of reading a page of *Passenger*, which then produces a new experience and so on, page by page, chapter by chapter, day by day, as *both* reader and story develop in a 'constantly mutating experience' (Paran, 2011).

The 'building' aspect of novel reading (discussed in Chapter 7) means that the experience of reading pages of the novel merges with the experience produced by having read other pages of the novel. These aspects of experience 'cross-fertilize' (a word which one of Hartley's [2002] participants used to describe the interactions of her reading circle). As already noted, both cognitive psychologists and literary theorists analyse the process by which the reader reads a piece of text, processes it into frames of meaning, and then uses these frames of meaning to process subsequent text. In this way, Iser stresses, reading replicates 'the process by which we gain [our own life] experience' (1972, p. 224). The above interpretation of Dewey's 'art as experience' model adds to this equation the development of the reader him- or herself during the reading process. The experience *of* reading creates experiences *from* reading, while also determining the next experience of reading. Novel reading, therefore, interweaves these aspects of reading as experience.

Within a reading circle, it is not just one intermingling of Dewey's three aspects of experience that takes place, but, crucially, each reader influences the lived reading experience of every other reader, changing one another in ways that will influence the next group reading experience. Beverley's life experience as a health-care assistant increased her interest in the medical aspects of the novel, which affected her enjoyment of, and confidence in, the reading process (including showing the novel to colleagues at work, and being identified as the member of the reading circle with the medical expertise). This in turn influenced the entire circle's understanding and enjoyment of the medical aspects of the novel. What they read next together (Milan's experience at the hospital, for example) then influenced Beverley to recognize better her patients' disorientation, and perhaps Katherine to get in touch with her mother. This gave them both slightly different experiences with which to read more of the novel, individually and as a group. Each time the circle read, each member brought a slightly different bank of individual experiences with them, and each time they finished reading and discussing as a circle, they had each gained more experience to take back into their 'outside' lives and influence their gathering of new life experience.

Seen in this way, any novel reading is heightened experience formation, and novel reading *within a reading circle* is experience formation further amplified. This has implications for contexts that value the gaining of life experience. In Auster's *Oracle Night* (2004), for example, the protagonist rewrites *The Time Machine* as a new Hollywood script. In his rewritten version, the citizens of the twenty-second century are required to mark their twentieth birthdays with a time-travel voyage:

> You begin two hundred years before your birth ... and gradually work your way home to the present. The purpose of the trip is to teach you humility and compassion, tolerance for your fellow men. (p. 106)

Auster's futuristic coming-of-age ritual, like novel reading within a reading circle, is an accelerated form of experience formation, designed to teach salient lessons. This brings us back to Dewey, this time to *Experience and Education* (Dewey, 1938), and his central 'belief that all genuine education comes about through experience' (Dewey, 1938, p. 25).

Chapter Summary

To write that 'reading is experience', or to speak of a 'reading experience', may be commonplace, but to conceptualize reading as experience means taking up a theoretical position which will influence how reading is researched. If reading is an experience, then it must be researched, at least sometimes, from the points of view of the readers themselves. Additionally, the term 'experience' has a familiarity which obscures its complexity. This chapter aimed to explore how individual and communal reading processes relate to notions of lived and past experience. Using data from the main case study, along with ideas from Bakhtin (1981),

Habermas (1984), Dewey (1934, 1938) and Auster (2004), I argued that novel reading, and particularly novel reading within a reading circle, is heightened, or 'extreme', experience formation. As members of the eighteenth- and nineteenth-century reading circles and mutual improvement societies understood, in this way reading circles can provide powerful educational (as well as social) opportunities.

Suggested Reading

Auster, P. (2004), *Oracle Night*. London: Faber and Faber.
One of many must-read Auster novels, *Oracle Night* examines the relationship between experience, humility and compassion.

Bakhtin, M. M. (1981), *The Dialogic Imagination* (C. Emerson & M. Holquist, trans.). Austin: University of Texas Press.
A highly influential work on the multiple voices of the novel.

Dewey, J. (1934), *Art as Experience*. New York City, NY: Perigee.
Dewey's philosophical work on the characteristics of works of art, and how art relates to experience.

Dewey, J. (1938), *Experience & Education*. New York City, NY: Touchstone.
A short book of Dewey's lectures on the relationship between education and experience.

The Open University (2010), *The Reading Experience Database (RED), 1450–1945*. Online database: http://www.open.ac.uk/Arts/RED/.
An interactive database of past 'reading experiences'.

Chapter 9

Reading Circles as 'Ideal Pedagogy'

In this chapter, I will take the findings of the main case study and use them, along with insights from previous chapters, to present the notion of reading circles as 'ideal pedagogy'. This is a move away from this particular case study and into a wider discussion of pedagogy. I will cover peer-teaching, negotiated syllabi, differentiation, the needs of first- and second-language speakers and the notion of citizenship education.

Peer-Teaching

Dewey stresses that for experience to be educative, it must be continuous and interactive (Dewey, 1938). The case study reading illustrates Dewey's view. It was certainly continuous, lasting for just over six months. It also involved constant peer-interaction, with members discussing ideas, explaining words and concepts and finishing one another's sentences week after week. Both O'Donnell-Allen's (2006) and Daniel's (2006) definitions of reading circles emphasize the importance of reading circles being peer-led and peer-managed. As discussed in Chapter 5, Long (2003) and Hartley (2002) report that reading circles in the United States and Britain are overwhelmingly peer-led affairs, even if many groups elect a leader for a particular session or hire an 'expert' from time to time. Though my role as teacher worked against this initially, the case study reading circle quickly became peer-led, an example of what education studies terms peer-work, peer-teaching and peer-assessment.

The importance of peer-interaction and collaborative learning is central to the ideas of good teaching which permeate studies of adult education (Derrick, Ecclestone, & Gawn, 2009; Derrick, Gawn, & Ecclestone, 2008; Gardner, 2006; Looney, 2008; Swain, Griffiths, & Stone, 2006). These studies stress that adults learn best when engaging in peer- and self-teaching and assessment. This is supported by the fact that the reading circles and mutual improvement societies of the late eighteenth and nineteenth centuries may have been the only educational option for some, but they were also the preferred educational option for many (see Chapter 5).

Unpicking this idea somewhat, Day's (2003) research on using reading circles in Australian primary-school English classes found that 'to relinquish teacher control' and encourage peer decision-making had the 'unexpected benefit[s]' of 'absolute enjoyment' and 'a deeper level of understanding' as 'students' ability to clarify, crystallize and justify their thoughts and ideas … improved dramatically' (pp. 10–11). Cumming-Potvin (2007) found reading circle work in middle-school Australian English classes to be effective because of its integral peer support, which scaffolded literacy development (p. 501). Even outside the adult context, peer-learning is identified as effective pedagogy.

'Scaffolding' (Bruner, 1983) is a useful way of expressing the in-built peer support of a reading circle. Hughes (2010) discusses the idea of scaffolding and its centrality to adult literacy pedagogy in her 'Writing' chapter of *Teaching Adult Literacy: Principles and Practice.* She focuses on how, when producing a piece of writing, adult literacy learners could experience 'cognitive overload' from so many different writing skills or sub-skills being drawn on at once, each potentially challenging for someone less confident with their writing. If one or more of these skills are 'scaffolded' by the teacher or other learners (for example, if learners are provided with key spellings), this can enable the learner to focus on implementing (and developing) one skill in particular (for example, paragraph structure).

This is particularly significant when we think about what is involved in reading longer texts, such as novels. An adult literacy learner may be able to tackle each of the individual skills/sub-skills involved in reading a novel (such as decoding words and sentences, inference and remembering what was read before), but without some of these skills being 'automatic' and/or without confidence in one's command of these skills, performing all of these skills at the same time may be too daunting or difficult. Usually, scaffolding refers to the support given or organized by a teacher; yet, within the case study reading circle, participants not only provided scaffolding *for themselves* (using their notebooks to record vocabulary or plot events, for example), but also, significantly, provided scaffolding *for one another* throughout each session. Participants helped one another decode, explained vocabulary, helped with remembering and interpretation and gave one another positive, reinforcing feedback on their interpretations and ideas, thus developing one another's confidence in interpretation. This allowed each participant to read *Passenger* despite their individual anxieties (Beverley had trouble decoding, Safia with vocabulary, Paula with remembering 'what was going on'). Together they managed to read what few would have felt confident tackling alone. This is the principle which has made reading circles an effective peer-led adult education option for centuries.

Negotiated Syllabi

Because the reading circle was peer-managed and involved peer-assessment, it can usefully be considered an example of a 'negotiated syllabus'. Breen & Littlejohn (2000) emphasize the importance of the curriculum emerging as a product of negotiation with learners, rather than being something imposed on those learners. They conceptualize 'negotiation' as being of three kinds arranged in a Russian-doll structure. The outer doll, 'procedural negotiation', aims to 'reach an agreement' about what to do in the classroom, how, why and/or when. A group may decide their main topic for the week, their learning outcomes for a series of sessions or to work towards a particular form of external accreditation. The middle doll, 'interactive negotiation', is the conversation, dialogue or communication processes undertaken in order to reach those decisions. The inner doll is 'personal negotiation', referring to the individual understanding, interpreting, reflecting and deciding, which allows the individual to make a genuine contribution to the group negotiation. Each of these aspects of negotiation are key to Breen & Littlejohn's process of negotiating a syllabus, their emphasis on learning being in the negotiation as well as led by it, and the sense of personal and group investment in (and responsibility for) the syllabus produced.

This model is a close match to the case-study reading circle work (and indeed to the workings of most of the other reading circles I spoke to this year). It was the group that decided that they wanted to read a novel using a reading circle approach. It was also the group that decided how to spend their forty minutes of weekly reading circle contact time, and what to do at home. Both of these are examples of procedural negotiation. These decisions were made through conversation (interactive negotiation), with time given for individuals to think through what they wanted, and encouragement to express those views and listen to the views of others (personal negotiation). This is also an example of *open-ended pedagogy* (Derrick, 2010): teaching activities which do not have closed or pre-defined objectives, but rather are open for participants to take their learning in the direction appropriate to them. If we see this reading circle as part of the tradition of reading circles started autonomously by groups of adults around the world, then this aspect of negotiated, open-ended pedagogy is unremarkable, simply part of the long and dominant mutual-improvement society tradition of adult education. However, if we see this reading circle in the light of most early twenty-first-century formal Anglophone adult literacy provision, this negotiation of syllabus becomes a radical pedagogic departure, with risks (such as the 'loss of teacher control' identified by Malchow Lloyd [2006]) as well as substantial and much-needed potential benefits, including a means to 'construct and reflect learning as an emancipatory process' and 'activate the social and cultural resources of the classroom group' (Breen & Littlejohn, 2000, pp. 21–22). This is reminiscent of the more learner-centred pedagogy of Hamilton & Hillier's (2006) first three English adult literacy policy phases, of Sticht's (2002) self-improvement tradition of United States adult literacy education, the philosophy behind the Scottish literacies 'Curriculum Wheel' (Leavey, 2005) and current Irish adult literacy provision (Ryan, 2010). It is also an old answer to a newly fashionable, or newly framed, issue: differentiation.

Differentiation

Differentiation has been *the* buzzword in post-compulsory education in England for most of the young twenty-first century. It relates to the complex task of recognizing difference (different needs, different experience, different interests, different 'abilities') while working towards the overall aim of equality of educational opportunity. Put another way, differentiation is simply the idea that in any teaching process, the learning methods, topics, tasks or outcomes should be adapted to meet the varied needs and interests of different learners. Depending on one's point of view, differentiation is therefore either overwhelmingly problematic (if not impossible) or a very normal, natural part of any teaching process.

The data from the reading circle case study indicate that reading circles offer opportunities for what I would term 'participant-led differentiation'. Participants decided together how to spend their communal time, as well as what to do at home, thus creating 'tasks' and 'outcomes' to match their own abilities, confidence and goals. For example, Aisha wanted to expand her vocabulary, while Paula wanted to improve her ability to remember the events in a longer text. Both of these participants shaped their own reading circle work accordingly. Aisha asked questions about items of vocabulary each week and used her personal notebook to record new words and definitions. In the group, Paula asked and answered questions about the story and took notes on each chapter as she read at home, to help her remember. Significantly, Katherine noticed this differentiation of goal and personal outcome:

> Beverley, for example, she was getting the medical point of view – she was fascinated by it and also it was a good book for her to read because she wasn't a book reader, she'd never read a book before ... There was another girl, a lady, in the class, who had difficulty with the words, but she really read well and understood a lot ... I'm really, really interested in how people think and how they see things ... how they create things in their minds and how they pull things out of books and out of situations. (Katherine final interview)

Reading circles, therefore, provide differentiation by activity (what members do), by topic (what members read and/or discuss) and by outcome (what members produce or gain from the process) by allowing adults to work individually and collaboratively according to their interests, needs and goals.

The Needs of First- and Second-Language Speakers

One particular kind of differentiation has been a long-standing challenge in adult literacy provision throughout the Anglophone world: meeting the needs of those for whom English is a native (and often only) language and meeting the needs of those who speak English alongside other languages, with varying degrees of confidence. There can therefore be substantially different needs to be met in one group, particularly around reading. The requirements of a first-language speaker who has difficulty decoding words are potentially very different from those of a second-language speaker who wants to develop vocabulary and grammatical accuracy and may have difficulty understanding why a native English speaker 'cannot read'. Likewise, the needs of a second-language speaker who is confident reading and writing in another language may be very different from a second-language speaker who finds reading and writing challenging in any language or who has never before accessed any formal educational provision.

This range of needs presented itself in the case-study reading circle, with Safia a learner confident in her literacy in two other languages, but newer to English and wanting to develop her reading and writing along with her vocabulary and grammar, and Beverley a native speaker (bilingual from an early age) who is confident with her vocabulary and grammar, but who was unable to read or write in any language five years ago and still finds decoding challenging. This was a key difficulty for me as a teacher when planning and teaching the 'normal' adult literacy provision elements of our weekly sessions. It was a very happy surprise, therefore, to see that the reading circle 'worked' with both sets of needs, and those in between. Participants who wanted to develop their English vocabularies did so, with the support of those with larger English vocabularies who enjoyed explaining word meanings as part of exploring the meaning of the novel (rather than as a potentially tedious game of providing definitions). Those who wished to develop their confidence in accurate speaking and listening did so in the discussions, offering their understanding of the developing story as an incentive to those listening to their, at times, less confident and slower speech. Those who had found decoding a challenge were able to call on the help of others to decode particular words, while the fact that they were helping with definitions gave a sense of a 'level playing field', with everyone having some needs alongside obvious, and useful, strengths.

This mutual exchange of expertise may seem utopian: what would have happened, for example, if there was someone who did not have any 'strengths' to offer the group? This is actually very unlikely. In a context where word, sentence and text-level linguistic and literacy skills; analytical skills; life experience of all kinds; study skills and social skills all contribute to the 'building up' of the 'story', everyone really does have something to offer the communal reading process. Crucially, a reading circle provides a range of activities broad enough to work for wide-ranging linguistic or literary 'levels'. A reading circle approach, therefore, is worth exploring as one means to differentiate effectively with mixed ESOL/literacy groups, just as the reading circles explored in Chapter 5 often met a spectrum of educational, personal and social needs.

Learning Words

Exactly how the case study reading circle members used their reading circle to learn words was discussed in Chapter 7, but I would like to return to both aspects – meaning and decoding – in the light of literature in the respective fields. Nagy (1997) argues for the importance of context, stressing that there are three types of context-related knowledge involved in learning – and using – items of vocabulary: linguistic knowledge, world knowledge and strategic knowledge. These are usually viewed as individual cognitive abilities, but applied to this case study they can be used to describe the group interaction, which provided (and developed) all three areas of knowledge. The text of the novel itself, along with the readers' shared linguistic knowledge, provides the linguistic context for learning new words. The novel and circle of readers also provide knowledge of 'the world', the developing world of the novel and the worlds of each participant. One participant worked in a hospital and could provide medical knowledge, one was familiar with classical music and another shared her knowledge of trams. Each helped the others to understand and use new words. Finally, together they developed their strategic (study skills) knowledge, using notebooks to record words in different ways and 'recycling' these words in group discussions. In this sense, this reading circle became an ideal environment for learning vocabulary in context.

However, theorists do not agree on the use of context in vocabulary learning. Sökmen (1997) questions this emphasis on context, specifically whether inferring from context alone is enough. Not only does she feel that relying on inference can be slow and confusing, but she argues that vocabulary needs to be learnt in such a way that it can be used in new and different contexts, which involves a broader understanding than may come from one context. Vocabulary, she feels, needs to be observed in numerous 'encounters' and 'recontextualized' by learners, used in new situations and contexts, for a 'deeper processing' to take place. Sökmen also stresses the importance of using explicit vocabulary teaching techniques such as dictionary work and 'semantic elaboration' (ways for learners to record and explore vocabulary in relation to other vocabulary).

This is precisely the process that occurred in this reading circle. Most new items of vocabulary reoccurred in the novel and/or the discussion, providing the 'numerous encounters' required to learn vocabulary. As noted above, participants themselves 'recycled' their newly learnt vocabulary. The vocabulary discussions involved negotiating a range of contexts (see examples of 'wholesome,' 'thimble' and 'accompany' in Chapter 7). Additionally, participants used dictionaries (English and bilingual) and recorded words in notebooks (using and developing strategic knowledge). Vocabulary, in this reading circle, was both inferred from context *and* peer- and self-taught explicitly and systematically.

With *Passenger* we were reading in the class ... and at home and we were talking ... We explain when we come back in class what happen and which words we don't know the meaning and we underline and then we discuss

… and we are writing the meaning in the book to learn and for the spelling practice. (Safia final interview)

Neither as teacher nor as researcher did I suggest that participants record words in notebooks or give any advice about learning vocabulary or practising spellings. The study skills that the majority of the participants used were peer- and self-developed and used within the reading circle to develop particular individual goals (such as vocabulary or spelling). These peer- and self-developed study skills are at the heart of strategic knowledge.

The other aspect of 'learning words' that was important to these participants was decoding words. Our reading circle involved no explicit reading instruction, and yet participants reported a greater confidence decoding words by the end of *Passenger.*

Reading words, you know spelling them out – sounding them. I'm definitely better at reading words now. (Paula final interview)
I can tackle more words now, try to say them out instead of being scared. (Beverley final interview)

In their final interviews, reading circle members discussed how listening to others read while following along (therefore reinforcing the written-spoken connection) helped their decoding. They also reported that reading aloud themselves allowed them to get help from others in the group, while developing decoding automaticity.

Reading aloud is hotly contested as a way of developing reading skills, in both adult literacy and EFL circles (Gabrielatos, 1996; Gibson, 2008; National Institute for Literacy, 2009) as well as school literacy (Ash, Kuhn, & Walpole, 2009). Accusations range from it merely being 'ineffective'– as it allocates only a small proportion of class time to any one learner's reading and provides listeners with poor models (Ash et al., 2009, p. 87) – to actively 'damaging students' social and emotional growth' due to potential 'embarrassment and anxiety' (p. 89). Others argue that reading aloud is simply not a useful skill: 'Except for students who want to be radio announcers, I'm not sure what it accomplishes' (National Institute for Literacy, 2009).

These data, or rather these reading circle members, answer the above charges. When one participant was reading, she was not only developing her own reading skills, but also those of everybody listening and following on in the text. Significantly, what the participants read aloud was usually (though not always) the text that they had already read at home, and so the reading and listening were often displaying, checking and reinforcing decoding work that was already attempted individually. The time taken by one participant reading aloud was used to develop (check and reinforce) the reading skills of all the participants, not just those of the person reading aloud. Supporting this observation, Gibson (2008) and Duncan (2009) argue that reading aloud can develop understanding of phoneme-grapheme correspondence in the listener as well as the reader. Seen in this way, reading aloud becomes a highly efficient use of time. Second, the argument that a 'less than fluent' reader does not provide a good model for listening peers is mistakenly to imagine that the world is composed of two types of readers – 'fluent' and 'not fluent' – and that learners can only learn from the fluent. However, surely all readers are on a spectrum of fluency, and connections between written and spoken words can develop from listening to readers on all parts of this spectrum? The assertion that a non-fluent reading is not a good model for listening peers also assumes that 'fluency' is a straight-forward marker, while I would argue that notions of 'fluency' – or what makes a reader, or an instance of reading – fluent are far from universally agreed. Chapter 2's review of reading in adult life supports this view; 'real life' adult reading practices are hugely varied. Additionally, for a reader with no confidence, listening to someone else reading with a similar lack of confidence can be encouraging, as Beverley explained: 'Everybody encourage everybody to read and the beauty of it is that when somebody finish reading, you can't wait to read'.

The case study reading circle members also spoke of how reading aloud, and listening to others read, developed rather than damaged their reading identities and made them 'stronger' (Beverley final interview), more confident readers. Finally, they argued, just as I have previously (Duncan, 2008, 2009), that not only does reading aloud help develop their reading (and reading identities), but it is also a common reading practice in itself. Participants explained that they would like to be able to read aloud to family members, at work or to enjoy more novels with others.

I am not, however, arguing that reading aloud is integral for reading circles. Though reading aloud seems to have played a large part in many of the eighteenth- and nineteenth-century reading circles and mutual improvement societies, the vast majority of the contemporary reading circles that Long (2003), Hartley (2002) and I spoke to did not do any reading aloud. It is also important not to go overboard and overstate the importance of reading aloud or to go anywhere near suggesting that *enforced* reading aloud is a good idea. At the *Alberto Manguel, Azar Nafisi & Daniel Pennac: The Rights of the Reader* Free the Word event (London, 12 April 2008), Daniel Pennac explained that in the 1970s, reading aloud was all but forbidden in French schools. Now, after a resurgence in enthusiasm for reading aloud, it is practically forbidden not to read aloud. Both positions, he remarked, are 'equally stupid'.

However, I am arguing that reading aloud can play in important role in reading circles, for two reasons. First, the commitment to a *peer-led* reading circle has to be complete: if members want to read aloud, they should read aloud and, if a reading circle is happening as part of a more formal educational offer, it is part of the teacher's job to think about *why*. For example, Cho & Choi (2008) worked with Korean school children learning English and found that the process of *listening to* a story read aloud 'awakens' pupils' interest in both stories and reading. Secondly, critics of reading aloud as an educational tool (whether in formal or informal educational settings) forget that reading aloud is a common literacy practice. People do indeed read aloud in daily life, whether a few lines of an email to a listening colleague, the delights of a menu in a new café or a lengthy passage from a holy book for religious workshop. Confident, fluent readers simply do not notice the frequency of these occurrences, but adult literacy learners are acutely aware of them and therefore often want to develop this aspect of reading.

Citizenship

Educational objectives around conforming to, contesting or simply exploring the individual's role as a local, national or global citizen are as old as reading instruction, and, as discussed in Chapter 4, are often the reason behind reading instruction. Citizenship education is fundamental to literacy in its various definitions. Reading and writing are, quite literally, about our place in relation to others (I read another's words; I write for someone else to read).

Yet the findings from the case study make a case for reading circles in particular (rather than literacy education more broadly) as a citizenship pedagogy. Participants explained that they learnt about the world, about others and about their own place in the world – what Gordon (2009) describes as 'consideration of the very nature of identity, their own identity and the identities of others' (p. 174). This kind of 'citizenship' education recalls Meek's (1988) and Rose's (2010) arguments for the study of literature as a political education (see Chapter 4). It also echoes Harvey & Daniels's (2009) arguments for the pedagogical benefits of what they call 'inquiry circles' for the teaching of all subjects in compulsory education. They stress the importance of learner autonomy, individual and communal research and the role of discussion in creating, testing and adapting ideas as central to a student's development in both individual subject areas and as an adult citizen. The very act of working within an inquiry circle, or reading circle, is training in participatory citizenship.

Chapter Summary

The above exploration of reading circles as ideal pedagogy is not a self-congratulatory claim that the case study reading circle represents the best way to realize the above notions of 'effective' pedagogy. Nor is it an argument that reading circles are the only or best way to develop adult reading. Rather, it was an attempt to use contemporary educational discourse to analyse what the case study participants felt they gained from their reading circle and to suggest why other adult literacy learners and teachers may want to experiment in a similar way. I argued that reading circles (within and without formal educational settings) allow adults to teach one another; determine what and how they learn; to work towards learning outcomes of their own choosing and based on their own particular language, literacy and other needs; to work together to develop their vocabularies and decoding abilities; and to negotiate what it is to be an adult citizen.

Suggested Reading

Derrick, J., Ecclestone, K., & Gawn, J. (2009), *Formative Assessment in Adult Literacy, Language and Numeracy*. Leicester: NIACE.
This book presents and explores research findings on formative assessment, including ideas on peer-interaction and collaborative learning.

Pennac, D. (2006), *The Rights of the Reader* (S. Hamp Adams, trans.). London: Walker Books.
Pennac's entertaining and insightful book presents the rituals, joys and fears of reading, and our rights as readers to skip, reread, 'mistake a book for real life', and, crucially, not to read at all.

Schmitt, N., & McCarthy, M. (eds) (1997), *Vocabulary: Description, Acquisition and Pedagogy*. Cambridge: Cambridge University Press.
Discusses how we learn the meanings of words.

Chapter 10

The Individual and the Communal

According to the main case study reading circle members, the imaginative act of reading allows us to gain new experience and to see things from others' points of view, bringing with it a triumphant sense of breaking out of the individual subjectivities within those hard little 'bone boxes' (Byatt, 1978, p. 279) that divide us from one another. With remarkable similarity, Long's (2003) female Texan reading circle participants reported this breaking down of individual subjectivities in the communal discussion of a book as central to the appeal of reading circles. Yet, is this a move into another individual subjectivity or a transition from an individual perspective to the communal?

From the perceived gulf between the individual cognition-based and the social practice-based approaches to literacy, to debates about whether individual silent reading or reading aloud is 'the norm', studies of reading, reading pedagogy, reading circles and the novel are riddled with tensions between the individual and the communal. In this chapter, I aim to examine these tensions as they run throughout the main case study data and the preceding chapters of this book. I would also like to interrogate how reading circles in particular epitomize reading as being at once individual and communal.

The history of the novel has been argued as a history of the philosophy of the individual. Lodge (1992) characterizes the novel as the first literary genre to claim to be telling new stories, born of individuals, rather than retelling the existing stories of a culture. Watt places the novel within the development of 'modern realism', which 'begins from the position that truth can be discovered by the individual through his senses; it has its origins in Descartes and Locke' (2000, p. 12), arguing that the novel evolved out of the (new) eighteenth-century twin cultural preoccupations of the ordinary and the individual, and is essentially a form exploring 'the primacy of the individual experience' (2000, p. 15). Eagleton (2005) presents the novel as born of, and dominated by, realism, representing 'the ordinary' while preoccupied with what 'lurks deep in the human psyche' (p. 11). Writing of the twentieth-century novelists he admires, Burgess (1967) devotes a chapter to 'Great Individuality', noting the dominance of 'the strong individual voice that shouts or sings alone' (p. 73).

The development of the novel as a literary genre, and one preoccupied with individuality, can be linked with the increasing dominance of silent and/or solitary reading. From at least the sixteenth century, silent reading was gradually becoming a more common practice in Europe, potentially (though not necessarily, see Chapter 2) because being able to read became more common and the need for the few readers to read to the many non-readers was gradually decreasing. Rose writes of the sixteenth-century religious and political figure Hendrik Niclaes's dislike for 'the learnt classes ... arrogantly enforcing a literal reading of the Bible'. Niclaes welcomed 'the untutored common reader' reading for himself using 'the new fashion for individual silent reading' (2010, p. 14). Both Niclaes and Rose stress the association of silent reading with individuality of thought. By the time the novel became the dominant popular literary form in the late eighteenth and early nineteenth centuries, silent reading was firmly established as a common practice (Pugh, 1978). It could therefore be argued that the novel was born of a philosophical interest in the individual, became popular at a time when reading as a silent, solitary activity was also becoming increasingly dominant and associated with individual thought, and remains a literary form enjoyed privately and concerned with individual psychology.

Those accessing forms of reading circles and mutual improvement societies from the eighteenth century onwards may have been reading, studying and learning as a group, but it could be argued that they were motivated to do so for individual gain – for their own individual educational advancement. Likewise, many contemporary reading circle members joined their groups for focused individual aims: for intellectual challenge or an intellectual life, to escape an existence dominated by housework, or for the motivation to read more and different books – an impetus to advance their individual reading habits (Hartley, 2002; Long, 1993, 2003).

The case study data support this view. Participants read individually at home or on public transport each week, kept individual notebooks based on individual needs and recounted their personal interpretations of the novel. Their novel reading was, therefore, at least partly, an individual experience. *Passenger* too revolves around the thoughts and feelings of one main character, Milan, and the reading circle discussion reflected this focus. Participants also stressed that they were learning to see from someone else's point of view, gaining another – but still *individual* – perspective. Katherine declared, 'it's someone else's vocabulary, somebody else's personality that you're reading', and Beverley explained that reading *Passenger* has 'given me the guideline of how I can see things from someone else's head' (Beverley final interview). *Passenger*'s content, how participants read the novel and their reflections on this reading process all undeniably highlight individual psychology: 'What's a novel? ... I'd say it's ... a quiet place to go ... into someone else's life' (Katherine final interview).

However, there is, of course, the other side. As much as the early development of the novel had 'the individual' as its subject, its production was the result of large communal – or community – shifts. Watt (2000) connects the development of the novel as a genre, and its rising popularity, with the development of the reading public, dramatically increasing in size from the late eighteenth and early to mid-nineteenth centuries. The factors that produced this increase in the reading public are various and interrelating: from the greater availability of books (in coffee houses and new libraries) to changes in working patterns and large-scale movements of population (from the countryside to the cities) following the Industrial Revolution, and from religious and political movements which emphasized freedom through education to changes in printing and taxation, which allowed for more affordable books and periodicals to become commonplace (Altick, 1957; James, 1973; Rose, 2002; Vincent, 1989, 2000; Webb, 1955).

This 'rise of mass literacy' occurred at a time when the novel was becoming the dominant literary genre, which resulted, at least in part, from a change in how literature was funded: a shift away from an individual-focused system of literary patronage towards the new public-taste-led publishing industry (Watt, 2000). By the mid-nineteenth century, decisions about what was published were dictated, for the first time, by the reading choices of 'the masses' (James, 1973).

Rose (2010) notes another communal aspect of reading. In 1872, reading the national press allowed labourers on strike at different ends of the country to see themselves as part of a larger political struggle around voting and trade unions. He argues further that larger numbers of working people reading canonical literary works (including novels and poetry) played a significant role in the growing national politicization of the 'working classes', citing nineteenth-century associations of literature with socialism, as the reading of literature brought (quoting Lord Lyttleton) 'freedom of thought [...] to rebel against custom and convention' (p. 37). This argument carries with it both the greater contention that the development of a print culture is linked to the 'disintegration of feudalism' (p. 25) because it created new communities which weakened the servant-master links of the oral networks, and, more controversially, that by definition great literature makes its readers 'militant and articulate' (p. 39).

Literary criticism too carries challenges to the idea that the novel is a genre of the individual. As discussed in Chapter 8, Bakhtin (1981) classifies the novel as 'multi-voiced discourse', arguing that it contains many voices, not simply those of direct character speech, but also those of the 'character zones' which divide the narrative linguistically and ideologically into inter-acting 'specific world views' (p. 292). In this analysis, the novel is a commu-nity of voices, shaping individual voices into a written representation of community. Culler (1975) also considers the novel a container of diversity: 'Fiction can hold together within a single space a variety of languages, levels of focus, points of view, which would be contradictory in other kinds of dis-course' (p. 261). For Culler, this is a unique quality of narrative fiction; other 'kinds of discourse' cannot hold together this diverse community of voices.

Irish short-story writer Frank O'Connor approached the novel as com-munity from a different angle, arguing that the main difference between a short story and a novel is that the main character of a novel must 'represent the reader in some aspect of his [the reader's] own conception of himself' but stressed that this can only happen within 'some relationship – hostile or friendly – with society as a whole' (O'Connor, 1963, p. 27). He argues that a novel, unlike a short story, must represent the communal, the society. In this light, *Passenger* is not really just about Milan, but about Milan and Roma, about Milan's girlfriends Karen and Murri, about Milan's orchestra and how it operates. It's about the media, about the worlds of academic research, medical hierarchy and scientific ambition.

Finally, and perhaps most fundamentally, novels were, and still are, read communally. Mullan (2006) cites evidence from Jane Austen's letters demonstrating that it was common for novels to be read aloud in families throughout the eighteenth century. He goes on to argue that novelists of this period wrote with the expectation that their novels would be read aloud, writing different characters' voices in anticipation of reader drama-tization using different accents. Altick describes 'twenty men and women gathering in a locksmith's shop to listen to the newest number of the *Pickwick Papers*, borrowed from a circulating library at *2d.* a day' (1957, p. 11). Novel reading was (and is), at least sometimes, a communal activity with one person reading aloud to a group of eager listeners, just as it was and is performed in reading circle formations. Families, work colleagues and friends read together, taking turns to read and discuss the latest novels. Novel reading has long been public, external, culturally visible and debated, and one answer to the 'why' of contemporary reading circles is that they are simply continuing this long-standing cultural tradition.

Silent reading may well be the dominant form of novel reading now, with the reading aloud of fiction mainly associated with parents reading to children, but we do not really have a good sense of how much reading aloud of novels goes on. Radio 4's *Book of the Week* and *Book at Bedtime* were two of British radio's most popular programmes in 2004 (both featuring in the top 25 most accessed radio programmes online) (BBC Press Office, 2004); audiobooks are gaining in popularity with the rise of MP3 technology (Piatkus, 2009), and now have their own review sections in the national press (see guardian.co.uk and timesonline.co.uk). Observing a teacher-training class at a London further education college last year, I overheard one woman tell another that she had started listening to audiobooks, loves the sound of sentences read aloud, but does not like 'strange' voices 'interpreting ... for me' and now likes to read novels aloud with her friends. Only one of the reading circles I spoke to read aloud, but what of the thousands I was unable to access? Adults may well be reading novels aloud to one another more than we realize.

In addition, it would be a mistake to assume that reading aloud is the only shape that communal novel reading takes. A reading circle, by definition, presents discussion as an essential part of novel reading (Daniels, 2006; Jackson, 1999; Long, 1993, 2003; Radway, 1994; Swann & Allington, 2009). More generally, Paran (2003), Long (2003) and Harvey & Daniels (2009) all argue that there is a basic human need to talk about what one has read. My data strongly support this view. In their final interviews, the case-study participants stressed how much they enjoyed reporting, clarifying vocabulary and interpreting together in their reading circle. Perhaps most significantly, as I argued in Chapter 7, their process of building the novel through group discussion was an example of reading as a communal cognitive process, rather than simply a communal practice.

Is novel reading, therefore, primarily individual or communal? The answer, predictably, is that the dichotomy is illusionary: echoing the dynamics of Nietzsche's (1872/1993) Apolline and Dionysiac, each needs and contains the other. O'Connor's (1963) distinction between the short story and the novel is really an argument that the novel's protagonist needs a society to stand against, a community to create him or her as an individual, and while print culture can be perceived as the bringer of many new communal groupings, print is also seen as 'the technology of individualism'(Rose, 2010, p. 25 quoting McLuhan, 1962, p. 158). Even Long's fight for the visibility of reading as a social act includes an acknowledgement that it is the relationship *between* the individual and the communal which is crucial. Radway (1994) shares Long's interest and expresses it thus:

> She is interested, finally, in the way reading group members use their reading, both individually and collectively, to negotiate their relationship to the culture and society within which they find themselves. (Radway, 1994, p. 293)

Pennac (2006) also recognizes this seeming paradox: 'We live in groups because we are sociable, but we read because we know we're alone. Reading offers a kind of companionship that takes no one's place'(p. 174). The novel concerns precisely this complex interplay between the individual and the communal, in content as well as in its publishing and reading processes. The enduring popularity of reading circles, as well as people reading alone in grateful isolation, is testament to this duality.

The case study participants discussed how the group experience has changed their reading identity, and therefore their own reading in five acts. They also described how group-scaffolding has helped them with the 'individual cognition' aspects of individual reading, such as decoding, assigning meanings to words, remembering and interpretation. Finally, the group made inferences together, feeding individual ideas into a group interpretation, and using the group interpretation as a basis for further individual reading. Participants discussed reading as gaining another perspective, what Wright (1982) (see Chapter 1) called 'a re-creation of identity ... an intersubjective process, in that it is the overtaking of another's meaning' (Wright, 1982, p. 149). The reading circle members used their reading to escape one subjectivity and access another, or several: the narrator, Milan, Roma, Karen or Murri. This shift, so valued by Long's (2003) interviewees, allows the reader to escape the self and understand what is outside of the self. The novel reader – whether reading alone, for others, or with others – is necessarily taking on other subjectivities, and therefore stepping outside his or her individual perspective to imagine the world outside. Reading circles are a clear enactment of this interplay between the individual and the communal, the pleasures and politics of which are discussed in the next chapter.

Chapter Summary

Within every other chapter of this book – and, arguably, within any study of reading or the novel – is a tension between the individual and the communal. Is reading primarily an individual or a communal act? Is the novel a genre of the individual or the group? Is the inter-subjective shift so discussed by reading circle participants and literary theorists a move from an individual subjectivity to a truly communal perspective or merely to another individual subjectivity? This chapter tackled this question, examining literature on the politics and philosophy of the novel genre, thoughts on how novels were and are read, and data from the main research case study itself. I used these ideas to argue that reading, and novel reading, cannot be purely individual any more than it can be truly communal. Reading, novel reading, and, even more so, novel reading within reading circles, are of (and about) the relationship between the individual and the communal, and help us tackle some of the great human questions: Who am I as an individual? What larger structures am I part of? And how can or should I live my life in relation to others?

Suggested Reading

Byatt, A. S. (1978), *The Virgin in the Garden*. London: Chatto and Windus/Penguin.
The first of Byatt's three novels about the Potter family (followed by *Still Life* and *Babel Tower*), each of which develops a meditation on human separation. In Chapter 31, Stephanie and Daniel lie in bed together after consummating their marriage, and Daniel reflects: 'skulls separate people. In this one sense, I could say, they would say, I lose myself in her. But in that bone box, she thinks and thinks, and I think in mine, things the other won't hear, can't hear, though we go on like this for sixty years.'

Mullan, J. (2006), *How Novels Work*. Oxford: Oxford University Press.
Based on Mullan's *Guardian* column, this is an examination of the novel as a literary genre and a cultural phenomenon. The introduction and 'beginning' chapter are particularly useful on the novel as a new(ish) literary form.

Lodge, D. (1992), *The Art of Fiction*. London: Penguin Books
Another newspaper article collection, this time from the *Independent on Sunday* and the *Washington Post*. Lodge identifies characteristics of the novel and explores them with reference to well-known works of literature: for example, 'intertexuality' through the work of Joseph Conrad.

Rose, J. (2010), *The Intellectual Life of the British Working Classes* (2nd edn). London: Yale University Press.

A seminal social history of the reading and education of working people in Britain from before the Industrial Revolution to the twentieth century.

Watt, I. (2000), *The Rise of the Novel.* London: Pimlico.
An influential examination of the social, economic, philosophical and political context of the birth and 'triumph' of the novel.

Chapter 11

The Pleasures and Politics of Novels and Reading Circles

Rebecca West (1928) famously called literature 'the strange necessity', arguing that literature satisfies the '"the What-is-it?" reflex' (p. 88). Literature is pleasurable (and important) because 'art is at least in part a way of collecting information about the universe' (p. 89). A group of adult literacy learners I interviewed a few years ago spoke, unprompted, about the pleasures of reading fiction. One of their key pleasures was to do with time: the pleasure of creating time for reading or escaping from a particular space and time through reading.

When it's a bad time, I just get a book and I read it.

When I read, I forget about all, I forget about this time, my environment – yes, I forget about it all when I'm reading.

They also spoke about how, as 'new' readers, they were acutely aware of the sense of control over time which being able to read can bring:

A story is there *the whole time*, you can read before you go to bed, you can read it *whenever you like*.

As a reader, one can decide what and when to read, communicating across time and space:

It [reading]'s like speaking, because I can't be with that person, then it is like them speaking but now it is in writing.

With striking similarity, Manguel comments on the seventh-century theologian Isidore of Seville believing 'that reading made possible a conversation across time and space'. He quotes from Isidore's *Etymologies*: 'Letters have the power to convey to us silently the sayings of those who are absent'(1996, p. 49).

Very much focused on their communal gatherings in one set space and time, the women of the Kalamazoo Library Association (Jackson, 1999) found pleasure in the 'delightful entertainment' of books, along with the structure and discipline of their routine. Both the Hamilton sisters (Sicherman, 1989) and the Brontë sisters (Teale, 2005) – contemporaries on either side of the Atlantic – found pleasure in using novels to lead the lives that reality denied them, as nineteenth-century middle-class women. Members of present-day reading circles around the world have included, as their key pleasures, sociability, intellectual challenge, access to a type of education, encouragement to read more, joys of a single-sex gathering and the development of individual and social identities.

The participants in the case study reading circle were equally forth-coming about what they found pleasurable, describing the joys of con-structing a story; of moving with the emotions of the central character; of the intellectual stimulation of the reading and discussion process; of their satisfaction of their achievement; of their ownership of the physical book, story and reading circle process; of companionship and sociability and, finally, of the joys of being inspired, to read more and to write their own stories. It is not hard to find examples of the diverse (but of course not exclusive) pleasures of reading, of novel reading and of reading circles in these data as from thousands of years of writings about reading.

However, the connection between reading and pleasure is far from straightforward. Trilling (1966) famously wrote of the uneasy relationship between pleasure and morality in European art (including literature). He argued that a wider 'devaluation of pleasure' (p. 82) and post-Romantic separation of art and politics meant that pleasure became (and remains) morally suspect, and art, including its pleasures, removed from, and irrele-vant to, 'serious' political or ethical contemplation. This dominant cultural thread, which few would deny, is seemingly at odds with the tradition which associates reading with the development of morality, from the medieval reading of sacred texts to the Victorian use of morality tales in reading primers, or a present-day notion of illiteracy as antisocial and potentially criminal behaviour. Yet, the linking of reading and morality is not predom-inantly a view that identifies reading as an art, but rather as social participa-tion: reading as a force of civilization, conformation and, at times, liberation. Novels, by contrast, were considered, for much of the eighteenth and nine-teenth centuries, as silly things for silly (usually female) pleasure-seeking minds. Is novel reading, therefore, echoing Trilling's broader ideas about art and, despite an enduring cultural association of reading with morality, removed from 'serious' ethical exploration? Put more simply, is novel reading only about accessing certain pleasures, or does it have a moral or ethical dimension?

Much has been written on ethics and the novel. Sartre (1967) argues that the taste of 'human freedom' provided by the 'building' acts of novel reading (see Chapter 7) necessarily makes it an ethical lesson, as the reader feels their 'freedom is indissolubly linked with that of all other men' (p. 46). Hillis Miller (1987) writes of the 'ethics of reading', stating that storytelling embodies the 'universal moral law' of action and consequence. Narrative, he argues, is necessarily an exploration of ethical equations, of the ethical implications of different courses of action. Booth (1988) similarly stresses the importance, or even inevitability, of ethical evaluation in literary study, given 'the unique value of fiction: its relatively cost-free offer of trial runs ... a relative freedom from consequence' (p. 485). While Sartre focuses on reading as an experience of freedom and its obligations, and Hillis Miller suggests that the cause-and-effect nature of narrative itself becomes a demonstration of ethics, Booth focuses on the reader's ethical training in 'trying out' courses of action with 'relative freedom from consequence'. These theorists are not arguing that reading, or reading novels, is *necessarily* a moral or ethical act, but rather that literature can encourage thinking about the ethical implications of human action.

Bettelheim (1975) presents literature as central to a child's moral education, 'helping him to find meaning in life' (Bettelheim, 1975, p. 3), including initiation into the polarities of good and evil. Fairy tales, Bettelheim argues, teach children the difference between 'good actions' and 'evil' through identification with the hero and demonstration of the fate of evil-doers. Though speaking of children, and fairy tales, this central idea is shared with Sartre, Hillis Miller and Booth: when we read we see how different lives are led, observe who does what and what happens to them, and thus gain moral/ethical understanding. Tedros spoke similarly in his initial interview:

When you read, it's like you're finding out something ... the challenges that happen in people's lives ... for you to see, for you to learn from it ... Like some people they put theirself in unnecessary situations, like getting on drugs or mixing in some world that they don't know ... and then later on they can't just walk away out of it. [You read] to make sure that you don't put yourself in that kind of position. (Tedros initial interview)

Novelists too have written of the ethical element of their craft, often explicitly linked to the relationship between the individual and the communal. Woolf (1929) stresses the importance of writers writing as models for the next generation and readers reading models from the previous generation. Forster (1927) argues that people read novels to find 'solace' and guidance in the 'visibility' of the lives of characters in novels. Orwell argued that the most significant motive for writing is 'political purpose' or a 'desire to push the world in a certain direction, to alter other people's ideas of the kind of society that they should strive after' (Orwell, 1946/2003, pp. 4–5). Chinese short-story writer Lu Hsun (or Lu Xun) (Hsun, 1918/1960) was a young man at medical school in Japan when his class was shown images of Chinese soldiers being massacred by the Japanese. He immediately left medical school to begin his career as a short-story writer because he felt this was the only way to save his country, so convinced was he of the role that literature plays in the ethical life of a nation. Woolf, Forster, Lu Hsun and Orwell believed that reading their fiction would have an effect – a cultural, emotional, moral, ethical, political effect – on their readers.

Manguel (novelist, essayist and historian of reading and libraries) locates this ethical potential of literature in its opening of possibilities or realizations within the mind of the reader:

> Books may not change our suffering, books may not protect us from evil, books may not tell us what is good or what is beautiful, and they will certainly not shield us from the common fate of the grave. But books grant us myriad possibilities: the possibility of change, the possibility of illumination. It may be that there is no book, however well written, that can remove an ounce of pain from the tragedy of Iraq or Rwanda, but it may also be that there is no book, however foully written, that does not allow an epiphany for its destined reader (2006, pp. 231–232).

Some novelists locate this ethical dimension specifically in ideas of truth and untruth. Irving (1993) writes of how as a teenager he and his friends made constant fun of 'Piggy Sneed' – an unfortunate man in their town – until one day this cruel mockery led to Sneed's death in a barn fire. Irving produced his first story as an attempt to rewrite Sneed's life and death, both reproducing and redeeming life's cruelties. He wrote that 'a writer's business is setting fire to Piggy Sneed – *and* trying to save him – again and again, forever' (p. 25) because 'the most truthful detail is what *could* have happened' (p. 9). Hemingway, too, spoke of the writer's 'sense of justice and of injustice' (p. 61) in terms of the creation of truths:

> From things that have happened and from things as they exist and from all things that you know and all those you cannot know, you make something through your invention that is not a representation but a whole new thing truer than anything true and alive, and you make it alive, and if you make it well enough, you give it immortality. (The Paris Review Interviews, 1958, p. 61)

The concept of 'a whole new thing truer than anything true' recalls the discussion of fiction and truth in Chapter 7 and Aisha's point that reading a novel allowed her to play with the possibility of something being true, and to learn from it, without the anxiety of knowing that it was 'really happening'.

Hemingway's emphasis on 'a whole new thing' and Irving's 'what could have happened' also suggest that we look again at the workings of imagination (one of the five acts of reading presented in Chapter 7). The term imagination was used by participants to express how they visualized the events of the novel 'like a film in your mind'. This was, however, only one part of their conception of imagination; the other, as for Sadoski & Paivio (2001) and Coleridge (1817/1986), is an act of creation, in this case the ability to get inside the minds of others for 'a freshness of sensation' (Coleridge, 1817/1986, p. 395). Ignoring the word 'imagination', Russian formalist Shklovsky (1965) called this creative freshness *ostranenie*, or 'defamiliarization', arguing (exactly as Wordsworth and Coleridge argued in their revolutionary *Preface to the Lyrical Ballads* 1802]) that the goal and glory of literature is to re-present the world that habit has blinded us to (Shklovsky, 1965). A work of literature allows us to lose our blinding familiarity so we can once more 'feel vividly and see clearly' (Wordsworth & Coleridge, 1802, p. 168). This cannot fail to inspire those developing their reading (and therefore help adults to learn to read), just as it motivated and encouraged the case study reading circle members.

Maxine Greene also links imagination to *ostranenie*, arguing of the educative powers of the arts for 'becoming wide-awake in the world. For me as for many others, the arts provide new perspectives on the lived world ... a startling defamiliarization of the ordinary' (Greene, 1995, p. 4). Like the participants in the main case study, Greene sees *ostranenie* as not only about 'transfiguring the commonplace' (Danto, 1981; Spark, 1961) so we can see *our* old familiars with the freshness of defamiliarization, but also about another kind of defamiliarization: seeing someone else's world, through that someone's eyes.

Seeing, or rather reading, the ordinary through the ordinary eyes of ordinary others is praised by Rose (2010) as the key to a political perspective and the importance of a national press. He quotes George Bourne who, arguing of the impact of the national press in the late nineteenth/early twentieth centuries, wrote 'the main thing is that the village mind should stretch itself, and look beyond the village' (p. 28). Case study participant Beverley echoes this sentiment:

> If you never read before, like me, I have no awareness of what's happening to those around me. I am just one fool on the street, don't know better about others. But the way I read the book it's given me a guideline of how I can see things from someone else's head. I can see things better. (Beverley final interview)

Novel reading can get us beyond the village, beyond the individual 'fool on the street' perspective, which necessarily has ethical/political implications.

Zunshine (2006) approaches this issue from the perspective of cognitive psychology and literary theory as she investigates 'why we read novels'. She uses the term 'mind reading' (taken from studies of autism [Baron-Cohen, 1997]) to describe the usual human ability (though less common in people with autism) to use external signs such as facial expressions or movements, to make inferences about the internal mental states of others. This ability, she argues, is both required to read a novel and further developed through novel reading, and is the basis of our ability to empathize with other human beings. 'Mind reading' seems to fit with the above ideas on imagination, on enjoying and developing the ability to see through someone else's eyes. Likewise, Zunshine's claim that novel reading develops empathy is echoed by Luis's argument that *Passenger* is about empathy. Luis argues that with Roma, Milan develops an empathy that was absent from his life before, and, reading *Passenger*, the reader too develops renewed empathy.

> Luis: It [*Passenger*]'s good for people, even people at sixteen. It teaches empathy – things that these days we often overlook, but are important for human beings – how to sympathize with somebody, how to help people, how to empathize with people.
>
> SD: Why does *Passenger* in particular develop empathy?

Luis: Because the relationship between the brother and the sister ... the empathy, some people don't see it, they are not capable of understanding other's problems. To give them empathy, to feel sorry for them, everyone feels better, so you know they're not alone in what they feel. (Luis final interview)

This was discussed within the reading circle as well:

He was a selfish young man and do things for himself and don't care but when he discovered his sister he become very caring. (Beverley 29 March 2009)

Beverley elaborates on how novel reading can develop empathy in its readers:

With a patient, my patient in the hospital, they are from their house, they come to an unknown setup ... and what's going to happen to them. It [*Passenger*] taught me a thing or two – that first thing in the morning I should go and say good morning to them – it taught me how the other person will be feeling, there on the other side of the bed. I'm here on this side, I'm OK, and they are there, and they're not well. In Milan's case, he have this thing ... this object in his body and he have no idea ... For me he's like a patient lying in the bed, not knowing who's going to come through that door in the morning ... I need to think what they are feeling. (Beverley final interview)

Reading as an imaginative act is an act of *ostranenie*, an act of seeing afresh by taking on other identities. These shifts in identity are cause – and effect – of the oscillation between the individual and the communal perspectives, which I am arguing is core to novel reading and amplified in the reading circle experience. Reading novels and taking part in reading circles (which scaffold the novel-reading process as well as heighten its communal nature) are acutely political acts because they educate us in the lives of others, thereby developing that often underrated by-product of empathy: compassion.

After describing his mind-map and how *Passenger*, for him, was about compassion, Luis explained why this is so important:

Sometimes we are narrow-minded and see things just from our point of view, and someone has to remind us to be open, to understand what happens to other people and understand other people. (Luis final interview)

FɪɢᴜʀE 6   Luis' mind-map.

Chapter Summary

Adults have found diverse pleasures in reading, in novel reading and in working in reading circles. These include pleasures of communicating with someone physically (or temporally) distant, pleasures of building a story, pleasures of temporarily 'becoming' someone else and pleasures of group discussion. The act of reading itself has also been associated with a moral development or moral duty – people have learnt to read in order to be good members of religious or other communities – while novel reading (like many artistic endeavours) has also been seen as frivolous, potentially immoral and certainly removed from serious ethical contemplation. In this chapter, I explored thinking on the potentially ethical dimension of novel reading: that it offers training in action and consequence, that it invites contemplation of possibilities of individual or social change and that it encourages the imaginative act of walking in someone else's shoes or seeing through someone else's eyes. In this way, I argued, novel reading, particularly in a reading circle formation, is necessarily – and potentially radically – a political act.

Suggested Reading

Bettelheim, B. (1975), *The Uses of Enchantment: The Meaning and Importance of Fairy Tales*. Harmondsworth: Penguin Books.
Bettelheim's psychoanalytical study of fairy tales.

Booth, W. C. (1988), *The Company We Keep: An Ethics of Fiction*. Berkeley, CA: University of California Press.
This is a hefty and satisfying argument for the importance of ethical criticism.

Gourevitch, Philip (ed.) (2007–2009), *The Paris Review Interviews, vols 1, 2, 3 & 4*. Edinburgh: Canongate.
A four-volume collection of the *Paris Review* interviews with poets, dramatists, short-story writers and novelists, full of ideas on reading and the writing process.

Greene, M. (1995), *Releasing the Imagination: Essays on Education, the Arts and Social Change*. San Francisco, CA: Jossey-Bass.
Widely read American philosopher's essays on the role of imagination in education.

Irving, J. (1993), *Trying to Save Piggy Snead*. London: Black Swan.
The title essay of Irving's collection of memories plays with ideas of what truth means to a novelist. It starts with the line, 'This is a memoir but please understand that (to any writer with a good imagination) all memories are false.'

West, R. (1928). *The Strange Necessity: Essays and Reviews*. London: Jonathan Cape.
Rebecca West's collected essays on literary criticism start with 'The Strange Necessity', her account of 'this mystery of mysteries': why 'art matters'.

Conclusion

This final chapter summarizes the implications of the main case study, along with the exploration of the first five chapters, in three categories: implications for novel reading, implications for reading circles and implications for the development of adult emergent reading. I would then like to return to the main arguments I hoped to make in this book before suggesting ideas for future research. Finally, I end with thoughts on an alternative to the now-dominant 'functional' view of literacy.

Summary of Implications

Implications for understanding novel reading

- Novel reading, like all reading, is five acts: a cognitive act, an educational act, an imaginative act, a communicative act and an affective act.
- Novel reading involves the reader 'building up' the *work* (Iser [1972]) or *story* (participants) through the cognitive, imaginative and affective work of inference; the creating, rejecting and adapting of 'frames of meaning' (Perry, 1979); as well as word-level decoding and vocabulary processing.
- Though often performed by a lone reader, the above 'building' can be carried out by a group, through discussion. Group members can talk through connections, memories, inferences and potential interpretations to create and adapt 'frames of meaning' together. *In this way, reading can be a communal cognitive process as well as a communal practice.*
- Novel reading is often a communal as well as an individual activity. Besides aspects of the reading *process* being potentially communal (see above), many people get together to discuss the novels they are reading or have read, listen to others reading novels to them, read novels aloud to others, recommend novels and receive recommendations – passing novels around social circles. These are all aspects of how novel reading can be a communal practice (as well as being an intensely individual one). These social forms of novel reading may well increase as other opportunities for communal gatherings decrease.

- Any work of art can be an experience (as Dewey [1934] argues), but novel reading is 'more' of an experience than most. The time it takes to read a novel and the active role of the reader (requiring the reader to 'input' experience in order to read) mean that novel reading interweaves Dewey's three aspects of 'art as experience'. The experiences that have produced the novel, the lived experience of reading the novel and the experiences that this reading produces intermingle in a reading process of acute experience formation. Within a reading circle, this produces an interpersonal process of experience formation.
- There is a juxtaposition between the self-evident truths of a novel and its declared untruth, a simultaneous reality and unreality central to the novel form. This means that readers can learn from novels without the anxiety of knowing that what they are reading is 'really happening'.
- The inter-subjective and experience-building aspects of novel reading can develop empathy, compassion and a potentially political perspective in readers (away from the 'one village' or 'one fool on the street' limited view). This is a function of the novel's oscillation between the individual and the communal, and is heightened in a reading circle approach.

Implications for reading circles

- Reading circles are by their very nature often invisible or obscured, leaving no traces in terms of funding applications or publications. It is therefore very difficult to determine how many reading circles are out there, now as in the past, who take part and for what purposes.
- Nevertheless, there is enough research to demonstrate that reading circles are (and have been for hundreds of years) a significant and common reading practice, as well as a potential pedagogy.
- In formal educational settings, reading circles can be an effective tool to develop peer-teaching and peer-assessment, learner autonomy and learner-led differentiation. Reading circles can also be model examples of open-ended pedagogy and negotiated syllabi (Breen & Littlejohn, 2000).
- For hundreds of years, reading circles (and other mutual improvement societies) have been used as informal educational provision by those who could not access other educational provision *and* by those who simply prefer(red) this mode of learning.
- Used in adult literacy/ESOL classes, reading circles can provide individually focused differentiation to meet varied language and literacy needs within one group (allowing one student to focus on a self-selected and

self-managed 'outcome' of widening vocabulary and another on phonic decoding, while still working together).

- Reading circles can provide opportunities for participants to read aloud, if they wish so, and therefore an opportunity for the reinforcement of decoding skills as well as the development of the practice of reading aloud.

- Reading circles can model, and scaffold, the interpretative aspects of novel reading, which can be challenging to less confident readers.

- Some people enjoy reading in a group, for the pedagogic reasons already listed, because readers like to talk about what they are reading (D. Gordon, 1999; Harvey & Daniels, 2009; Paran, 2003) and because talking about a book is an opportunity to talk about the other things that we long to talk about, including who we are or who we want to be (Long, 2003).

Implications for developing adult emergent reading

- There is no single right way to teach or learn reading, for children or for adults. For more than three thousand years, children and adults have learnt and been taught to read using a diverse and evolving range of methods.

- Adult emergent readers often want to 'learn words', a process involving increasing the range of words they can both understand and decode. Reading circles can be a way of working on this.

- Adult emergent readers may find the peer-scaffolding of a reading circle a supportive environment in which to develop a range of reading skills (for all five acts of reading), from decoding, learning words and remembering what was read before (in a longer text), to reading clearly to others, and from guessing the meaning of a word from its visualized context to interpreting action and characters in an emotional engagement.

- Adult emergent readers may find reading aloud and/or listening to others read aloud a useful tool in developing decoding skills. They may also want to develop their confidence reading aloud in order to read to others in family, social, work or religious contexts.

- We all have a reading identity, and the reading identities of many adult emergent readers are based on a deficit (what I cannot do or am scared to do). This identity is as much of a barrier to being able to read a text as a lack of particular reading skills. Therefore, the role of adult literacy education is to develop this reading identity (into someone who can read different texts, can try even more texts and can recommend books

to others) as well as developing reading skills (such as decoding or inference). A reading circle, where participants can contribute to communal
reading according to their own strengths or confidence levels, is one way
to do this.

- The complex pleasures and ethical discussions inherent in novel reading are likely to be as important for adult emergent readers as for any of
  us. Adult literacy teachers should not shy away from literature because of
  fears of associations with elitist politics or worries that a particular text is
  'too hard'. Texts can be adapted and tasks can be graded.
- Adult literacy teaching (in some contexts more than others) may be in
  danger of losing the learner-centred pedagogy, and philosophy, which
  dominated during the 1960s, 1970s, 1980s and 1990s. A reading circle
  – and other forms of 'negotiated syllabi' (Breen & Littlejohn, 2000) and
  peer-assessment (Derrick et al., 2009) – could a provide much-needed
  reminder that the only adult literacy curriculum is what literacy means
  to each learner.

A Return to the Arguments

The above implications are the product of this book's investigation into reading circles, novel reading and adult reading development. As part of this
investigation, I hoped to make four arguments, one primary and three secondary: that reading circles should be used in, and as, adult literacy provision; that we need to research reading by talking to readers themselves; that
adult literacy teachers should learn something of the history of literacy use
and literacy pedagogy; and that adult literacy provision should regain its
alignment with broader models of adult education, including the mutual
improvement society approach. I would like to return to each of these here.

A reading circle and adult literacy provision

The primary argument of this book is that reading circles should be used
in, and as, adult literacy provision. The historical, ethnographic and educational examination of reading circles in Chapter 5 demonstrated that for
hundreds of years adults have formed themselves into reading circles (and
other mutual improvement societies) of their own accord. They – we –
have done this in order to teach and learn from one another, to gain different perspectives, to pass the time, to challenge one another, for
particular kinds of company, and to read, think and create ideas (creating

culture) communally. Evidence from educational research suggests that a reading circle approach can develop a range of reading, writing, speaking and listening skills, along with the confidence and social skills needed to operate in a democratic group. The findings of the main research case-study indicate that a reading circle creates an environment of amplified experience formation conducive to learning. I argued that reading circles were therefore potentially 'ideal pedagogy': encouraging peer-learning through negotiated syllabi and open-ended pedagogy, providing opportunities for differentiation (including differentiating between first- and second-language needs), developing decoding and vocabulary skills, and encouraging a citizenship education in the form of better understanding the lives of others.

Yet perhaps the strongest argument for using a reading circle approach within adult literacy provision comes from the fact that reading circles are a distinctly *adult* approach to learning, participant-led and self-managed. A reading circle approach may be popular in secondary and even primary schools, but this is usually a slightly different and more teacher-monitored process (see Chapter 5). Reading circles that are formed within existing adult literacy provision need to take their lead from the reading circles which adults form and have formed autonomously for hundreds of years. Even with teacher scaffolding and monitoring, reading circles can be learner-led and managed.

This means, of course, that within existing, formal adult literacy provision, I would recommend that a teacher facilitates a reading circle only if groups really want to read longer texts together and like the idea of a reading circle. A reading circle should never be enforced. Within existing formal provision, teacher involvement is a question of staging. For the first few weeks, months or even the first book, a reading circle could be more teacher-controlled, but gradually teacher-scaffolding should fade, leading to complete participant autonomy. It is also important to remember that in this context (a reading circle within a scheduled adult literacy class) the learners have probably joined the class to do other things, such as develop their punctuation or spelling, and so it is important that the reading circle takes up *part* of the class time, but not all. The division between the 'usual' provision and the reading circle could be emphasized by different seating arrangements.

The main research case study worked with a group labelled as E3/L1 in the English adult literacy core curriculum system. This is a 'level' where learners can often read shorter pieces and more regular or common words with confidence, but wish to develop their reading of longer texts, their decoding of less common or less regular words, and their confidence in writing and discussion. However, a reading circle approach can also be used with less confident (or 'beginner') readers, with attention to the choice of reading material. Texts produced specifically for adult literacy learners, such as the English Gatehouse series (www.gatehousebooks.co.uk) or Pat Neuman's Canadian series (http://library.nald.ca/learning/browse/author?name = Pat + Neuman) may work best. A reading circle with 'beginner' readers would also require different teacher-scaffolding. For example, I have taken a similar approach with a 'beginner' group, reading Pat Neuman's *The Blanket* (2003) over four weeks. I first read *The Blanket* aloud myself and we discussed it at length before learners read sections in pairs. Then some learners read sections aloud to the group, pausing after every page for a group discussion of the unfolding narrative. Gradually, more and more learners joined in with the reading and everyone was engaged in the discussion. A reading circle approach is worth trying within any form or level of adult literacy provision.

There are, however, other ways to use reading circles as part of an adult literacy offer. Reading circles for adults less confident in their literacy can be organized in community centres or libraries. In this model, a librarian or teacher could set up the reading circle, perhaps joining the circle for the first few sessions, but then withdraw to leave the group to self-run. This model is more autonomous and has implications for funding: as Rado & Foster (1995) noted, it is potentially a lower-cost offer (there is no regular paid teacher). However, we should not forget that many adults join adult literacy provision to develop skills which may not be so easily developed in reading circle formation (and some may simply not want to join a reading circle), and therefore such reading circles should not be seen as a replacement for 'regular' provision, but rather an addition.

Finally, reading circles are set up entirely autonomously by small groups of people all around the world in order to develop reading and other skills. These groups, like any reading circles, develop literacy skills while enjoying the social aspects of communal reading. Case study participant Beverley told me of a reading circle she knew of that sat under a tree every Sunday and developed one another's literacy by reading short passages from the Bible. Though most members of the group were 'new readers' (as she called them), the group had enough of the Bible committed to memory to be able to work together to decode each word. This truly was education '*of* the people' rather than '*for* the people' (Radcliffe, 1997): a reading circle started, and run, by a group of adults who wanted to develop their literacy alongside religious worship. I am arguing, therefore, that a reading circle approach can be used as part of adult literacy development in three ways: within existing formal adult literacy provision, as semi-formal, supported provision in community centres or libraries, and as informal, self-organized, peer-learning.

Researching reading as experience: what it feels like to read

One theoretical perspective underpins this research and book: that reading can and should be researched by accessing the first-person perspectives of readers themselves. In Chapter 1, I noted that 'the reader perspective' could be seen as one way that reading is defined and researched, that only by talking to readers can we possibly find out what reading feels like. In Chapter 6, I expanded this idea, arguing that reading is an experience and therefore its research can never be complete without accessing the perspectives of those doing the experiencing. From this theoretical position, any attempt to make a distinction between what reading 'really is' and what its readers 'think it is' is false. Reading *is* what it is to readers. If we want to know more about how adult literacy can be learnt and taught, we need to talk to adult literacy learners, many of whom have thought about it a great deal. Adult literacy learners bring their adult knowledge, skills and experience to their literacy work and are therefore an invaluable, though often underused, resource for gathering insights into adult literacy teaching and learning. I also noted that working from the reader perspective is one way to maintain an interdisciplinary stance, to keep listening to all the diverse disciplines that research reading.

Likewise, if we want to find out what novel reading involves, we need to talk to novel readers, and if we want to find out how reading circles work, we need to talk to reading circle members. The main research case study involved talking and listening to the reading circle members, also adult literacy learners, and using their ideas to generate implications for adult reading development, reading circles and novel reading. This is only one way to research reading, and we certainly need people to keep researching reading in all the other ways as well (including cognitive psychology, ethnography, social history and literary theory), but it has provided, for me at least, valuable pieces of this ever-expanding puzzle.

Why history?

Another secondary argument concerns history: what should we, as adult literacy teachers, know about the history of literacy use and learning? Before I started the research for this book, I probably would have thought very little, but now I feel that adult literacy teachers should have at least some grounding in this history for three reasons. First, learning about the history of reading pedagogy provides us with a much-needed perspective on the present-day 'reading wars' in primary education and our equivalents in adult literacy. All the methods for the teaching of reading that we debate now have been debated – and combined – for not decades but (in most cases) centuries. It is important that we understand this before we enter the debate.

Second, a historical understanding of who reads, what they read, why they read and when they read, provides a crucial perspective on literacy use, one which can help us better understand our learners. This is particularly important as a defence against the present-day idea that it is abnormal not to be able to read and write. This is a very recent (not to mention geographically specific) notion born of illogical leaps: that teaching everyone to read and write will automatically mean that everyone will be able to read and write, or that if someone cannot read and write (or cannot to the levels of our present-day expectations) then the 'system' has 'failed them', or – worse – they have failed us. We need history to remind us that these expectations and judgements are incredibly recent and should be treated with suspicion (see the next argument).

Third, the social history of literacy is part of our developing field of adult literacy studies. It is not enough for us only to focus on literacy as a social practice (however important this is); we need to *learn more* to become better teachers. We need to learn about linguistics; we need to learn about the psychology of reading; we need to understand what literary theory has to offer; and we need to study the social history of reading, for the reasons noted above, and also because it is (if we look carefully enough) simply very interesting.

Adult literacy teaching and traditions of adult education

My final argument relates to each of the others. Adult literacy provision should be positioned within a broad adult education provision that is designed to meet a range of adult learning needs and desires. This argument has three aspects. First, adult literacy provision is not an answer to a problem, either individual or social. As noted above, history tells us that the idea that everyone *should* be able to read and write, and at a certain 'school-leaving-age' standard, is a relatively new one. Universal schooling does not equal universal literacy, not because school has necessarily 'failed' us (though this does happen), but rather because how we grapple with the written code is highly individual due to our greatly differing cognitive affinities. Some of us are 'tone deaf' and others have 'perfect pitch'. Some of us have tremendous hand-eye coordination and are expert cricketers; others (like me) find it hard to catch a ball, however big or slow-moving. Some of us find reading and writing very easy, some struggle a little and some struggle much harder.

We will therefore always need well-funded, well-organized, and well-taught adult literacy provision to support those adults who want help with their reading and writing, not because those with 'low' literacy are an economic liability, but because they want to develop their literacy (just as others may want to learn Italian or learn how to sew). This is the second element of the argument. Adult literacy provision, as part of a wider adult education offer, should be state-funded and supported in such a way as to recognize the individual nature of 'progression' and motivation: we need a provision based on needs and desires related to a diversity of life practices, not fixated on a narrow notion of 'employability'. What the reading circle members gained from their circle related to a range of life practices, from work to child-rearing, from how they relate to others socially to a personal need to write about the past (see Chapter 7).

Finally, we need to remember that adult literacy provision, as part of adult education more broadly, is about more than formally organized and funded classes. This is just one form, and tradition, of adult education. The other, as argued in Chapter 5, is the mutual improvement society model of collective autodidactism. Adults can teach one another in peer-learning groups; adults have done this in the past, both when they had no other educational opportunities and when they did. The multitudes of contemporary reading circles are inheritors of this tradition, and we should not forget that these frequently have explicit educational – as well as social – motivations. By their very nature we (as teachers) cannot form these reading circles *for* 'learners', but we (as adults) can join them, support them and recognize them as an important educational tradition which can support adult literacy needs just as they can support many other human needs.

Call to Action

This book has a very limited scope. My aim was to address novel reading, reading circles and adult emergent reading development. I was interested in analysing typical characteristics of reading circles, and novel reading more generally, but was less interested in trying to claim that these characteristics were unique to novel reading or reading circles. This book, therefore, offers ideas on what novel reading can be, what a reading circle approach can offer and what adult emergent readers can get out of a reading circle approach. It is not an 'advantages vs. disadvantages' analysis of reading circles. Likewise, I have used these data to argue that novel reading, particularly in a reading circle formation, can develop empathy and political/ethical thinking in terms of the individual's relationship with the communal. I believe these data demonstrate this to be the case. However, it would be wrong to argue that novel reading always develops these things, or that novel reading is the only way to develop empathy and ethical contemplation. As already discussed, this is clearly not true.

When I presented this case study to a group of adult literacy teachers, some responded that a reading circle can work with this particular literacy 'level' but would not work with less confident, more 'beginner' readers. I have already argued that I think it can work. However, this was not something addressed in the main case study itself. The case study was a study of one reading circle with one group of adult literacy learners, reading one novel. A case study of a reading circle of a different group of adult literacy learners, or this group of learners but using a different text, or a reading circle of a different sample of people (art-school students, for example) would have produced different data and slightly different implications.

A case study working with a 'lower level' literacy group, a group firmly within ESOL provision, a group of bilingual adults reading in two different languages, or groups from other sections of adult education would offer additional insights into reading circles. A case study of a reading circle reading non-fiction texts (such as history or biography) – or indeed non-narrative text (such as cook books) – would make a fascinating research study, as would a case study of a present-day mutual improvement society (such as the science group discussed in Chapter 5). Additionally, further studies of those often-obscured reading circles formed and meeting all the time – what do they do and why? – would be as valuable as it would be challenging. These are some calls to action.

Recently, I happened upon an interview with a consultant medical psychiatrist, David Fearnley, talking about his use of a reading circle within a high-security mental health facility (Davis, 2009). His reading circle was remarkably similar to the main case study: meeting once a week, reading a novel and reading aloud. Fearnley also noticed improvements in reading circle members' literacy alongside *something else*: increased confidence, happiness, self-respect and respect for others. As a psychiatrist, he was particularly interested in where this 'something else' came from: 'I wonder if it's that people feel safer with a book. Whether it's impersonal or they feel they can be themselves more' (p. 36). This seeming paradox of novel reading being both impersonal (it is not about us, after all) and potentially a way to 'be ourselves more' echoes Iser's (1972) oscillation between the 'real me' and the 'alien me' of the literary reading process (see Chapter 1). It also recalls Long's (1993, 2003) argument that reading circles are a way for people to talk about the things they want to talk about, in the way they want to talk about them: a very particular mixture of the personal and impersonal.

This idea is developed later in the interview. Analysing the pleasures of reading aloud in the circle, Fearnley explains: 'The group allows you to listen to other people speaking' (p. 37). Reading this line, I was first struck by how strange it was to talk about reading aloud as *speaking*, when surely reading aloud and speaking are quite different acts. Next, I thought that this was perhaps a doctor's perspective – perhaps some members of the circle did not speak at all in their day-to-day lives, but did in fact read aloud, therefore gaining speaking practice, exercising their voices. Finally, I realized that 'other people' may refer not to other reading circle members, but rather to the characters in, or narrator of, the novel. In this way, reading aloud is a conjuring of voices. When we read aloud we lend our voices to others, making the 'speaking and listening' of reading aloud an oral and aural enactment of reading's intersubjective processes. This would also be a fascinating area for future research.

Final Thoughts

UNESCO (United Nations Educational, Scientific and Cultural Organization) has worked to establish and consolidate literacy programmes around the world, believing that literacy is key to a nation's economic development. Their emphasis is on 'functional literacy', the reading and writing required to participate in one's society, with participation usually meaning being employed within that society and therefore helping to further national economic growth (Barton, 2007). The idea of 'functional literacy' has dominated the Anglophone national literacy campaigns ever since. This is particularly evident in the present focus on 'employability'. The discourse of 'functional literacy' implies another, alternative literacy lurking in the shadows: non-functional, non-essential, frivolous. This may be the literacy of writing a diary, the literacy of reading love letters, the literacy of writing poetry on the back of a bus ticket, or the literacy of reading circles. This may be the literacy enjoyed by those writing policies of functional literacy for the masses. One of the great unspoken objections to using literature in formal adult literacy provision is that it is *not* 'functional': it is unnecessary or inappropriate.

Yet, as Rose (2002), Meek (1988, 1991), Paran (2008), Pennac (2006) and the case study reading circle participants have argued, reading, discussing and writing about literature can develop the reading, writing and discussion skills which are the basis for any kind of literacy, any kind of 'function' and any kind of job. Equally importantly, reading and discussing literature may fulfil a 'function' which models of functional literacy ignore: the intersection between the personal, political, emotional and spiritual. One week in March 2009, the reading circle members were discussing Milan's attempt to explain the concept of death to Roma. The word 'metaphysical' featured in the text and they talked through its meaning, coming to ideas of 'more than' the physical. Later the same evening, marvelling at Roma's musical talent and her ability to influence Milan's life, Katherine interjected, 'She's metaphysical! Roma is metaphysical!' This struck me as a particularly apt way of expressing the (faint) uncertainty around Roma's physical reality combined with the unquestionable reality of her sisterly function in Milan's emotional life: the co-presence of these two different types or levels of truth.

This may also be an apt way to express the breadth and significance of literacy outside the 'functional', and reintroduce a Freirean idea of literacy as transformative, not only allowing each individual to transform their lives (if they so desire), but also to recognize a communal human obligation to improve or transform the lives of others. The ghost complement to 'functional literacy' might therefore not be 'frivolous' literacy but 'metaphysical' literacy: literacy serving artistic, philosophical, political, emotional and spiritual purposes – all those purposes craved by reading circle members. The identification of metaphysical literacy as complement to functional literacy is not to express a split, an 'either or' model, where some literacy is 'functional' while other is 'metaphysical'. Instead, I wish to express a *co-presence*: all literacy is both functional and metaphysical. The meanings, uses and values of literacy are broader than those functions we observe one another performing as we scuttle around our homes, streets and workplaces. Any example of literacy is at once functional *and* metaphysical, individual *and* communal, transformative *and* transfiguring. This view may help us to further our understanding of literacy and its role in human life.

Glossary

Action research: See **practitioner research.**

Affective: Referring to emotions or attitudes; reading as an affective act means reading as an emotional act or an act related to confidence.

Alphabetic method: A method of teaching reading popular from Ancient Greek and Roman times until (at least) the nineteenth century. The alphabetic method involves learning and chanting the alphabet, combining letters into syllables and then 'spelling out' words (saying the names of each letter and then reading the word) in significant (often religious) texts. See Chapter 3.

Book club: Another term for a **reading circle.**

Book group: Another term for a **reading circle.**

Canon: The group of texts or works valued by a particular society or societal domain. Shakespeare is firmly established as part of our early twenty-first century English literary canon. The works of Jane Mace are central to our developing adult literacy canon.

Case study research: A research methodology that involves using a detailed examination of a particular case to learn something about that case, or, potentially, to draw generalizations about a wider situation or phenomenon. Some consider a case study to be a choice of sampling, rather than a methodology. However, I would argue that it is a methodology because the use of a case study is a decision about what is useful to research, what we can learn from and why.

Codex: The arrangement of bound pages that we now call a book. The word 'codex' can also be used to refer to a bound manuscript (written by hand) as opposed to a printed book.

Cognitive: Relating to processes of thought, such as the processing and storing of information; reading as a cognitive act means reading as a process of mind or brain.

Cognitive psychology: The branch of psychology interested in developing our understanding of **cognitive** processes. Cognitive psychologists are one group of researchers who undertake a great deal of reading research.

Comprehension (reading comprehension): Usually refers to the reading skill (or sub-skill) of understanding the meaning of a phrase, a sentence, a paragraph or an entire text. This could include both understanding explicit meanings and inferring implicit meanings.

Critical reading: Reading that focuses on asking questions of who wrote the text, for whom the text has been written and why, how the text is positioning the author and how the text is positioning the reader(s).

Decoding: Refers to the reading skill (or sub-skill) of identifying a printed word and turning that printed word into a spoken word and/or unit of meaning. Decoding could refer to a reader's ability to translate a **grapheme** into a **phoneme**, a written syllable into a spoken syllable, a whole written word into a whole spoken word or meaning – or indeed an entire passage into spoken language or meaning.

Deep orthography: A writing system is said to have a deep orthography when there are complex, multi-way relationships between *phonemes* and *graphemes*. English has a deep orthography: one phoneme can be represented by several different graphemes, and one grapheme can represent several different phonemes. By contrast, some writing systems have **shallow orthographies**.

Ethnography: The study of people, human societies or cultures. An ethnographic approach emphasizes obtaining an insider perspective, through entering and living within a group of people (often for years), or otherwise accessing the perspectives of the members of the group. **Social practice theory** is associated with an ethnographic approach.

Experience: The act of living 'through', or living something, or what one gains or gathers from that lived experience: 'I would like to experience dawn in the desert' or 'He has a lot of professional dance experience.' This book is based on the notion that reading is, among other things, an experience.

Fiction: A term used to classify texts; fiction refers to a text that declares itself as not literally true, a text imagined or created by its author. See Chapter 4 for a detailed discussion.

Grapheme: The smallest unit of written language; in the case of English, a letter, or group of letters, representing one **phoneme**. Some people also consider punctuation marks and emoticons graphemes.

Grounded theory: An approach to research where the researcher is not aiming to test a pre-existing theory, but rather to use data to build new ideas or knowledge. Grounded theory also often involves a certain method of coding data; see Chapter 6 and the work of Strauss & Corbin (1990).

Katharsis (or **catharsis**): This is a key concept in Aristotle's *Poetics*: the audience of a tragedy experience a purification of excesses of pity and fear by experiencing versions of these emotions in the tragic imitation.

Language experience: An approach to developing reading or writing skills where a learner tells a story and the teacher (or another person) scribes that story (word for word). The resulting text is then used for teaching reading or writing. This approach has been popular in British adult literacy education since the 1970s. See the work of Jane Mace and Wendy Moss.

Literacy: Today, the term 'literacy' most commonly refers to reading and writing, making literacy a subset of language. In the past, it has referred to being able to read and write in Latin (rather than the vernacular), and the term is also used today as a synonym for competency, for example, 'computer literacy' or 'cultural literacy'.

Literary theory: The theorizing, or study, of **literature** or the nature of 'literariness'.

Literature: Written **fiction: novels,** poetry, short stories and plays. The term 'literature' also often connotes a judgement of value (of being 'highbrow') or the sense of belonging to an established canon. See Chapter 4 for a detailed discussion.

Literature circle: Another term for a **reading circle**.

Morphophonemic: The present-day English writing system can be considered morphophonemic because it combines a phonemic orthography (a spelling system based to some extent on phoneme-grapheme relationships) with a morphemic orthography (where individual morphemes maintain the same spelling even when they are pronounced differently in different words). For example, the morpheme 'ed' to indicate the past simple tense represents three different phonemes or phoneme combinations: /t/ (as in 'matched'), /d/ (as in 'walked') and /ə(schwa) + d/ (as in 'beloved', when pronounced as three syllables).

Mutual improvement societies: Popular in the late eighteenth and nineteenth centuries, mutual improvement societies were groups of people who met for the purposes of reading, discussion and self-education. Mutual improvement societies can be seen as a type of **reading circle**. See Chapter 5.

Neuroimaging: The process/techniques/technology used to produce images of the structure and functions of the brain. Neuroimaging (or neuro-imaging) has revolutionized reading research by allowing researchers to identify which sections of the brain are active at which stages of the reading process.

Novel: A book-length piece of written, fictional **prose**. See Chapter 4 for a detailed discussion.

Pedagogy: The study of education or approaches to teaching. This word has its origins in the Greek 'ped' referring to children. Some theorists of adult education use the term 'androgogy' to refer to the study of adult learning or teaching. However, in this book, I have used the word pedagogy in its most common, general sense of 'the study of teaching' (for adults or children).

Phenomenology: A branch of literary, philosophical and social science research theory associated with an interest in the world as experienced in individual consciousnesses.

Phoneme: A basic sound unit in a particular language. There are 24 consonant phonemes in most accents of English. By most counts, there are 20 vowel phonemes in Received Pronunciation English, 13 in Scottish Standard English and 16 in Standard American.

Phonics: A shorthand for phonic instruction; phonics refers to the teaching of phoneme-grapheme correspondences as part of reading instruction.

Polysemy: The concept of a word or phrase having multiple potential meanings.

Practices: Practices refer to things done, or performed, often on a regular basis. Reading practices, for example, are the types of reading someone does. My reading practices include reading emails for work and reading novels for pleasure. The Social Practice theorists are particularly interested in reading practices.

Practitioner research: A research methodology used by teachers (or other practitioners) to scrutinize an aspect of his or her own practice, or own teaching situation. Also called **action research**.

Prose: In opposition to verse (poetry), prose is writing in 'normal' sentences, following accepted punctuation conventions. **Novels** are works of **fiction** in prose. This book is written in prose, not in verse.

Qualitative research methods: Research methods that focus on non-numerical qualities rather than numbers. Qualitative research aims to provide a more detailed description of the 'why' and 'how'. Qualitative research often involves observation, interviews or focus groups.

Quantitative research methods: In contrast to qualitative methods, quantitative research methods involve the collection numerical data and use of statistical methods of analysis. See Cohen, Manion & Morrison (2007) for a more detailed examination of **qualitative** and quantitative methods.

Rasa: Sanskrit term often translated as 'taste', 'mood', or 'flavour', used to describe the emotional experience of the audiences of Ancient Sanskrit drama. Most dramatic theorists wrote of eight varieties of rasa: romantic/erotic, comic, violent/furious, peaceful/compassionate, repulsed, terrified, heroic and marvellous/wondrous.

Reading: The act, activity or experience of gaining meaning, pleasure, information or perhaps something else from a piece of writing. See Chapter 1 for some of the ways reading is defined and researched.

Reading circles: Groups of people gathered to read and discuss books (often novels) communally.

Scientific studies of reading: Studies of reading that aim to follow scientific, positivist principles of research. These are usually **quantitative** studies, and are performed by the disciplines of **cognitive psychology** or neuroscience. There is also a journal called 'Scientific Studies of Reading'.

Semi-structured interviews: Interviews where the interviewer has established a framework for the interviews (perhaps some question prompts or potential questions) but aims to improvise in the interview situation. Semi-structured interviews are distinct from structured interviews (where the researcher works through a pre-set list of questions) and unstructured interviews (where the interviewer uses no prompts and simply improvises a conversation).

Shallow orthography: A writing system where one **phoneme** is represented by one **grapheme**, and one **grapheme** represents one **phoneme**, or very close to this. Spanish and Russian have shallow orthographies. English, by contrast, has a **deep orthography**.

Social history of reading: The study of reading that looks at reading practices historically: who read, when, how, what, with whom and so on. Social history is the type of history more concerned with people's daily lives than with the great leaders, treaties and wars. This includes the increasingly popular 'history of the book'.

Social practice theory: The idea that literacy is a social practice, something performed for a particular reason in a particular context. This is in opposition to a skills-based approach to literacy, which defines literacy as a set of cognitive skills, located within an individual. However, most people would agree that a social practice approach and a skills-based approach should in fact be complementary rather than opposing. See Chapter 1.

Sociology: The study of society, societies, communities and people in groups. **Social practice theory** is a sociological approach to literacy.

Subvocalization: The act of 'saying' sounds or words 'in one's head' or 'under one's breath' while reading, believed by some to be a stage in the development of fluent silent reading.

Tabulae: The wooden, stone or wax tablets used for writing in Ancient Greece and Rome. Pre-Christian Roman texts were primarily **tabulae** and **volumen**.

Verse: Verse refers to poetry as opposed to **prose**; for example, 'I have a good verse translation of the *Odyssey*, which I prefer to the recent prose translation'. A verse (or a stanza) is a group of lines of a poem or song.

Vocalization: 'saying' words (or anything) 'out loud', using our vocal chords. In the context of reading, vocalization means saying a written word aloud, or **decoding** a written word into a spoken word.

Volumen: What we would now call scrolls: the most common form of extended text in Ancient Greece and Rome. Volumen had to be read using both hands, one hand holding the rolled up scroll and the other unrolling it as one read.

Whole word approach: An approach to reading instruction, where people are encouraged to memorize and recognize whole words as single units, rather than decoding the **phoneme/grapheme** correspondences. This approach became popular in Europe in the seventeenth and eighteenth centuries.

References

Albin, M. (2009). The Islamic book. In S. Eliot & J. Rose (Eds), *A Companion to the History of the Book* (pp. 165–176). Oxford: Wiley-Blackwell.

Allende, I. (1996). Two words (M. Sayers Peden, Trans.). In K. Figes (Ed.), *The Penguin Book of International Women's Stories* (pp. 212–219). London: Penguin.

Altick, R. D. (1957). *The English Common Reader: A Social History of the Mass Reading Public 1800–1900*. Chicago, IL: The University of Chicago Press.

Anderson, P. L., & Corbett, L. (2008). Literature circles for students with learning disabilities. *Intervention in School and Clinic, 44*(1), pp. 25–33.

Applebee, A. N. (1974). *Tradition and Reform in the Teaching of English: A History*. Urbana, IL: National Council of Teachers of English.

Aristotle. (1996). *Poetics* (M. Heath, Trans.). Harmondsworth: Penguin Books.

Asch, S. E. (1946). Forming impressions of personality. *Journal of Abnormal and Social Psychology, 41*, pp. 258–290.

Ash, G. E., Kuhn, M. R., & Walpole, S. (2009). Analysing "inconsistencies" in practice: Teachers' continued use of round robin reading. *Reading & Writing Quarterly, 25*(1), pp. 87–103.

Atwood, M. (1989). Reading blind: The best American short stories 1989. In M. Atwood (Ed.), *Writing with Intent: Essays, Reviews, Personal Prose 1983–2005* (pp. 68–79). New York, NY: Carroll & Graf Publishers.

—. (2005). Review: Reading Lolita in Tehran: A Memoir in Books by Azar Nafisi. In M. Atwood (Ed.), *Writing with Intent: Essays, Reviews, Personal Process 1983–2005* (pp. 317–321). New York, NY: Carroll & Graf Publishers.

Auster, P. (2004). *Oracle Night*. London: Faber and Faber.

Bailey, I. (2006). Overview of the adult literacy system in Ireland and current issues in its implementation. In NCSALL (Ed.), *Review of Adult Learning and Literacy* (Vol. 6, pp. 197–240) (online).

Baker, J. M. (1993). The presence of the name: Reading scripture in an Indonesian village. In J. Boyarin (Ed.), *The Ethnography of Reading* (pp. 98–138). Berkeley, CA: Univerisity of California Press.

Bakhtin, M. M. (1981). *The Dialogic Imagination* (C. Emerson & M. Holquist, Trans.). Austin: University of Texas Press.

Baron-Cohen, S. (1997). *Mindblindness: An Essay on Autism and Theory of Mind*. Cambridge, MA: The MIT Press.

Barr, D. (2009). The importance of reading aloud. *Timesonline*, 24 March 2009.

Barton, D. (2004). What is ethnography? *Reflect, 1*, 29.

—. (2007). *Literacy: An Introduction to the Ecology of Written Language* (2nd ed.). Oxford: Blackwell Publishing.

Barton, D., Hamilton, M., & Ivanic, R. (Eds). (2000). *Situated Literacies: Reading and Writing in Context.* London: Routledge.

BBC Press Office. (2004). Millions flock to BBC Radio Online [Electronic Version]. *BBC Press Releases.* Retrieved 26 October 2009.

Becker, H. S. (1984). *Writing for Social Scientists.* Chicago, IL: University of Chicago Press.

Benjamin, W. (1936/1969). The work of art in the age of mechanical reproduction. In H. Arendt (Ed.), *Illuminations.* New York, NY: Schochen Books.

Besser, S., Brooks, G., Burton, M., Parisella, M., Spare, Y., Stratford, S., et al. (2004). *Adult Literacy Learners' Difficulties in Reading: An Exploratory Study.* London: NRDC.

Bettelheim, B. (1975). *The Uses of Enchantment: The Meaning and Importance of Fairy Tales.* Harmondsworth: Penguin Books.

Booth, W. C. (1988). *The Company We Keep: An Ethics of Fiction.* Berkeley, CA: University of California Press.

Boyarin, D. (1993). Placing reading: Ancient Israel and Medieval Europe. In J. Boyarin (Ed.), *The Ethnography of Reading* (pp. 10–37). Berkeley, CA: University of California Press.

Boyarin, J. (1993). Voices around the text: The ethnography of reading at Mesivta Tifereth Jerusalem. In J. Boyarin (Ed.), *The Ethnography of Reading* (pp. 212–237). Berkeley, CA: University of California Press.

Brandt, D. (2001). *Literacy in American Lives.* Cambridge: Cambridge University Press.

Breen, M. P., & Littlejohn, A. (2000). The significance of negotiation. In M. P. Breen & A. Littlejohn (Eds), *Classroom Decision-Making: Negotiation and Process Syllabuses in Practice* (pp. 5–38). Cambridge: Cambridge University Press.

Brooks, G. (1984). Teaching silent reading to beginners. In G. Brooks & A. K. Pugh (Eds), *Studies in the History of Reading* (pp. 85–96). Reading: University of Reading School of Education.

Brooks, G., Burton, M., Cole, P., & Szczerbinski, M. (2007). *Effective Teaching and Learning: Reading.* London: NRDC.

Brown, M. P. (2009). The triumph of the codex: The manuscript book before 1000. In S. Eliot & J. Rose (Eds), *A Companion to The History of the Book* (pp. 179–193). Oxford: Wiley-Blackwell.

Brumfit, C. J., & Carter, R. (1986). Introduction: English literature and English language. In C. J. Brumfit & R. Carter (Eds), *Literature and Language Teaching* (pp. 2–21). Oxford: Oxford University Press.

Bruner, J. (1983). *Child's Talk: Learning to Use Language.* Oxford: Oxford University Press.

Burgess, A. (1967). *The Novel Now: A Guide to Contemporary Fiction.* New York, NY: W. W. Norton & Company

Burke, S. J., & Brumfit, C. J. (1986). Is literature language? or Is language literature? In C. J. Brumfit & R. Carter (Eds), *Literature and Language Teaching* (pp. 171–176). Oxford: Oxford University Press.

Burns, B. (1998). Changing the classroom climate with literature circles. *Journal of Adolescent & Adult Literacy, 42*(2), pp. 124–128.

Burton, M. (2007a). *Oral Reading Fluency for Adults.* London: NRDC.

—. (2007b). *Reading.* Leicester: NIACE.

Burton, M., Davey, J., Lewis, M., Ritchie, L., & Brooks, G. (2008). *Improving Reading: Phonics and Fluency.* London: NRDC.

Byatt, A. S. (1978). *The Virgin in the Garden.* London: Chatto and Windus/Penguin.

Caplan, D. (2004). Functional neuroimaging studies of written sentence comprehension. *Scientific Studies of Reading, 8*(3), pp. 225–240.

Carter, R. (1986). Linguistic models, language, and literariness: Study strategies in the teaching of literature to foreign students. In C. Brumfit & R. Carter (Eds), *Literature and Language Teaching* (pp. 110–132). Oxford: Oxford University Press.

—. (1997). *Investigating English Discourse: Language, Literacy and Literature.* London: Routledge.

Cavallo, G. (1999). Between volumen and codex: Reading in the Roman World (L. G. Cochrane, Trans.). In G. Cavallo & R. Chartier (Eds), *A History of Reading in the West* (pp. 64–89). Cambridge: Polity.

Cavallo, G., & Chartier, R. (1999). Introduction (L. G. Cochrane, Trans.). In G. Cavallo & R. Chartier (Eds), *A History of Reading in the West* (pp. 1–36). Cambridge: Polity.

Chinn, C. A., Anderson, R. C., & Waggoner, M. A. (2001). Patterns of discourse in two kinds of literature discussion. *Reading Research Quarterly, 36*(4), pp. 378–411.

Cho, K. S., & Choi, D. S. (2008). Are read-alouds and free reading "natural partners"?: An experimental study. *Knowledge Quest, 36*(5), pp. 69–73.

Clanchy, M. T. (1984). Learning to read in the Middle Ages and the role of mothers. In G. Brooks & A. K. Pugh (Eds), *Studies in the History of Reading* (pp. 33–39). Reading: University of Reading School of Education.

—. (2009). Parchment and paper: Manuscript culture 1100–1500. In S. Eliot & J. Rose (Eds), *A Companion to the History of the Book* (pp. 194–206). Oxford: Wiley-Blackwell.

Clark, C., Osborn, S., & Ackerman, R. (2008). *Young People's Self-perceptions as Readers: An Investigation Including Family, Peer and School Influences.* London: The National Literacy Trust.

Clarke, G. (2008a). Introduction. In S. Grylls (Ed.), *Six Book Challenge 2008: The Impact on Readers.* London: The Vital Link/The Reading Agency.

—. (2008b). Reading should be a pleasure. *Reflect, 11*, 15.

Cohen, L., Manion, L., & Morrison, K. (2007). *Research Methods in Education* (6th ed.). London: Routledge.

Coleridge, S. T. (1817/1986). Biographia Literaria. In M. H. Abrams (Ed.), *The Norton Anthology of English Literature* (5th ed., Vol. 2, pp. 386–405). London: W. W. Norton & Company.

Coltheart, M., & Jackson, N. E. (2001). *Routes to Reading Success and Failure: Towards an Integrated Cognitive Psychology of Atypical Reading.* Macquarie: Macquarie Monographs in Cognitive Science.

Cope, B., & Kalantzis, M. (Eds). (2000). *Multiliteracies: Literacy Learning and the Design of Social Futures.* London: Routledge.

Coulmas, F. (2003). *Writing Systems: An Introduction to Their Linguistic Analysis.* Cambridge: Cambridge University Press.

Cowan, S. (2010a). London: Personal email communication to Sam Duncan, 14 September 2010.

—. (2010b). *Literacy in Britain During the Enlightenment*. Paper presented at the Institute of Historical Research, Senate House, University of London, 4 June 2010.

Cowie, B. (2008). *Passenger*. London: Old Street Publishing.

Crowther, J., Hamilton, M., & Tett, L. (Eds). (2006). *Powerful Literacies*. Leicester: NIACE.

Cuddon, J. A. (1991). *Dictionary of Literary Terms and Literary Theory*. Harmondsworth: Penguin.

Culler, J. (1975). *Structuralist Poetics: Structuralism, Linguistics and the Study of Literature*. London: Routledge & Kegan Paul.

Cumming-Potvin, W. (2007). Scaffolding, Multiliteracies, and Reading Circles. *Canadian Journal of Education, 30*(2), pp. 483–507.

Dakin, J. C. (1991). The prevalance of mutual improvement societies in adult education in New Zealand 1870–1915. *International Journal of Lifelong Education, 10*(3), pp. 243–254.

Daniels, H. (2006). What's the next big thing with literature circles? *Voices from the Middle, 13*(4), pp. 6–15.

Danto, A. C. (1981). *The Transfiguration of the Commonplace: A Philosophy of Art*. Harvard, MA: Harvard University Press.

Davis, P. (2009). Interview: Talk to me, Phil Davis in conversation with David Fearnley. *The Reader, 34*(Summer), pp. 31–38.

Day, C. (2003). *Reading and Responding in Literature Circles*. Marrickville, Australia: Primary English Teaching Association, PEN.

Day, D., & Ainley, G. (2008). From skeptic to believer: One teacher's journey implementing literature circles. *Reading Horizons, 48*(3), pp. 157–176.

Derrick, J. (2010). London: Personal communication with Sam Duncan, 7 December, 2010.

Derrick, J., Ecclestone, K., & Gawn, J. (2009). *Formative Assessment in Adult Literacy, Language and Numeracy*. Leicester: NIACE.

Derrick, J., Gawn, J., & Ecclestone, K. (2008). Evaluating the "spirit" and "letter" of formative assessment in the learning cultures of part-time adult literacy and numeracy classes. *Research in Post-Compulsory Education, 13*(2), pp. 173–184.

Dewey, J. (1934). *Art as Experience*. New York, NY: Perigee.

—. (1938). *Experience & Education*. New York, NY: Touchstone.

Draper, J. A. (1989). A selected chronology of literacy events. In M. C. Taylor & J. A. Draper (Eds), *Adult Literacy Perspectives* (pp. 15–23). Ontario: Culture Concepts.

Duncan, S. (2006). Voices on the Page. *Reflect, 6*, pp. 18–19.

—. (2008). What are we doing when we read aloud? *Reflect, 11*, p. 24.

—. (2009). 'What are we doing when we read?' – Adult literacy learners' perceptions of reading. *Research in Post-Compulsory Education, 14*(3), pp. 317–331.

—. (2010). *What Are We Doing When We Read Novels? – Reading Circles, Novels and Adult Reading Development*. EdD Thesis, Institute of Education, London.

Duncan, S., & Mallows, D. (Eds). (2007). *Voices on the Page: Stories and Poems by Adults in Skills for Life Learning*. Warrington: New Leaf with NRDC.

Dundas, P. (1994). Indian Civilisation – Sanskrit Drama. Unpublished Lecture. University of Edinburgh.

Eagleton, T. (1996). *Literary Theory: An Introduction.* Oxford: Blackwell.

—. (2005). *The English Novel: An Introduction.* Oxford: Blackwell.

Eco, U. (1983). *The Name of the Rose.* London: Vintage.

Edgren, J. S. (2009). China. In S. Eliot & J. Rose (Eds), *A Companion to the History of the Book* (pp. 97–110). Oxford: Wiley-Blackwell.

Editors of the Paris Review. (1957). Interview with Truman Capote: The Art of Fiction. In P. Gourevitch (Ed.), *The Paris Review Interviews, 1* (2007 ed., pp. 15–33). Edinburgh: Canongate.

—. (1984). Philip Roth: The Art of Fiction. In P. Gourevitch (Ed.), *The Paris Review Interviews 4* (2009 ed., pp. 203–235). Edinburgh: Canongate.

English, R., Robinson, A., Mathews, D., & Gill, M. (2006). Literature circles in action. *Teacher* (170), pp. 36–40.

Excellence Gateway. (2008). Interactive Online Skills for Life Adult Literacy Core Curriculum. Retrieved 31 July 2009, from http://www.excellencegateway.org. uk/sflcurriculum.

Feather, J. (2009). The British book market 1600–1800. In J. Rose & S. Eliot (Eds), *A Companion to the History of the Book* (pp. 232–246). Oxford: Wiley-Blackwell.

Fergus, J. (1996). Provincial servants' reading in the late eighteenth century. In J. Raven, H. Small & N. Tadmore (Eds), *The Practice and Representation of Reading in England* (pp. 202–225). Cambridge: Cambridge University Press.

Figes, K. (Ed.). (1996). *The Penguin Book of International Women's Stories.* London: Penguin Books.

Fish, S. (1980). *Is There a Text in This Class?: The Authority of Interpretive Communities.* Cambridge, Massachusetts: Harvard University Press.

Forster, E. M. (1927). *Aspects of the Novel.* Harmondsworth: Penguin.

Fowler, K. J. (2004). *The Jane Austen Book Club.* London: Penguin Books.

Fowler, R. (1977). *Linguistics and the Novel.* London: Methuen.

Freebody, P., & Luke. (1999). Further Notes on the Four Resources Model [Electronic Version]. From http://www.readingonline.org/research/lukefreebody.html.

Freeborn, D. (1998). *From Old English to Standard English* (2nd ed.). Basingstoke: Palgrave.

Freire, P. (1978). *Cultural Action for Freedom.* Harmondsworth: Penguin.

—. (1985). *The Politics of Education: Culture, Power, and Liberation* (D. Macedo, Trans.). New York, NY: Bergin & Garvey.

Gabrielatos, C. (1996). Reading allowed (?): Reading aloud in TEFL. *Current Issues* (8), pp. 7–9.

Gardner, J. (2006). *Assessment and Learning.* London: Sage.

Garnham, A. (1987). *Mental Models as Representations of Discourse and Text.* Chichester: Ellis Horwood.

Garnham, A., & Oakhill, J. (1992). Discourse processing and text representation from a "mental models" perspective. In A. Garnham & J. Oakhill (Eds), *Discourse Representation and Text Processing* (pp. 193–204). Hove: Lawrence Erlbaum Associates.

Gawn, J., Derrick, J., Duncan, S., & Schwab, I. (2009). *Teaching Reading to Adults: A Pack of Resources and Ideas for Literacies tutors.* Glasgow: The Scottish Government.

Gebre, A. H., Rogers, A., Street, B., & Openjuru, G. (2009). *Everyday Literacies in Africa: Ethnographic Studies in Literacy and Numeracy Practices in Ethiopia.* Kampala, Uganda: Fountain Publishing.

Gee, J. P. (1996). *Social Linguistics and Literacies: Ideology in Discourses.* London: Taylor & Francis.

Ghose, M. (Ed.). (2007). *Exploring the Everyday: Ethnographic Approaches to Literacy and Numeracy.* New Delhi: Nirantar and ASPBAE.

Gibson, S. (2008). Reading aloud: A useful learning tool? *ELT Journal, 62*(1), pp. 29–36.

Gillray, J. (Artist). (1805). *The Plum Pudding in Danger* (artwork).

Gilroy, M., & Parkinson, B. (1996). Teaching literature in a foreign language. *Language Teaching* (29), pp. 213–225.

Good, M., Hollin, F., Simpson, A., Steeds, A., Clary, H., Henderson, S., et al. (2001). *Adult Literacy Core Curriculum:* The Basic Skills Agency.

Goodwyn, A. (2005). The subject of English: Putting English in perspective. In A. Goodwyn & J. Branson (Eds), *Teaching English: A Handbook for Primary and Secondary School Teachers* (pp. 1–17). London: Routledge.

Gordon, D. (1999). Practical strategies: Reading and responding in authentic ways to reading – Reading Club Groups. *Literacy Learning: Secondary Thoughts, 7*(2), i–viii.

Gordon, J. (2009). Sound[']s right: Pupils' responses to heard poetry and the revised national curriculum for English. *Curriculum Journal, 20*(2), pp. 161–175.

Gould, J. E. (1961). *The Chautauqua Movement: An Episode in the Continuing American Revolution.* Albany, NY: State University of New York Press.

Graff, H. J. (1979). *The Literacy Myth: Literacy and Social Structure in the Nineteenth-Century City.* New York, NY: Academic Press.

Green, A., & Howard, U. (2007). *Skills and Social Practices; Making Common Cause.* London NRDC.

Greenaway, P. (1996). *The Pillow Book* (film).

Greene, M. (1995). *Releasing the Imagination: Essays on Education, the Arts and Social Change.* San Francisco, CA: Jossey-Bass.

Gregory, E., & Williams, A. (2000). *City Literacies: Learning to Read Across Generations and Cultures.* London: Routledge.

Grylls, S. (2009). *Six Book Challenge 2008: Impact on Readers.* London: The Vital Link/ The Reading Agency.

Habermas, J. (1984). *The Theory of Communicative action, Reason and the Rationalisation of Society* (Vol. 1). London: Heinemann.

Hall, G. (2005). *Literature in Language Education.* Basingstoke: Palgrave MacMillan.

Halliday, M. A. K., & Hasan, R. (1989). *Language, Context, and Text: Aspects of Language in a Social-Semiotic Perspective.* Oxford: Oxford University Press.

Hamesse, J. (1999). The scholastic model of reading (L. G. Cochrane, Trans.). In G. Cavallo & R. Chartier (Eds), *A History of Reading in the West* (pp. 103–119). Oxford: Polity.

Hamilton, M. (1996). Literacy and adult basic education. In R. Fieldhouse (Ed.), *A History of Modern British Adult Education* (pp. 142–165). Leicester: National Institute of Adult Continuing Education.

—. (2005). *Living History – Adult Literacy and the Politics of Change.* Paper presented at the NRDC Autumn Lecture Series Institute of Education, University of London, 8 November 2005.

Hamilton, M., & Hillier, Y. (2006). *Changes Faces of Adult Literacy, Language and Numeracy: A Critical History.* Stoke on Trent: Trentham Books.

Harrison, J. (1974). *A Right to Read: Action for a Literate Britain*. London: The British Association of Settlements.

Hartley, J. (2002). *The Reading Groups Book* (2002–2003 ed.). Oxford: Oxford University Press.

Harvey, S., & Daniels, H. (2009). *Inquiry Circles in Action: Comprehension & Collaboration*. Portsmouth, NH: Heinemann.

Haviland, R. M. (1973). *Survey of Provision for Adult Illiteracy in England*. Reading: Centre for the Teaching of Reading, University of Reading.

Heath, S. B. (1983). *Ways with Words: Language, Life and Work in Communities and Classrooms*. Cambridge: Cambridge University Press.

Hellinga, L. (2009). The Gutenberg Revolutions. In S. Eliot & J. Rose (Eds), *A Companion to the History of the Book* (pp. 207–219). Oxford: Wiley-Blackwell.

Herbert, P., & Robinson, C. (2001). Another language, another literacy? Practices in northern Ghana. In B. Street (Ed.), *Literacy and Development: Ethnographic Perspectives* (pp. 121–136). London: Routledge.

Hillis Miller, J. (1987). *The Ethics of Reading*. New York, NY: Columbia University Press.

Holland, N. (1975). *5 Readers Reading*. London: Yale University Press.

—. (1978). A transactive account of transactive criticism. *Poetics* (7), pp. 177–189.

Houston, R. A. (2002). *Literacy in Early Modern Europe: Culture and Education 1500–1800*. London: Longman/Pearson Education.

Howard, U. (2006). Literary literacy. *The Guardian*, 20 May, London.

Howe, N. (1993). Cultural Construction of Reading in Anglo-Saxon England. In J. Boyarin (Ed.), *The Ethnography of Reading* (pp. 58–79). Berkeley, CA: University of California Press.

Hsun, L. (1918/1960). *Selected Stories of Lu Hsun* (H.-Y. Yang & G. Yang, Trans.). New York, NY: Norton.

Huey, E. B. (1908/1968). *The Psychology and Pedagogy of Reading*. Cambridge, MA: MIT Press.

Hughes, N. (2010). Writing. In N. Hughes & I. Schwab (Eds), *Teaching Adult Literacy: Principles and Practice* (pp. 209–263). Maidenhead: Open University Press.

Hughes, N., & Schwab, I. (Eds). (2010). *Teaching Adult Literacy: Principle and Practice*. London: Open University Press.

Hunter, K. (2003). *Literature Circles and Book Clubs: Variations on a Theme* (Winter). Victoria, Australia: School Library Association of Victoria.

Individual authors. (1976–1986). *Write First Time*. The Federation of Worker Writers and Community Publishers (FWWCP)

—. (1984). *Yes I Like It: Poems by New Writers*. Manchester: Gatehouse.

Irvine, R. (2010). English literary studies: Origins and nature. In D. Cavanagh, A. Gillis, M. Keown, J. Loxley & R. Stevenson (Eds), *The Edinburgh Introduction to Studying English Literature* (pp. 16–24). Edinburgh: Edinburgh University Press.

Irving, J. (1993). *Trying to Save Piggy Snead*. London: Black Swan.

Iser, W. (1972). The reading process: A phenomenological approach. In D. Lodge (Ed.), *Modern Criticism and Theory* (pp. 211–228). London: Longman.

Jackson, M. L. (1999). *A Delightful Entertainment: Study Groups as part of the Kalamazoo Ladies' Library Association*. Paper presented at the Annual Meeting of the Popular Culture and American Culture Association.

Jakobson, R. (1960/1988). Linguistics and poetics. In D. Lodge (Ed.), *Modern Criticism and Theory* (pp. 32–57). London: Longman.

James, L. (1973). *Fiction for the Working Man 1830–50*. Harmondsworth: Penguin University Books.

Johnson Cain, A., & Benseman, J. (2005). Adult Literacy in New Zealand. In NCSALL (Ed.), *Review of Adult Learning and Literacy* (Vol. 5, pp. 155–185) (online).

Jones, H. M. F., & Marriott, S. (1995). Adult literacy in England, 1945–75: Why did it take so long to get 'On the Move'? *History of Education, 24*(4), pp. 337–352.

Just, M. A., & Carpenter, P. A. (1977). Reading comprehension as eyes see it. In M. A. Just & P. A. Carpenter (Eds), *Cognitive Processes in Comprehension* (pp. 109–139). Hillsdale, NY: Lawrence Erlbaum Associates.

—. (1980). A theory of reading: From eye fixations to comprehension. *Psychological Review, 4*(87), pp. 329–354.

Katz, C. A., Kuby, S. A., & Hobgood, J. M. (1997). Trapped in a month of mondays (middle school). *Journal of Adolescent & Adult Literacy, 41*(2), pp. 152–155.

Kelly, T. (1952). The Origin of Mechanics' Institutes. *British Journal of Educational Studies, 1*(1), pp. 17–27.

Kendall, A. (2008). 'Giving up' reading: Re-imagining reading with young adult readers. *Research and Practice in Adult Literacy, 65*(Spring/Summer), pp. 8–13.

Kim, M. (2004). Literature Discussions in Adult L2 Learning. *Language and Education, 18*(2), pp. 145–166.

King, C. (2001). I like group reading because we can share ideas: The role of talk within the literature circle. *Reading, 35*(1), pp. 32–36.

Kress, G., & Mavers, D. (2005). Social semiotics and multimodal texts. In B. Somekh & C. Lewin (Eds), *Research Methods in the Social Sciences* (pp. 172–179). London: Sage.

Kvale, S. (1996). *Interviews: An Introduction to Qualitative Research interviewing*. Thousand Oaks: Sage.

Leavey, J. (2005). Adult Literacies: The Scottish approach. *Reflect, 1*, pp. 22–25.

Leech, G. N., & Short, M. H. (1981). *Style in Fiction: A Linguistic Introduction to English Fictional Prose*. London: Longman.

Lindsay, A., & Gawn, J. (2005). *Developing Literacy: Supporting Achievement*. Leicester: NIACE.

Lloyd, S. L. (2004). Using comprehension strategies as a springboard for student talk. *Journal of Adolescent & Adult Literacy, 48*(2), pp. 114–124.

Lodge, D. (1992). *The Art of Fiction*. Harmondsworth: Penguin.

Long, E. (1993). Textual interpretation as collective action. In J. Boyarin (Ed.), *The Ethnography of Reading* (pp. 180–211). Berkeley, CA: University of California Press.

—. (2003). *Book Clubs: Women and the Uses of Reading in Everyday Life*. Chicago, IL: University of Chicago Press.

Looney, J. (2008). *Teaching, Learning and Assessment for Adults – Improving Foundation Skills*. Paris: Organisation for Economic Co-operation and Development.

Luchins, A. (1957). Primacy–recency in impression formation. In I. C. Hovland (Ed.), *The Order of Presentation in Persuasion*. New Haven, CT: Yale University Press.

Lukacs, G. (1978). *The Theory of the Novel* (A. Bostock, Trans.). London: Merlin Press.

Macdonald, D. (1961). *Masscult & Midcult.* New York, NY: Partisan Review/Random House.

Mace, J. (1979). *Working with Words: Literacy Beyond School.* London: Writers and Readers Publishing Cooperative in association with Chameleon

—. (1992). *Talking About Literacy: Principles and Practices of Adult Literacy Education.* London: Routledge.

—. (1995). Reminiscence as literacy: Intersections and creative moments. In J. Mace (Ed.), *Literacy, Language and Community Publishing: Essays in Adult Education* (pp. 97–117). Clevedon: Multilingual Matters.

Mace, J., Smith, M., & Aylett, P. (Eds). (1990). *If It Wasn't for This 2nd Chance.* London: National Federation of Voluntary Education Schemes, Cambridge House.

Maddox, B. (2001). Literacy and the market: The economic uses of literacy among the peasantry in north-west Bangladesh. In B. Street (Ed.), *Literacy and Development: Ethnographic Perspectives* (pp. 137–151). London: Routledge.

Malchow Lloyd, R. (2006). Talking books: Gender and the responses of adolescents in literature circles. *English Teaching: Practice and Critique, 5*(3), pp. 30–58.

Maley, A. (1989). Down from the pedestal: Literature as a resource. In R. Carter, R. Walker & C. J. Brumfit (Eds), *Literature and the Learner: Methodological Approaches.* Basingstoke and London: Modern English Publications/The British Council.

Manguel, A. (1996). *A History of Reading.* New York, NY: Viking.

—. (2006). *The Library at Night.* London: Yale University Press.

Manguel, A., Nafisi, A., & Pennac, D. (2008). *Alberto Manguel, Azar Nafisi & Daniel Pennac: The Rights of the ReaderEvent* at the Free the Word! International PEN Festival of World Literature, Southbank Centre London, 12 April 2008.

Martin III, R. L. (2009). North America and Transatlantic Book Culture to 1800. In J. Rose & S. Eliot (Eds), *A Companion to the History of the Book* (pp. 259–271). Oxford: Wiley-Blackwell.

McKay, V. (2007). Adult Basic Education and Training in South Africa. In NCSALL (Ed.), *Review of Adult Learning and Literacy* (pp. 285–310) (online).

McLuhan, M. (1962). *Gutenberg Galaxy: The Making of Typographic Man.* Toronto: University of Toronto Press.

McRae, J. (1991). *Literature with a Small 'l'.* London: Macmillan.

McShane, S. (2005). *Applying Research in Reading Instruction for Adults: First Steps for Teachers.* Washington DC: National Institute for Literacy, The Partnership for Reading and National Center for Family Literacy.

Meadows, G. (2008). Literacy: An end in itself? *Reflect, 11*, pp. 16–17.

Meek, M. (1988). *How Texts Teach What Readers Learn.* Stroud: The Thimble Press.

—. (1991). *On Being Literate.* London: The Bodley Head.

Monaghan, E. J. (1989). Literacy Instruction and Gender in Colonial New England. In C. N. Davidson (Ed.), *Reading in America: Literature & Social History* (pp. 53–80). Baltimore, ML: The Johns Hopkins Univerisity Press.

—. (2005). *Learning to Read and Write in Colonial America.* Boston, MA: University of Massachusetts Press.

Monaghan, E. J., & Barry, A. L. (1999). *Writing the Past: Teaching Reading in Colonial America and the United States 1640–1940: An Exhibition.* Paper presented at the 44th Annual Conference of the International Reading Association.

Moser, C. (1999). *Improving Literacy and Numeracy: A Fresh Start.* London: DfEE Publications.

Moss, W. (2005). Theories on the Teaching of Reading to Adults. *RaPAL, 56*(Spring), pp. 23–27.

Mullan, J. (2006). *How Novels Work.* Oxford: Oxford University Press.

Murakami, H. (1993). *Hard-Boiled Wonderland and the End of the World* (A. Birnbaum, Trans.). London: Vintage.

—. (2005). *Kafka on the Shore* (P. Gabriel, Trans.). London: Vintage.

Murphy, G. R. S. J. (1989). *The Saxon Savior: The Germanic Transformation of the Gospel in the Ninth-Century Heliand.* New York, NY: Oxford University Press.

—. (1992). *The Heliand: The Saxon Gospel.* New York, NY: Oxford University Press.

Nafisi, A. (2004). *Reading Lolita in Tehran.* London: Fourth Estate Ltd.

Nagel, T. (1974). What is it like to be a bat? *The Philosophical Review, LXXXIII*(4), pp. 435–450.

Nagy, W. (1997). On the role of context in first- and second-language vocabulary learning. In N. Schmitt & M. McCarthy (Eds), *Vocabulary: Description, Acquisition and Pedagogy* (pp. 64–83). Cambridge: Cambridge University Press.

Nation, I. S. P. (2001). *Learning Vocabulary in Another Language.* Cambridge: Cambridge University Press.

Nation, K. (2006). Reading and genetics: An introduction. *Journal of Research in Reading, 29*(1), pp. 1–10.

National Adult Literacy Database. (2010). National Adult Literacy Database Library. Accessed 2010, *http://library.nald.ca/learning* (online).

National Institute for Literacy. (2009). [Assessment 1921] Basic Reading Skills Discussion list. From 27 May 2009 *www.nifl.gov/pipermail/assessment/2009/001950.html.*

Neuburg, V. (1989). Chapbooks in America: Reconstructing the popular reading of early America. In C. N. Davidson (Ed.), *Reading in America: Literature & Social History* (pp. 81–113). Baltimore, ML: The Johns Hopkins University Press.

Neuman, P. (2003). *The Blanket.* Pembina Valley: The National Literacy Secretariat Human Resources Development Canada.

Nietzsche, F. (1872/1993). *The Birth of Tragedy* (S. Whiteside, Trans.). Harmondsworth: Penguin Books.

Noordman, L. G. M., & Vonk, W. (1992). Readers' Knowledge and Control of Inferences in Reading. In A. Garnham & J. Oakhill (Eds), *Discourse Representation and Text Processing* (pp. 373–391). Hove: Lawrence Erlbaum Associates.

O'Connor, F. (1963). *The Lonely Voice: A Study of the Short Story.* London: Macmillan.

O'Donnell-Allen, C. (2006). *The Book Club Companion: Fostering Strategic Readers in the Secondary Classroom.* Portsmouth, NH: Heinemann.

O'Leary, J. D. (1991). *Creating a Love of Reading.* Ottawa, ON: National Literacy Secretariat.

Openjuru, G. L., & Lyster, E. (2007). Christianity and rural community literacy practices in Uganda. *Journal of Research in Reading, 30*(1), pp. 97–112.

Orwell, G. (1946/2003). Why I write. In *Shooting an Elephant and Other Essays.* Harmondsworth: Penguin.

Ostler, N. (2005). *Empires of the Word.* London: Harper Perennial.

Paran, A. (2003). Bringing the outside world into the classroom: Ways of making reading lessons less of a tedious task. *English Teachers' Association Switzerland (ETAS) Journal, 20*(2), pp. 26–28.

—. (2006a). *Critical Necessities: Literature in Foreign Language Teaching.* Institute of Education, University of London.

—. (2006b). The stories of literature and language teaching. In A. Paran (Ed.), *Literature in Language Teaching and Learning* (pp. 1–10). Alexandria, VA: Teachers of English to Speakers of Other Languages.

—. (2008). The role of literature in instructed foreign language learning and teaching: An evidence-based survey. *Language Teaching, 41*(4), pp. 465–496.

—. (2011). London: Personal communication with Sam Duncan, 15 January 2011.

Parkes, M. B. (1999). Reading, copying and interpreting a test in the early middle ages (L. G. Cochrane, Trans.). In G. Cavallo & R. Chartier (Eds), *A History of Reading in the West* (pp. 90–102). Oxford: Polity.

Pennac, D. (2006). *The Rights of the Reader* (S. Hamp Adams, Trans.). London: Walker Books.

Perfetti, C. A., & Bolger, D. J. (2004). The brain might read that way. *Scientific Studies of Reading, 8*(3), pp. 293–304.

Perry, M. (1979). Literary dynamics: How the order of a text creates its meanings [with an analysis of Faulkner's "A Rose for Emily". *Poetics Today, 1*(1/2), pp. 35–361.

Petrucci, A. (1999). Reading to reading: A future for reading (L. G. Cochrane, Trans.). In G. Cavallo & R. Chartier (Eds), *A History of Reading in the West* (pp. 345–367). Cambridge: Polity.

Piatkus, J. (2009). Fresh Opportunities [Electronic Version]. *Thebookseller.com, 22.10.09.* Retrieved 26 October 2009.

Poldrack, R. A., & Sandak, R. (2004). Introduction to this special issue: The cognitive neuroscience of reading. *Scientific Studies of Reading, 8*(3), pp. 199–202.

Pugh, A. K. (1978). *Silent Reading: An Introduction to Its Study and Teaching.* London: Heinemann.

Purcell-Gates, V. (1997). There's reading ... and then there's reading: Process models and instruction. *Focus on Basics: Connecting Research and Practice, 2*(A).

Purcell-Gates, V., Jacobson, E., & Degener, S. (2004). *Print Literacy Development: United Cognitive and Social Practice Theories.* Cambridge, MA: Harvard University Press.

Quick Reads. (2010). Online Resource. Accessed 2010, http://www.quickreads.org.uk.

Radcliffe, C. (1986). Mutual improvement societies in the west riding of yorkshire, 1835–1900. *Journal of Educational Administration and History, 18*(2), pp. 1–16.

—. (1997). Mutual improvement societies and the forging of working-class political consciousness in nineteenth-century England. *International Journal of Lifelong Education, 16*(2), pp. 141–155.

Rado, M., & Foster, L. (1995). Strategies for expanding learning opportunities for NESB adult literacy learners. *Prospect, 10*(3), pp. 59–74.

Radway, J. (1994). Beyond Mary Bailey and Old Maid Librarians: Reimagining readers and rethinking reading. *Journal of Education for Library and Information Science, 35*(4), pp. 275–296.

Raven, J. (1996). From promotion to proscription: Arrangements for reading and eighteenth century libraries. In J. Raven, H. Small & N. Tadmore (Eds), *The Practice and Presentation of Reading in England* (pp. 175–201). Cambridge: Cambridge University Press.

Raven, J., Small, H., & Tadmore, N. (1999). Introduction. In J. Raven, H. Small & N. Tadmore (Eds), *The Practice and Representation of Reading in England* (pp. 1–21). Cambridge: Cambridge University Press.

Rayner, K., & Pollatsek, A. (1989). *The Psychology of Reading*. Englewood Cliffs, NJ: Prentice Hall.

Reber, A. S. (1995). *The Penguin Dictionary of Psychology*. Harmondsworth: Penguin.

Ren, G.-Q., & Yang, Y. (2010). Syntactic boundaries and comma placement during silent reading of Chinese text: Evidence from eye movements. *Journal of Research in Reading*, *33*(2), pp. 168–177.

Rimmon-Kenan, S. (1989). *Narrative Fiction: Contemporary poetics*. London: Routledge.

Robson, C. (2002). *Real World Research*. Oxford: Blackwell.

Rodrick, A. B. (2001). The importance of being an earnest improver: Class, caste, and self-help in mid-Victorian England. *Victorian Literature and Culture*, pp. 39–50.

Roemer, C. (2009). The papyrus roll in Egypt, Greece and Rome. In S. Eliot & J. Rose (Eds), *A Companion to the History of the Book* (pp. 84–94). Oxford: Wiley-Blackwell.

Rose, Jim. (2006). '*Independent Review of the Teaching of Early Reading*'. Department for Education and Skills, March, London.

Rose, Jonathan. (2010). *The Intellectual Life of the British Working Classes* (2nd ed.). London: Yale University Press.

Rosenblatt, L. (2005). *Making Meaning with Texts: Selected Essays*. Portsmouth, NH: Heinemann.

Ryan, M. (2010). London: Personal communication with Sam Duncan, 16 September 2010.

Sadoski, M. (1998). Mental imagery in reading: A sampler of some significant studies. *Reading onlinewww.readingonline.org* (International Reading Association).

Sadoski, M., & Paivio, A. (2001). *Imagery and Text: A Dual Coding Theory of Reading and Writing*. Mahwah, NJ: Lawrence Erlbaum Associates.

Salvino, D. N. (1989). The word in black and white: Ideologies of race and literacy in antebellum America. In C. N. Davidson (Ed.), *Reading in America: Literature & Social History* (pp. 140–156). Baltimore, ML: The Johns Hopkins University Press.

Sarris, G. (1993). Keeping slug woman alive: The challenge of reading in a reservation classroom. In J. Boyarin (Ed.), *The Ethnography of Reading* (pp. 238–269). Berkeley, CA: University of California Press.

Sartre, J.-P. (1967). *What Is Literature?* (B. Frechtman, Trans.). London: Methuen

Sastri, G. (1960). *A Concise History of Classical Sanskrit Literature*. Oxford: Oxford University Press.

Schmitt, N. (2000). *Vocabulary in Language Teaching*. Cambridge: Cambridge University Press.

Schwab, I. (2010). Reading. In I. Schwab & N. Hughes (Eds), *Teaching Adult Literacy: Principle and Practice*. London: Open University Press.

Shaffer, M. A., & Barrows, A. (2009). *The Guernsey Literary and Potato Peel Pie Society.* London: Bloomsbury.

Shaw, D. J. (2009). The book trade comes of age: The sixteenth century. In J. Rose & S. Eliot (Eds), *A Companion to the History of the Book* (pp. 220–231). Oxford: Wiley-Blackwell.

Shklovsky, V. (1965). Art as technique (L. T. Lemon & M. J. Reis, Trans.). In D. Lodge (Ed.), *Modern Criticism and Theory* (pp. 15–30). London: Longman.

Shohet, L. (2001). Adult learning and literacy in Canada. In NCSALL (Ed.), *Review of Adult Learning and Literacy* (Vol. 2, pp. 1–37) (online).

Short, M. H., & Candlin, C. N. (1986). Teaching study skills for English literature. In C. J. Brumfit & R. Carter (Eds), *Literature and Language Teaching* (pp. 89–109). Oxford: Oxford University Press.

Sicherman, B. (1989). Sense and sensibility: A case study of women's reading in late-Victorian America. In C. N. Davidson (Ed.), *Reading in America: Literature & Social History* (pp. 201–225). Baltimore, ML: The Johns Hopkins University Press.

Small, H. (1996). A pulse of 124: Charles Dickens and a pathology of the mid-Victorian reading public. In J. Raven, H. Small & N. Tadmore (Eds), *The Practice and Representation of Reading in England* (pp. 263–290). Cambridge: Cambridge University Press.

Sökmen, A. J. (1997). Current trends in teaching second language vocabulary. In N. Schmitt & M. McCarthy (Eds), *Vocabulary: Description, Acquisition and Pedagogy* (pp. 237–257). Cambridge: Cambridge University Press.

Southwold Museum. (2010). The Sailor's Reading Room. Retrieved December 2010, http://www.southwoldmuseum.org/Sea%20popups/readingroom_popup.htm.

Spark, M. (1961). *The Prime of Miss Jean Brodie.* London: Macmillan.

Stake, R. E. (1994). Case studies. In N. K. Denzin & Y. S. Lincoln (Eds), *Handbook of Qualitative Research.* London: Sage.

—. (1998). Case studies. In N. K. Denzin & Y. S. Lincoln (Eds), *Strategies of Qualitative Inquiry* (pp. 86–109). London: Sage.

Sticht, T. (2002). The rise of adult education and literacy system in the United States: 1600–2000. In NCSALL (Ed.), *Review of Adult Learning and Literacy* (Vol. 3, pp. 1–26) (online).

—. (2004). Literacy frees the world. *Reflect, 1* (online).

Strauss, A. (1987). *Qualitative Analysis for Social Scientists.* Cambridge: Cambridge University Press.

Strauss, A., & Corbin, J. (1990). *Basics of Qualitative Research: Grounded Theory Procedure and Techniques.* London: Sage.

Street, B. V. (1984). *Literacy in Theory and Practice.* Cambridge: Cambridge University Press.

Stringer, E. T. (1999). *Action Research.* London: Sage.

Stuart, M. (2005a). *Learning to Read.* Paper presented at the Professorial Lecture Series, Institute of Education, University of London, 11 October 2005.

—. (2005b). Phonemic analysis and reading development: Some current issues. *Journal of Research in Reading, 28*(1), pp. 39–49.

Sutherland, S. (2003). Wider reading Pairs @ MGC: An old idea and a new solution. *Literature Enrichment,* Winter 2003.

Svenbro, J. (1999). Archaic and classical Greece: The invention of silent reading (L. G. Cochrane, Trans.). In G. Cavallo & R. Chartier (Eds), *A History of Reading in the West* (pp. 37–63). Cambridge: Polity.

Swain, J., Griffiths, G., & Stone, R. (2006). Integrating formative/diagnostic assessment techniques into teachers' routine practice in adult numeracy. *Research and Practice in Adult Literacy, 59*, pp. 17–20.

Swann, J. (2009). *The Discourse of Reading Groups.* Paper presented at the International Conference on the Book 2009.

Swann, J., & Allington, D. (2009). Reading groups and the language of literary texts: A case study in social reading. *Language and Literature, 18*(3), pp. 247–264.

Swicord, R. (2007). *The Jane Austen Book Club* (film).

Tadmore, N. (1996). 'In the even my wife read to me': Women, reading and household life in the eighteenth century. In J. Raven, H. Small & N. Tadmore (Eds), *The Practice and Representation of Reading in England* (pp. 162–174). Cambridge: Cambridge University Press.

Taylor, A. (1996). Into his secret chamber: Reading and privacy in late medieval England. In J. Raven, H. Small & N. Tadmore (Eds), *The Practice and Representation of Reading in England* (pp. 41–61). Cambridge: Cambridge University Press.

Teale, P. (2005). *Brontë.* London: Nick Hern Books.

The Book Club Bible. (2007). London: Michael O'Mara Books Limited.

The Editors of the Paris Review. (1958). Interview with Ernest Hemingway: The Art of Fiction. In P. Gourevitch (Ed.), *The Paris Review Interviews, 1* (Vol. 1). Edinburgh: Canongate.

The Open University. (2010). *The Reading Experience Database (RED), 1450–1945.* Accessed 15 October 2010, Online database: http://www.open.ac.uk/Arts/RED/.

The Reading Agency. (2009). Invitation to Join Chatabout: Online communication with Sam Duncan.

Thompson, E. P. (1964). *The Making of the English Working Class.* New York, NY: Pantheon.

Thomson, A. (2010). What is literature? In D. Cavanagh, A. Gillis, M. Keown, J. Loxley & R. Stevenson (Eds), *The Edinburgh Introduction to Studying English Literature* (pp. 3–15). Edinburgh: Edinburgh University Press.

Tinajero, A. (2010). *El Lector: A History of the Cigar Factory Reader* (J. E. Grasberg, Trans.). Austin, TX: University of Texas Press.

Tomlinson, B. (1998). Seeing what they mean: Helping L2 readers to visualise. In B. Tomlinson (Ed.), *Materials Development in Language Teaching* (pp. 265–278). Cambridge: Cambridge University Press.

Tomlinson, P. (1989). Having it both ways: Hierarchical focusing as research interview method. *British Educational Research Journal, 15*(2), pp. 155–176.

Trilling, L. (1966). The fate of pleasure. In *Beyond Culture: Essays on Literature and Learning.* London: Secker & Warberg.

Trubeck, A. (2010). How the Paperback Novel Changed Popular Literature. From 31 March 2010, *Smithsonian.com.*

Tusting, K. (2000). New literacy studies and time: An exploration. In D. Barton, M. Hamilton & R. Ivanic (Eds), *Situated Literacies: Reading and Writing in Context* (pp. 35–51). London: Routledge.

Vincent, D. (1989). *Literacy and Popular Culture: England 1750–1914.* Cambridge: Cambridge University Press.

—. (2000). *The Rise of Mass Literacy: Reading and Writing in Modern Europe.* Oxford: Polity.

Watt, I. (2000). *The Rise of the Novel.* London: Pimlico.

Webb, R. K. (1955). *The British Working Class Reader 1790–1848: Literacy and Social Tension.* London: George Allen & Unwin.

West, R. (1928). *The Strange Necessity: Essays and Reviews.* London: Jonathan Cape.

Wickert, R., Searle, J., Marr, B., & Johnston, B. (2007). Opportunities, transitions, and risks: Perspectives on adult literacy and numeracy development in Australia. In NCSALL (Ed.), *Review of Adult Learning and Literacy* (Vol. 7, pp. 245–284) (online).

Wolf, M. (2008). *Proust and the Squid: The Story and Science of the Reading Brain.* Cambridge: Icon Books.

Woodin, T. (2008). "A beginner reader is not a beginner thinker": Student publishing in Britain since the 1970s. *Paedagogica Historica, 44*(1), pp. 219–232.

Woolf, V. (1929). *A Room of One's Own.* Harmondsworth: Penguin.

Wordsworth, W., & Coleridge, S. T. (1802). Preface to lyrical ballads. In M. H. Abrams (Ed.), *The Norton Anthology of English Literature* (Vol. 2, pp. 155–170). London: W. W. Norton & Company.

Wright, E. (1982). Modern Psychoanalytic Criticism. In A. Jefferson & D. Robey (Eds), *Modern Literary Theory: A Comparative Introduction* (pp. 145–165). London: B. T. Batsford Ltd.

Wyss, H. E. (2000). *Writing Indians: Literacy, Christianity, and Native Community in Early America.* Amherst, MA: University of Massachusetts Press.

Yang, A. (2001). Reading and the non-academic learner: A mystery solved. *System, 29*(4), pp. 451–466.

Yin, R. K. (2003). *Case Study Research: Design and methods* (3rd ed.). London: Sage.

Ying Lao, C., & Krashen, S. (2000). The impact of popular literature study on literacy development in EFL: More evidence for the power of reading. *System, 28*(2), pp. 261–270.

Zakaluk, B. L. (1991). Book Bridges: Its first phase – An evaluation. *Junior League of Winnipeg (Manitoba), 1*(1), p. 105.

Zakaluk, B. L., & Wynes, B. J. (1995). Book Bridges: A family literacy programme for immigrant women. *Journal of Adolescent & Adult Literacy, 38*(7), pp. 550–557.

Zunshine, L. (2006). *Why We Read Fiction: Theory of Mind and the Novel.* Columbus, OH: The Ohio State University Press.

Index